Pu*blish*ng
Chil**ren's **oks

by Harold D. Underdown

ALPHA

A member of Penguin Group (USA) Inc.

To Ann, of course. —H. U.

Copyright © 2004 by Harold D. Underdown and Lynne Rominger

All rights reserved. No part of this book shall be reproduced, stored in a retrieval system, or transmitted by any means, electronic, mechanical, photocopying, recording, or otherwise, without written permission from the publisher. No patent liability is assumed with respect to the use of the information contained herein. Although every precaution has been taken in the preparation of this book, the publisher and author assume no responsibility for errors or omissions. Neither is any liability assumed for damages resulting from the use of information contained herein. For information, address Alpha Books, 800 East 96th Street, Indianapolis, IN 46240.

THE COMPLETE IDIOT'S GUIDE TO and Design are registered trademarks of Penguin Group (USA) Inc.

International Standard Book Number: 1-59257-143-3
Library of Congress Catalog Card Number: 2003113806

06 05 04   8 7 6 5 4 3 2 1

Interpretation of the printing code: The rightmost number of the first series of numbers is the year of the book's printing; the rightmost number of the second series of numbers is the number of the book's printing. For example, a printing code of 04-1 shows that the first printing occurred in 2004.

Printed in the United States of America

Note: This publication contains the opinions and ideas of its author. It is intended to provide helpful and informative material on the subject matter covered. It is sold with the understanding that the author and publisher are not engaged in rendering professional services in the book. If the reader requires personal assistance or advice, a competent professional should be consulted.

The author and publisher specifically disclaim any responsibility for any liability, loss, or risk, personal or otherwise, which is incurred as a consequence, directly or indirectly, of the use and application of any of the contents of this book.

Most Alpha books are available at special quantity discounts for bulk purchases for sales promotions, premiums, fund-raising, or educational use. Special books, or book excerpts, can also be created to fit specific needs.

For details, write: Special Markets, Alpha Books, 375 Hudson Street, New York, NY 10014.

Publisher: *Marie Butler-Knight*
Product Manager: *Phil Kitchel*
Senior Managing Editor: *Jennifer Chisholm*
Senior Acquisitions Editor: *Renee Wilmeth*
Development Editor: *Ginny Bess Munroe*
Copy Editor: *Keith Cline*
Illustrator: *Chris Eliopoulos*
Cover/Book Designer: *Trina Wurst*
Indexer: *Angie Bess*
Layout/Proofreading: *Becky Harmon, Donna Martin*

Contents at a Glance

Appendixes

Contents

Foreword

In this honest and precise book on writing for children, Harold has managed to cram in almost everything about writing and illustrating books for children and getting them published there is to know.

With so much to cover, it's surprising that there were only three things about which I wish he'd said a little more: joy, gathering, and ducks.

I know this is an odd list. But read on a bit and see what I mean.

Joy. Too many writers talk about the difficulties of writing. How it takes blood and bile. How it is enormously difficult and lonely. How no one in his or her right mind would plan to make a living at it.

But I always want to come down on the side of joy.

Think of it: You will be writing down stories, poems, anecdotes, and information that might change lives.

I always told my children that they should leave the world a little better than they found it. Some might say it's an easy task, given in what awful shape the world is now. But I believe they have taken that mother line to heart. They are good, moral adults, and in their work do make a difference to the world.

Well, I am not modest about it. I get enough letters from children whose lives I have changed with my fictions and my poetry to know that it happens. On a small scale—certainly. One reader at a time—absolutely.

Art can work miracles.

Story can.

Now about *gathering,* here is what I mean.

My son Adam, his wife Betsy, and their little children Alison and David live in Minne-apolis. When I travel there, I know I will visit with family. Have good meals. See friends. Indulge in amusing conversations. Lots of fun music. (Adam is in two bands.)

What it doesn't mean is writing.

I can still accomplish daily things like keeping up with e-mail and phone calls.

But I do no writing.

Still, I consider these kinds of trips "gathering days." Good writing is made up of details. So on these hours away from the computer, away from actual writing, I become a collector of details. Some I collect actively, most passively.

The sweet talcum smell of the baby's neck, under the chin. How John, who plays backup guitar in Adam's Irish band, sweats in large discontinuous swatches on his T-shirt. The silhouette of my daughter-in-law holding Alison and how they pat one another on the back simultaneously. The damp Minnesota heat that leaves moist patches, like tears, under my eyes. The exact arch of a Catalpa tree leaning over the street.

It may look as if a writer uses such stuff to keep her away from the actual hard work of writing. And in fact many authors will tell outsiders just that. But do not be fooled. It is actually all grist to the mill.

For example, while I am speeding through the latest Dick Francis novel, I am also noting how he keeps his story moving, how the arc of his telling forces the reader to keep going. Reading the latest issue of *Cricket* or Richard Peck's Newbery Award novel I am taking in what is considered the best writing today. Working crossword puzzles, I am discovering new words. Watching TV, I am practicing dialogue. Listening to local gossip, I invest in character.

As I say in *Take Joy: A Book for Writers:*

> I never turn off my writer's head. Conversations are stuffed in there, the chalky sweet smell of paper-white roses, the sharp fishiness of herring fillets, the rough crumble of unharled stone, the way a rose bush points its wayward fingers upward in its search for some new purchase, how the ruined towers of a castle take on extra life against a gray sky, the feel of my granddaughter's small wriggly hand in mind.

> All this and more will be returned to me when I need it in a scene or a poem or as a central metaphor for a story.

> I didn't know that when I began writing. I thought any time away from the typewriter was wasted time. Then my husband and I spent nine months camping in Europe and the Middle East and I started throwing images of what I had seen into my stories. That's when I understood how important gathering days are for writers.

Finally, there are those *ducks.*

Often I feel as if my writing time is slowly being nibbled away by ducks. Other writers have made similar complaints. Life, we all say, simply gets in the way.

But then on reading a biography about Emily Dickinson, where she's shown making tea cakes and writing letters, helping in the house and playing with her nephew, etc., I realize that we writers still must live in the real world. That means cakes, letters, bills, clogged toilets, etc. That means reading other people's books, watching TV, doing crossword puzzles, chatting on the phone. That means taking children to school, to the orthodontist, to choir practice, to basketball games. That means working till 3, till 5, till 8, till midnight. That means vacuuming the living room of cat hairs, dog hairs, husband's hairs. That means running to the grocery store, the paint store, the shoe store. That means going to the doctor, the dentist, the hair salon.

What that means is life.

Besides, without life, what's there to write about?

Jane Yolen

Jane Yolen is the award-winning author of more than 200 books for children, young adults, and adults. Ms. Yolen's best-known title, the critically acclaimed *Owl Moon* (Putnam/Philomel), illustrated by John Schoenherr, won the prestigious Caldecott Medal for 1988. Among Jane Yolen's many other awards are the Catholic Library Association's 1992 Regina Medal for her work in children's literature and the University of Minnesota's Kerlan Award for the body of her work. She has also received numerous state awards, including New York's "Charlotte," Nebraska's "Golden Sower," and New Jersey's "Garden State Children's Book Award."

Introduction

I speak at children's book conferences, and I run a personal website on the world of children's publishing, and over and over again people ask me about how to get started, where the publishers are, how to get feedback on a manuscript, what you should have in a portfolio, and about other problems with which writers and illustrators struggle as they try to establish themselves. It's hard to find all the basic information about this cozy but mystifying world. And that, quite simply, is why I wrote this book—to bring together all that information. What you have in your hands is, I hope, a resource that lays out all the basics, takes you some steps beyond the basics, and points you in the correct direction when you are ready to learn still more.

Different people, of course, may have different ideas about what the basics are, or need different kinds of information at different times. So I've written dozens of definitions of publishing terms and taken a philosophical look at how your motives can affect your work. I've dissected the parts of a book and sketched a mini-history of children's publishing. I provide help in understanding contracts and sample letters to accompany manuscripts. And I've included many places to turn to for more information.

I love being involved in children's books, but know from personal experience that there's a lot to keep up with. I hope this book helps you to do that, to spend more time writing or illustrating, and to need to take less time trying to figure it all out.

How to Use This Book

The world of children's book publishing can be confusing and complicated to those unfamiliar with its traditions and procedures. I've organized this book into five parts to unravel the complexities for you, guiding you through the maze to your ultimate goal—publication—and beyond.

Part 1, "Where to Begin?" provides suggestions and information about moving your ideas from your imagination onto paper—the first steps of their journey to publication.

Part 2, "Finding Out What's Possible," explores the many faces of children's publishing. From board books for toddlers to historical novels for young adult readers, the kinds of children's books have different audiences, approaches, needs—and, of course, publishers.

Part 3, "Out into the World," gives you guidance in getting your work from your desk or drawing table to the right company, and to the right editor or art director at that company.

Part 4, "Working with a Publisher," explains what happens after you sign on the dotted line. If you think the hard part is over when the publisher sends you a contract, these chapters are especially for you!

Part 5, "My Book Is Published! Now What?" discusses the many events that move your book up the sales chain. From publicity appearances to reading for school children, there are many opportunities for you to increase your book's presence in the marketplace. And I take a look further ahead, to building a career and dealing with such disappointments as out-of-print books.

I've also developed a glossary of terms used in children's publishing, a resource list of books, magazines, organizations, and websites, and sample letters and guidelines. You'll find all these in the appendixes.

Extras

Sidebar boxes throughout the book highlight interesting information and important details.

Playground Stories

These anecdotes from, and profiles of, children's authors and publishers give you an inside view of the children's publishing world.

Can You Keep a Secret?

In these boxes, you'll find suggestions, tips, and resources to help you present yourself as a pro.

Vocabulary List

These boxes explain terms and lingo common in the children's publishing industry.

Class Rules

These boxes provide warnings and cautions.

Acknowledgments

I am always telling artists and writers that a book is a team effort. This one was no different, both in creating the original edition and this revised edition. Neither would have happened without the help of dozens of people. Renee Wilmeth contacted me to start the book off and helped me shape the outline, Lynne Rominger came onboard to help make the first edition happen. Debbie Romaine was an editor's editor (quite literally). Finishing the text of the first edition while I was working full-time was tough, but Debbie made it possible. Ginny Bess, my editor for the second edition, played a similarly important role.

Many others contributed their expertise and experience in e-mails and phone conversations, some of which I've quoted directly, others of which contributed to the thinking that shaped the book. They include Jennifer Armstrong, Bruce Balan, Susan Campbell Bartoletti, Miriam Bat-Ami, Carmen Bernier-Grand, Larry Dane Brimner, Evelyn Coleman, Sneed Collard, Bev Cooke, Elizabeth Devereaux, Muriel L. Dubois, Jennie Dunham, Lisa Rowe Fraustino, Sandy Ferguson Fuller, Charles Ghigna, James Cross Giblin, Lois Grambling, Megan Halsey, Tony Johnston, Elaine Landau, Grace Lin, Diane Mayr, Stephen Mooser, Josephine Nobisso, Jules Older, Larry Pringle, Dana Rau, Deborah Kogan Ray, Pam Muñoz Ryan, Mary Ann Sabia, Aaron Shepard, Tema Siegel, Alexandra Siy, Donna Spurlock, Ginger Wadsworth, Jan Wahl, Rozanne Lanczak Williams, Carolyn Yoder, and Jane Yolen. If I talked with you and you're not on this list, blame my record-keeping, not my lack of gratitude.

I interviewed a number of people by phone or e-mail and appreciate the time they took to deal with my sometimes lengthy lists of questions. So my special thanks to Emma Dryden, Beth Feldman, Bernette Ford, Jennifer Greene, Regina Griffin, Kate Jackson, Margaret K. McElderry, George Nicholson, Paula Quint, Mary Ann Sabia, Susan Sherman, and Christine Tugeau—and also to my work colleagues, for putting up with my sometimes distracted air while working on the book.

My family and friends have been remarkably tolerant of my absence from their lives during the work on the first edition and during the revisions, and of my aura of preoccupation on the rare occasions when I came to the surface.

My thanks above all to my wife, Ann Rubin, who not only encouraged me to take on this project when it first was offered, but never once expressed regret at having done so, and even continued to encourage me. As an artist, not a publishing insider, she also brought perspective into what was truly important on the many occasions when I got lost in the details. Most of all, her confidence that what I might want to say was worthwhile kept me going. This book would not have happened without her.

And for the revised edition, I offer rueful thanks to our daughter, who though not yet two has been very accepting of the sad reality that sometimes daddy had to work during our usual weekend time together. I hope that she will be proud of it when she is old enough to read it.

Special Thanks to the Technical Reviewer

The Complete Idiot's Guide to Publishing Children's Books, First Edition, was reviewed by an expert who double-checked the accuracy of what you'll learn here, to help us ensure that this book gives you everything you need to know about writing your story, getting your children's story into the hands of a publisher, working with a publisher, and building a career. Special thanks are extended to Alison James.

Ms. James is an author of novels and picture books, a translator, and a founder and organizer of the Kindling Words conference and Writers Colony.

In addition, Miriam Bat-Ami, Toni Buzzeo, Jennie Dunham, Megan Halsey, Jane Kurtz, Ann Tobias, and Christine Tugeau commented on revised materials.

Trademarks

All terms mentioned in this book that are known to be or are suspected of being trademarks or service marks have been appropriately capitalized. Alpha Books and Penguin Group (USA) Inc. cannot attest to the accuracy of this information. Use of a term in this book should not be regarded as affecting the validity of any trademark or service mark.

Part 1

Where to Begin?

If you're not a part of it, children's publishing can be a confusing world. Part 1 gives you the basics so you can get started with what you want to do: write or illustrate books for children, and then get them published.

This part kicks off with ways to get you writing, shows you how to find the best, most popular, and most recent children's books, and takes a look at how your motives can affect the work you do. Then you're taken from your immediate world—your office space and how to get organized—to the big world of publishing and what is happening there right now. Finally, you get a detailed guided tour of a book, so you can call each book element by the correct name.

That's a lot to cover, so hold on to your hat, and turn the page!

Chapter 1

Adults Rule the World

In This Chapter

- What this book is all about
- Some basics about children's books
- The importance of taking yourself seriously
- An introduction to the challenges of writing and illustrating for children

Welcome to a wonderful and challenging world, the world of children's books. I gave this chapter a title that pushes against the subject of this book just to remind all of us of a strange paradox at the heart of children's publishing. We are at work creating books for children, but everyone involved in producing and then buying them, with rare exceptions, is an adult. Even if in your mind you are creating for a child you know well—your own child, or the child you once were—for your work to become a book it must go through the hands of many adults.

Getting Started

So you want to write or illustrate a children's book (or both!). Maybe you already have. Maybe you've sent your work out to a few publishers and it's come back to you. Or maybe you've been working for a few years, and had some success, but want to push on ahead. Getting started is hard, and so is continuing, so I've filled this book with information, advice, resources, and stories of success and failure.

Piercing the Static

Picture the thousands of manuscripts and art samples that children's publishers receive every year as static. You've got to pierce that static. To do that, you need four things:

- You need to work hard on your illustrating or your writing and keep striving to improve it.
- You need to learn as much as you can about the publishing world.
- You need to be persistent—over years if necessary.
- You need some luck.

That's a tall order. Many people never do get published. I aim to help you get through the static so you can have a chance of being among those who do.

No One Best Way

You may be looking for the best way to get published. If so, I want you to know up front that there isn't one. There are as many ways as there are people, and that can be both frightening and freeing. It's frightening, because you'll have to figure out some things for yourself. It's freeing, because it allows you to be yourself. The good news is that in this book you'll learn about options you might not have considered—types of writing or illustrating to try, ways to approach publishers, kinds of publishers to investigate—and you'll learn how to chart your own path. Keep going down that path! If you don't, you won't reach the end of it.

It Takes Time

I hope you'll come to understand the value of patience. As you'll see in some of the stories, writing or illustrating for children is not the simple task that some outsiders assume. It's far more like becoming a brain surgeon than just starting a hobby, in fact. It takes years and years before you become a real practitioner, in which you learn many things and refine your technique and gradually get better.

So don't be too hard on yourself, and don't look over your shoulder to compare yourself to others. Deal with the challenges in front of you, whatever they may be, and after that you can worry about the next ones. As you learn and grow, and improve, you may not even notice your progress, but a day may come when you look up and find that you're on the top of that hill that only a short while earlier had looked like it was unclimbable.

> **Playground Stories** _____
>
> It can take longer than you might expect to feel that you have arrived. So said Simms Taback, illustrator, in his acceptance speech for the Caldecott Medal, the most prestigious award for illustrators. (His speech was published in the July/August 2000 issue of *The Horn Book Magazine*.) "What's really wonderful about getting this award is that I feel like a relative newcomer to the world of illustration, as if I have only just arrived as a practitioner of this craft. But actually, I have been illustrating for 40 years." He goes on to cite missteps and bad luck that kept him from feeling that he had ever "made it."

Lots to Learn—Start Here

There is a lot to learn. Children's book publishing is a big business. There are many kinds of publishers, and many kinds of books, and right ways and wrong ways to do even such a simple thing as write a cover letter. This is a world unto itself, and you need to know the jargon and the shared assumptions of the people in it if you are going to have a better chance of succeeding.

Books and Publishers

Writing or illustrating itself is hard enough. But if you are to go from a few sketches or a neatly typed manuscript to an actual book, you need to make sense of the children's publishing industry. You need to figure out what kind of work you are doing and what publishers might be a good match for you.

Picture Books and Chapter Books

There are many kinds of children's books, and we'll go into them in the chapters in Part 2, but to start with you need to understand a basic distinction. Picture books are books in which the pictures and words tell the story together. Often they have pictures on every page, and are read to children by the adults in their lives. Chapter books, on the other hand, have chapters. They may also have pictures, but the pictures aren't as important. The words tell the story. And these books are usually meant to be read by children or teenagers themselves.

Both of these basic types get divided into smaller categories. Do you have to know exactly what you've written, or the age group of the children for whom you want to illustrate? No, and sometimes a publisher will have a different idea about your work than you do. But it helps to know the basics, because some publishers only publish one type or the other. So you'll need to learn about them, too.

So Many Publishers!

At first glance, it may seem like there are hundreds of publishers all over the country. Or it can seem like there are only five, and they're all in New York. It's tricky to sort them all out, especially because in the last decade publishers have bought out other publishers in what seems like a never-ending dance of mergers and acquisitions. Actually, though five or six very large publishers may seem to dominate the market, there are many other publishers around the United States and Canada, and we are going to help you find them.

Kinds of Publishers

Different publishers, and sometimes different divisions of the same company, create very different kinds of books. A company selling books to libraries takes a different approach than one that sells its books in bookstores, or one that puts its books in racks in drugstores. Depending on what you want to write, you've got to find the right match. *Trade* publishers aim for the bookstores for the most part, though some also sell to schools and libraries. *Mass market* publishers target a wider audience, and find it in supermarkets and other general retail stores. Beyond books, magazines and electronic publishing beckon, too.

You'll read a lot more about these different markets later in the book.

Vocabulary List

Trade books sell mostly in bookstores, but some may also go into the "institutional" market—schools and libraries. **Mass market books** are for the masses, and are sold in warehouse stores, racks in newsstands, supermarkets, and similar outlets. Trade books are usually more expensive than mass market ones.

Putting Away Childish Things

As you read this book, and as you start to have contact with publishers, writers, and librarians, you'll find that children's publishing isn't all fluffy kittens and sad-eyed puppies. It may not be quite so cutthroat as some businesses, but it is a business, and, to repeat a wry aphorism I've heard several times, "It's a bunny-eat-bunny-world." Be prepared for this.

Take It Seriously

Begin by taking what you are about to do seriously. This is not a hobby or a pastime, or something you can succeed in by working on it only during your summer vacations. On the other hand, you don't have to define success by making money from your writing. As many will tell you, you may never be able to quit your day job. Creating books for children is not easy and takes time, space, and dedication. As I'll detail later in this Part, it's important to set aside a space and time, and remember that you need and deserve this.

Can You Keep a Secret? _____

How big is children's publishing? Estimates suggest about $2 billion in sales annually, with 5 publishers—Random House, Penguin Putnam, HarperCollins, Scholastic, and Simon & Schuster—accounting for about half. There are 4,000 to 5,000 new books published each year, half by the big guys. But hundreds (maybe thousands) of smaller companies publish books, too, right down to individuals who publish their own books.

Art and Commerce

Remember, too, that at the end of the process, at least if you want to get published, is a book or magazine or something similar that someone (actually thousands of some-ones) will have to decide to buy. You're an artist, but you're not creating one idiosyn-cratic work that needs to find only one buyer, or that you might even be keeping for yourself. Book publishing lies in an interesting middle area between art and commerce, between pure self-expression and the manufacture of millions of such useful but generic items as pencils and bars of soap. There's room for creativity, but you need to find an audience (your market), and a publisher will help you do that.

"When You Grow Up, Will You Write for Adults?"

Once you reach the point of identifying yourself as a writer or illustrator for children, it won't be long before you run into the condescension of those who assume that they, too, could write or illustrate wonderful children's books, if they could just find the time. Or those who exclaim that it's just wonderful that you've taken up such a charm-ing hobby: "Painting pretty pictures for the little ones! How sweet ...."

Sadly, many people don't understand that creating books for children is as significant, challenging, and absorbing as any other form of creative endeavor, from investigative journalism to spoken-word poetics, or from advertising design to land-form sculpture.

The attitude of these benighted souls seems to be that children aren't as mature or intelligent as adults, and so it must be easier to illustrate or write for them. Don't slide unaware into becoming one of the people who believes this. You are doing serious work, work that actually is harder than similar work for adults. After all, you aren't creating for someone just like you, though perhaps you are keeping in mind the child you used to be. It can be tricky to write or illustrate (or edit, for that matter) for this "other": Adults publishing for other adults can use their own reactions as guides to how their audiences will react. You can't do that. Be proud of what you are doing.

What This Book Can Do for You

Just how am I going to help you deal with the issues I've been discussing, as well as teach you what you need to learn? The following sections explain what I realistically can and cannot do for you.

The Whole Picture

I've worked hard to give you a comprehensive overview of this field. I don't just give you information about children's book publishers—I look at magazines and educational publishing, too. I get you started with tips on getting your manuscript or art samples to the right publishing companies, follow up with guidance on revision and contract negotiation, and help you complete the process through marketing and self-promotion. In short, I've tried to cover everything that someone just getting started would need to know, and then go beyond that and provide useful information for those already published. Of course, I'll be happy to hear from you if there's something you think I've left out and you want to suggest for the next edition—I provide contact information in Appendix B.

No Magic Formula

Looking for guidance on writing? I give you help on getting started writing, on examining your motives for writing, and on getting feedback. But I don't tell you *how* to write. There are so many different kinds of children's books, and I'm covering so much other information, that a how-to-write section would have become a series of oversimplified formulas. You could use them, and end up with formulaic stories, but there's nothing an editor dislikes more than formulaic stories. Fortunately, there are already many great books that explain how to write different kinds of children's books. I've listed many of them in Appendix B.

X Marks the Spot

The many books, websites, and other sources for more help that I identify in the appendixes and throughout make this book a treasure map to the many places you can go for more detailed and advanced information. You could find those places yourself, of course. But there are hundreds of books on publishing and on children's books, and as many websites. I've checked them out and organized them and made some judgments on which ones are worthwhile, so that you don't have to take the time out from your writing to do a lot of digging.

How Others Did It

A book full of advice and information would be pretty dry and hard to understand without real-life stories. I don't include these just for the human interest, though that would be enough of a reason. I include them because there's no better way to learn how to move forward in children's publishing than to hear how others have done it—or failed to do it, as the case may be. You'll read stories and tips from extremely successful people, and from others just getting started, from people who've succeeded in many areas, and from others who've specialized. And when it's called for, you'll read stories from publishing insiders too, so you can begin to get to know the people with whom you may be working.

A Vade Mecum

In a way, this is a most old-fashioned kind of a book, a *vade mecum*. This is a reference manual, a book that "goes with me." I don't expect you to read it from cover to cover, though I've set it up so that you could if you wanted to. I think you're more likely to read some of it, put it on your shelf, pull it down to look something up, look through it again a year or two from now, and perhaps find that a section that hadn't seemed relevant at first has become critically important. I hope this book will *go with you* as you learn and move ahead with your career.

Know the Forest, Not the Trees

Though I've packed it full of specific information—the trees—I hope this book will most of all help you begin to get to know the forest of children's book publishing. The strange ecosystem that is children's publishing changes slowly, even though individual trees may come and go. From the trees in this book—individual publishers, editors, types of books—you'll begin to put together an understanding of how the forest works, so that when you venture into new and uncharted parts of it you'll be less likely to get lost and go hungry. You'll know where to look for food and how to watch out for danger. You'll know how to survive, even if you don't recognize all the trees.

No Guarantees

One thing I can't offer you in this book is a guarantee. There are thousands of aspiring authors and illustrators out there, and I know from talking to some of them that you can follow the "rules" (or even find creative ways to bend them) and work for years and still not get published. If all you want is to get published by a well-known publisher, in fact, you might want to give up now. That desire isn't going to be enough to get you there. You have to want other things, too—to do exciting work for children, and to build a career. You also have to like what you are doing, and stick to it, have some talent, and, even then, understand that you might not make it. If the journey is worth it in itself, I'm here to help you choose your supplies and maybe even be one of your traveling companions. But if the trip's only worth it if you arrive at your destination, think twice about setting off.

Above all, be inspired by the example of a J. K. Rowling, but don't be disappointed if a career like hers doesn't evolve for you. With the amazing worldwide sales of millions of copies that the Harry Potter books have achieved, she did what no other author, whether for adults or for children, has ever done. Ever! Don't measure your success, or lack of it, against hers—or against the success of any other author or illustrator. Your personal best is what matters.

The Least You Need to Know

- You're starting out on a long and interesting road. Don't try to rush it.

- Getting a children's book published takes persistence.

- Understand the difference between picture and chapter books and between trade and mass market.

- Take yourself seriously, and take illustrating or writing for children seriously.

- Use this book as a reference manual and a starting point—I can't fit in all the answers, but I'll help you find them.

I Don't Know What to Say! And What Comes Next

In This Chapter

- ◆ How to find a direction
- ◆ How to use a journal to explore your interests
- ◆ Why writing must be practiced and how to do it
- ◆ What you need to do to write and how to create the time and space
- ◆ What to do when you think you're finished

There are few things as terrifying as a piece of blank paper staring up at you. How can you overcome that? Writers, even established writers—maybe even *especially* established writers—don't just sit down and write.

I'm going to suggest ways to fill that page: how to discover what you want to write, if you're unsure, and how to practice your writing and imagining skills, in much the same way you might practice skiing or hitting a golf ball. These are getting-started exercises. Once you're writing, you'll want to fit your writing into the specific formats and types of children's books. To do that, turn to Chapters 9 and 10. In this chapter, you'll also learn about the conditions you need to write without distractions, and how to keep working on your writing until it's truly ready.

You Are What You Read

Do you have the writing bug, but you just don't know what to write? Ask yourself what you like to read. Go over to your bookshelves, and take a careful look at your books. Which books sit there, never opened? Which ones have cracked bindings, well-thumbed pages, and little notes in the margins? Can you see certain kinds of books you usually read, or are your favorites fiction, nonfiction, light, heavy—all over the map? Most important of all, do you read books for children? If you don't, but think you want to write them, then start reading them. Find out what you like to read. That's probably the kind of book you will write.

In your reading, as in your writing, rule one is to write what you want to write, not what you think you should. "Shoulds" clog the mind and get in the way of the clear thinking you need to do your best writing, so run away from them.

Let's say you've noticed that you really like to read books that present science to a general audience, such as Lewis Thomas does for adults. Then try reading science books for children to see if such books interest you. Almost any kind of book you like as an adult points to a similar kind for children:

Can You Keep a Secret?

Your ninth-grade English teacher may have instilled in you a deep respect (and fear?) for the classics, but that doesn't mean that you have to go out and try to write one, at least not yet. Creativity is hard enough; do like the pros do and write what you like to write, not what your family says you should.

- ◆ Like romance novels? So do teenagers.

- ◆ Enjoy science fiction? Children do, too.

- ◆ Biographies grab you? Libraries grab them.

- ◆ Prefer magazines? So do many children.

Check Chapter 3 for help in finding particular kinds of children's books. Rest assured, you'll find something to write. But don't be too hasty and start by writing a specific type of book for a specific audience. First you need to explore ways of generating raw material, get in some practice, and set up the habits and schedule that will keep you going.

Dear Diary

Just about everybody has kept a diary at some time or another. If you haven't, don't feel bad, because most diaries cover mundane events, or, if written by a teenager, feelings that are very important to the diarist but probably to no one else. Now that you are writing, however, you should seriously consider keeping a diary that goes by a grander name—a *journal*.

A journal can be many things. You can use it to write about whatever is on your mind at the time. You can use it to record things you've observed that interest you, from the changing of the cloud patterns in the sky to the changing of emotions in the teenagers sitting next to you on the bus. You can use it to note ideas, remember sentences that come to you, transcribe snippets of dialogue, or to do pen portraits of interesting characters. You can use it to explore your feelings about writing, or your reactions to books you've read. More practically, you can keep track of when you write, for how long, and how effectively, so that you can figure out your best writing times.

Vocabulary List

The word *journal* is related to the French word for "day," *jour*. As that implies, a journal is a blank book to write in daily. Your journal should be as much a part of your life as a cup of coffee in the morning or the evening news.

If you're going to get the most out of your journal, you need to use it regularly. It's good to keep it with you so you can jot something down whenever you want to, but don't stop there. Make an appointment with yourself to write in your journal every day. Try to make it be the same time. If you can't, make sure that you find times when you won't be interrupted.

Writing every day can be difficult to maintain, especially without a structure. Don't feel bad that you aren't inspired; give yourself a break and give yourself a structure. Take a month to explore your feelings about your parents and your siblings, or to note down some key memories from a particular year of your childhood. Or give yourself a theme of the day:

◆ Monday for family

◆ Tuesday for friends

◆ Wednesday for writing

◆ Thursday for the natural world

◆ Friday for planning

◆ Saturday for fun

◆ Sunday for spirituality

Choose whatever topics are most important to you. What matters is that you make your journal your own, and that you be as honest with yourself in it as you can be. Make a point of reading back through it from time to time. Gradually, ideas and areas of interest will start to emerge and become clearer. Also, with the added practice of writing in a journal, your writing will benefit.

Practice Makes Perfect

A journal isn't the only way you can practice your writing. There are many ways in which you can work not only on improving the quality of your writing but also on your fluency. Getting words down on paper so that you can go back and revise later is a challenge to every writer, so the more easily and rapidly you can write, the better.

Writing exercises will also help you get started on a particular project. No writer starts a manuscript without a considerable amount of what is called "prewriting," meaning brainstorming, outlining, and the like. Jennifer Armstrong, a published author of fiction and nonfiction, observes:

> I spend a lot of time on preparation. Lots of notes, lots of outlining, lots of character sketching. (This of course all depends on what I'm writing.) Not until I really know where the book is going do I begin writing prose.

Our schools often leave us with the idea that good writers are able to sit down and write, producing something that's very close to its final form. That doesn't happen very often. To write well, there's a lot you have to do first, and as you'll see a little later in this chapter, more to do once you've come up with a first draft.

Playground Stories

Look into some general-purpose writing books. Natalie Goldberg's *Writing Down the Bones* and *Wild Mind: Living the Writer's Life* are great sources of inspiration and practical exercises. Ignore the New Age vocabulary if it bothers you. Or check out Jessica Wilbur's *Totally Private and Personal: Journaling Ideas for Girls and Young Women*. In spite of the title, it's great for people of any age and either gender. Take the time to browse through the general writing section in your local bookstore for books like these.

As you'll discover when you spend a little time exploring the titles about writing in a good bookstore, there are many ways to work on your writing. Here are a few.

Don't Stop

Writing without stopping to edit yourself or rethinking is difficult to do, but you can learn to do it. Give yourself five minutes to write, without stopping, without going back and correcting a word or a spelling. If you can't think of anything to write, just write "I can't think of anything to write," and keep going. Use a pen, a pencil, a type-writer, or a computer. The tool doesn't matter, so long as you feel comfortable with it. Do this every day, in your journal or not, as you choose.

After you've had some practice with this technique, try varying it. Give yourself a topic to start off with, or a writing prompt (a sentence to complete), and see where it leads you. Write "I love to write children's books because …" or maybe "I'm scared to write children's books because …." After some use of this technique, you may find that your conscious mind lets go a little, and you start writing things that surprise you. Like speakers practicing speaking off-the-cuff on impromptu subjects, this free, sustained writing can loosen you up and raise the overall quality of your writing. You'll still be revising, but from a higher level. (My thanks to Natalie Goldberg for these ideas.)

Visualize

Clear, concise description is a joy, and difficult to achieve, whether you are writing about a dark and stormy night or a new scientific discovery. Practicing visualization can help you improve your skills at description.

Settle on a scene you'd like to visualize, perhaps from your childhood, perhaps more recent, but not one that's right in front of you. Close your eyes, and conjure it up. Take some time to bring as much of it to your mind's eye as possible. If it's a room, imagine yourself walking around in it, looking under things, behind things, maybe even out the window. If you imagine yourself outside, walk around there, too. Settle on the limits of your scene. After you've looked your fill, listen. What sounds belong in your scene? What do you smell? What do you feel: the temperature of the air, the textures of the objects around you? If there's something edible, what do you taste?

After you feel you've fully placed yourself in your chosen scene, open your eyes and write. Describe it as fully and evocatively as you can. Don't edit! As with the previous exercise, just keep writing. After you have finished—and you could go on for pages and pages—you can go back and edit. You might use this to help you imagine a setting for a story, or you might just use it for practice. But try it again, with a different place. With practice, your ability to picture places familiar and unfamiliar will improve, and so will your ability to describe them.

Memories

Many writers for children draw on childhood experiences and memories as the raw material of their writing. Even if that is not your intention, even if you plan to write only about American history or biology or sports, being in touch with your own childhood and the feelings that you had then can only improve your ability to connect with your audience.

Think about an important milestone in your childhood, maybe the moment when you first succeeded in tying your own shoelaces, or the moment when you walked up to the chalkboard and wrote the right answer to a difficult math problem, or the moment when you said something clever at lunch and you noticed that cute boy (or girl) smiling. Visualize it. Write about it. Or remember the time you got lost in the big department store, or the time you had a fight with the playground bully, or the time you saw the girl (or the boy) you had a crush on dancing with someone else at the school dance, and obviously enjoying herself. Visualize that and write about it.

You may then develop something from your memory explorations. One or more of them could become the basis for a scene in a novel, or for an entire picture-book story. Or these explorations might help you understand what interests you in the world around you and find ways to present information to excite the child, you, and—we hope—your audience.

This Is Your Life

You have a life beyond writing, and your family and your day job can make it difficult to find time to write. But your day-to-day life can be an opportunity, too.

In the time you must spend in the rest of your life, do what Jane Yolen calls "gathering." Observe your family or your co-workers. Take in the scene outside your window. Watch for details that could bring a character or scene to life—how someone tugs at the top button of his shirt when explaining; the oil that leaks from the old car, making rainbow patterns when it rains. Make notes, mentally or physically. And of course, notice how other writers tell a story, describe a setting, or reveal a character.

Like your childhood memories, your entire life can be grist for your writing mill.

Get a Feel for It

Do you think you're ready to write that story? Maybe you already have. Whether you have or not, here's a different kind of exercise that will help you get a feel for the form of a children's book.

Can You Keep a Secret? _____

Looking for some guidance on writing specific kinds of children's books? There are already many wonderful books that provide just that help. Two I recommend are Katherine Paterson's *The Invisible Child: On Reading and Writing Books for Children,* and Uri Shulevitz's *Writing with Pictures: How to Write and Illustrate Children's Books.* But you should choose a how-to book *you* love. You'll find more possibilities in Appendix B.

Choose a favorite children's book and head to your typewriter or word processor. And all you have to do is to type it up, breaking the paragraphs where they break in the book. If it's a picture book, do the whole thing. If it's a novel, do a chapter or part of it.

Spontaneity or Results?

Now you're ready to be creative. So wait for inspiration to strike, and then get to work. You may be waiting a long time. Writers—accomplished writers—learn early that writing sometimes has to go ahead without inspiration. Writing is work: flashes of insight followed by the labor of translating that insight into words, and then revision (tips follow). Just like any other job, if you plan to succeed and turn in the goods, you need to put your nose to the grindstone.

But unlike those lucky people in 9-to-5 jobs, writers don't have supervisors breathing down their necks to get the job done—especially unpublished writers without deadlines. Your first book will result entirely from your own willpower. And even after you've got a book contract or established yourself as a full-time children's book author, you still won't have anyone hovering over you with a whip each morning, yelling, "Write!" You also won't have anyone telling you that your break ran too long. In one word, the profession you've chosen takes *dedication*. You need to look at your writing as you would any other job and set up a schedule.

Sitting behind a computer day-in and day-out in your bathrobe, barely showered, slaving away on a manuscript that might sell to a publisher or might not, isn't super glam. It's easy to procrastinate. Even established writers have times when washing the dog seems more urgent than writing. To succeed in the solitude of writing, consider these tips:

◆ Set a schedule and stick to it. Say to yourself, "I'm going to write every day from this time to that time," and do it. If you can only manage 15 minutes, that's okay. Just make it every day. Post your schedule on the refrigerator, and ask your family to respect it.

◆ Remove distractions, including children. Many, many parents hope to juggle the needs of their writing and of their children. But writing is a job. Any established writer will tell you that you can't concentrate on children and writing at the same time.

Class Rules

Although I'm emphasizing the importance of setting up time to write, don't leave out time to goof off, as Barbara Seuling notes in *How to Write a Children's Book and Get It Published*. If you feel guilty about doing things other than writing, sooner or later writing will become a drag. Give yourself writing time, yes, but give yourself nonwriting time, too.

Can You Keep a Secret?

Jennifer Basye Sander, an author of more than 20 books and the mother of 2 small boys, hires a baby-sitter for several hours a day while she writes. If that's beyond your budget, call on grandparent day care, trade baby care with friends and neighbors, or talk your spouse into taking the kids for a day every weekend. And you can squeeze in more writing whenever the kids are asleep. Be creative about making time for your writing.

- ◆ After you establish a schedule, every so often give yourself a change of scenery. When you write full-time from home, you'll find yourself turning into Howard Hughes if you don't get out of the house sometimes. So take a notepad and pen to your local coffeehouse or library and write there. Stick to your schedule, just write somewhere other than home.

- ◆ Let your neighbors and friends know you're working, not watching old movies. If you don't, you may find yourself the block baby-sitter or errand runner. Be firm and practice saying, "I'm sorry, but I'm working; I can't pick up your dry cleaning for you or baby-sit your son."

- ◆ Let the answering machine pick up the phone, and don't answer the door. You aren't home, you're writing.

Other than these few tips, there really isn't much more to say about time management. You just need to do it—write! If you want it (the finished book) badly enough, you'll do it.

Do It Again!

Remember when you were in school you'd sit down and write an essay straight through from start to finish and hand it in? Professional writers don't work like that. You spend a good amount of time first getting ready to write—researching, brainstorming, outlining—you write, and then you revise. And it's no exaggeration to say that most writing is revision. Because a lot of that happens after you start working with an editor, I go into the different parts of that process in Chapter 23. But as you get started, be aware that you should be going back and revising everything you write.

Read it over, maybe out loud. Ask if the story does what you want it to do. If it doesn't, dig in and change it. Remember—it's always easier to revise than to write. Of course, you can go too far with revision. There's a point where more revision is just avoiding the dreaded time when you show your work to someone else. How do you know when you've reached that point? You'll have to learn your own work habits, but watch out for revisions that don't change much. Are you changing a word here and there on each round, just tinkering? Or are you switching back and forth between two approaches? Both of these are clues that you're really done with the piece, for now, and that it's time to see what someone else thinks of it. Before you send it to a publisher, get some good feedback on it, as you will learn how to do in Chapter 4.

The Least You Need to Know

- Knowing what you like to read will help guide you in discovering what you might like to write.

- Systematic use of a journal can help you grow as a writer.

- Creativity exercises will help you explore your interests and improve your writing.

- Set a schedule for yourself.

- Revise, revise, revise—but know when to stop.

Chapter 3

Survey Course: The World of Children's Literature

In This Chapter

- Why your audience is so important
- Find out where to learn about the different areas of children's literature
- Learn about which children's books are most respected by librarians and other adults
- Discover good ways to learn what children like to read

Crucial to writing or illustrating for children is acquiring an understanding and knowledge of what children want to read, have read, and continue to read. You need to immerse yourself in the world of children's literature. Just as it's not enough to think you have a good idea for a business and then plunge yourself and your money into it, it's not enough to assume children's books are the right thing for you. What would you do in the case of a business? You'd research your prospects. Check out the competition. Look at how a similar business might have thrived in the past. The same goes for children's books. You need to immerse yourself.

Try It, You'll Like It

Remember how Mom used to nudge you into exploring new foods? "Try it. You'll like it," she'd say, as she'd thrust avocados or a new casserole on your plate. And as you grew up, you found many new favorites by listening to her, right? Well, children's literature is kind of like trying foods. There is no one right way to write or illustrate or one group who will be your audience. You'll find many reading levels, age groups, styles of writing and illustration, and audiences. As a result, the tone you use in a book for a witty and worldly sixth-grade boy probably isn't the same tone you'd employ in a picture book for a toddler. Case in point: *Island of the Blue Dolphins* (an historical novel by Scott O'Dell) and *Goodnight Moon* (a picture book by Margaret Wise Brown, illustrated by Clement Hurd) are both considered classics of children's literature, but clearly the audience for each is vastly different.

To really get a feeling for what works for a toddler, 10-year-old, or early teen, you must get to know the various books out there and how the publishers differentiate the genres. Don't rely on your memories of the books you read as a child. Publishing is different today and is changing all the time.

How do you learn about books and genres? Find out what critics and librarians deem the best of the best in books for kids. Now, don't overreact. You don't need to go out and get a Ph.D. in children's literature. I'm just suggesting a crash course in finding your way to the reading rainbow.

The Classics

Who can forget his favorite bedtime story? I loved Virginia Lee Burton's *Mike Mulligan and His Steam Shovel.* My toddler daughter loves Molly Bang's *Ten, Nine, Eight.* Many titles endure the test of time and generations of readings: *Make Way for Ducklings, Curious George, Charlotte's Web.* Even more recent books, from picture books like Dr. Seuss's *Oh, the Places You'll Go,* Liz Rosenberg's *Monster Mama,* and Chris Van Allsburg's *The Polar Express* to novels by Judy Blume, Virginia Hamilton, or Lloyd Alexander, now rank as classics.

 Class Rules ⎯⎯⎯⎯⎯⎯⎯⎯⎯⎯⎯⎯⎯⎯⎯

> Don't assume that books you loved as a child are actual classics or would be loved by children today. New classics come along, and old ones retire. People tend to believe that "the classics" are a fixed pantheon, but in fact every generation adds and subtracts to suit new tastes, conditions, and assumptions about what is good for children.

Although you may rattle off the titles of adult classics—such as *The Great Gatsby, Great Expectations,* or *The Odyssey*—getting to know titles throughout the many age levels and genres in the children's area may prove more difficult. Here's an introduction to this world—we zero in on the many kinds of children's books in Chapters 9 and 10.

Ask a Librarian

If you haven't read a children's book in 30 years, and don't know where to start, go ask your local children's librarian to show you around the world of classic children's literature. Children's librarians are experts on the classics and the very latest new books, and chances are they'll enjoy sharing their expertise with you. Follow these steps to ensure you receive some good take-home reading material:

◆ Make sure you hold an active library card. You'll want to check out titles to read and study.

◆ Call the library and ask whether a children's resource specialist or a librarian specializing in children's literature is available at the location. If so, ask to speak to that person. If not, find out who handles the children's books.

◆ If your local branch doesn't have a children's area, find out about a branch or a main library that does. Call them.

◆ After you have the librarian on the phone, explain that you are researching children's literature and, when convenient, would like the librarian to give you an overview of the classics, as well as pull several examples within different categories and age levels for you to check out and read. Make the appointment and keep it.

If your local library doesn't have much of a children's collection, or is too far away for easy access, your local school is an alternative resource. If your children attend school, you have a very good reason to find out what books the kids are reading at what level and to ask about other recommended books.

Playground Stories

This chapter advises you to consult experts, children, bestseller lists, and "best of" lists, but personal experience says that all of this should lead in one direction: developing your own taste. When I was getting started in children's publishing, which wasn't as long ago as you might think, I read Alison Lurie's *Don't Tell the Grown-Ups: The Subversive Power of Children's Literature.* This had a big influence on my developing tastes, because the book provided support for ideas I already had.

Finding the Very Best

Newspapers, magazines, and even television shows often put together "best of" lists that you can consult for guidance. Some come out at the end of the year, while others are more occasional. For example, *School Library Journal*, one of the nation's most respected reviewers of children's books, got together a panel of experts as the millennium approached to determine the "100 Significant Books" of the twentieth century. The list was published in their January 2000 issue. Here are a some examples from the list you might not know:

♦ *Tuck Everlasting*, by Natalie Babbitt

♦ *FreightTrain*, by Donald Crews

♦ *And Then What Happened, Paul Revere?*, by Jean Fritz

♦ *Shapes and Things*, by Tana Hoban

♦ *Chicka Chicka Boom Boom*, by Bill Martin Jr. and John Archimbault

♦ *The Alfred Summer*, by Jan Slepian

If you want to learn more, consult a guide book. Consider Anita Silvey's *The Essential Guide to Children's Books and Their Creators*. She's the former editor of the *Horn Book Magazine*, a highly respected children's book journal. Her guide compiles hundreds of entries on noted authors and illustrators, plus essays on specific genres. It's a great book to keep with you throughout your career.

Hot! Do Touch That!

Beyond immersing yourself in the classics, you also need to know what's hot now—what kids are reading and parents are buying for their kids today—besides *Harry Potter*, please! After all, there are thousands of new children's books published every year in the United States and Canada. Old standbys do retain steady sales year after year, but it's worthwhile to keep a finger on the pulse of kids' immediate reading preferences. It may seem like an overwhelming endeavor as you explore all the new titles bursting forth from the publishers, but there remain ways to streamline your mission. Follow the leader as we return to the library.

Back to the Library

Start again with a live source. Perhaps when you return all those classics that you checked out, you should ask the librarian to show you the hot titles of today. If the books are really hot, there may be a waiting list at the library for specific titles. Join the list—but at least you get an idea of what kids are enjoying nowadays. You might also ask for "Children's Choices," a list created by the International Reading Association and the Children's Books Council, which the library might have on hand.

Can You Keep a Secret?

What books do children themselves like? You could poll everyone under the age of 18 in your neighborhood. Or for a wider perspective, get your hands on the annual IRA/CBC "Children's Choices" list. You can find the latest list on the website of the Children's Book Council at www.cbcbooks.org/. Children in schools all over the United States vote for this list annually.

Here a Bookseller, There a Bookseller

Another great way to get up to date on the latest and greatest books for kids is by visiting the children's section of your local bookstore. Just by virtue of filling the shelves, employees in this department will know what's selling. They see what children and young adults pluck from the rack—and they may have noticed that these self-selected titles are quite different from what parents and grandparents are buying. Bookstore staff also may perform during story times at the stores and gain a good idea of those picture books that keep little ones interested.

Lynne went undercover in the children's department of a major superstore and asked the department supervisor a few questions. She asked first for hot young reader choices—books to give an elementary school student to read. The employee immediately said, "Anything with a timeless theme—like friendship or conflict—how about *The Wind in the Willows* by Kenneth Grahame? Or if you're interested in something more contemporary, I see a lot of kids buying titles from Lemony Snicket's *A Series of Unfortunate Events*." So we got a classic (*The Wind in the Willows* is on the *School Library Journal's* list of 100!) *and* a contemporary bestseller for kids. Similarly, when asked about picture books, the bookseller pulled everything by Margaret Wise Brown (*Hello!*, *Goodnight Moon*, *Runaway Bunny*), the classics,

Can You Keep a Secret?

Another way to find out about what's hot in the bookstores is to consult the bestseller lists. Both *Publishers Weekly* and *The New York Times* produce children's bestseller lists. Of course, in many cases the books on these lists are the ones with name recognition or big promotion budgets, but it doesn't hurt to learn about that side of things, too.

and a warm, new book called *No Matter What* by Debi Gliori that the bookseller offered as a title preschoolers really liked at story time.

Booksellers also meet with sales representatives from all the book publishers, who provide overviews of all the new titles launching each season. Pick the brain of a bookseller; you'll probably find yourself wading through piles of really wonderful new literature and classic stuff, too. Incidentally, Lynne bought *No Matter What*—to the delight of her twins, who ask for a nightly reading now.

Stop, Look, and Listen: Talk to Children

Most children tend to be honest and direct, so talk to children. Ask the kids of your uncles, cousins, neighbors, and friends what they like to read—and ask your own kids, too. If they feel comfortable with you, they'll call 'em like they see 'em—though they do like to make adults happy, so don't telegraph the answers you want to hear when discussing books with them. Don't suggest possible titles, and don't settle for what they read in school. Ask them what they read when they can choose the book. Children's tastes can outweigh any marketing plans. The initial popularity of the Harry Potter series came from word-of-mouth through kids, not what the publisher did. That's kid power!

If you're able to gather up a group and talk about certain books, do it. Perhaps a teacher you know will welcome you as a guest storyteller, or you might even become a regular volunteer. Bring a stack of various picture books and read for half an hour to first graders. Read the books beforehand, so you can keep your eyes on the children and not on the page. Gauge their interest and reaction to the material. Be careful of your delivery. You don't want to bore the kids with a monotone reading, but you also don't want to slant their reaction by giving an animated show either. This experience will help you gauge reactions if you ever try out your writing on children, a tricky thing to do that is discussed in more detail in Chapter 12.

It all comes down to this: You want to write or illustrate for children. So get to know what they find amusing, interesting, or fascinating.

CAUTION

Class Rules

Children's honesty is expressed by their bodies. If you're reading a picture book to a toddler, and she starts to squirm, she's not interested. Now you need to find out why. Try different books and see which she prefers. You can do the same thing with older children; just be sure you pay attention to their body language, not what they tell you afterward.

The Least You Need to Know

◆ Recognize that there are various styles of writing and illustrating for children. There is a difference between what a toddler enjoys and what a teen enjoys, but they are both categorized as children's literature.

◆ Study myriad works—from classic picture books to contemporary young adult novels. You can't illustrate or write for kids if you don't know what they read.

◆ Get help on your quest for kids' literature by asking a librarian, bookseller, or child to lead you toward what's out there and what's selling.

◆ Start to develop a sense of what children like, and how it's different from what adults want them to like.

Chapter 4

Why Create a Children's Book—and Why Not?

In This Chapter

◆ Why a desire for money and fame can let you down

◆ How your wishes for children can affect the way you work

◆ Why (and why not) self-expression and a love of the craft can be a good way to go

◆ How likely you are to succeed

◆ How some others have succeeded

We all have reasons for doing what we do, whether that's becoming a parent or having another slice of cake. That's good—if we didn't have reasons, we wouldn't do it. But when we don't understand our own motives, they can affect what we do in unexpected and possibly damaging ways. And that's bad.

This happens with children's books, too. The motives and reasons that lead us to work on children's books are as varied and different as people are, of course, but those who have been in the business for a while will tell you that they all boil down to one or a combination of a few. Some want fame or money. Others want to teach children something or to make them feel good about themselves. Still others write or illustrate as a means of self-expression.

This chapter covers motives and explains the effects they can have. You'll learn how your motives can affect the work you do, for better and for worse, and how they can affect your ability to stay in the field for the long haul.

I Want Money, but I'll Settle for Fame

If you judge by what you read in the newspapers and see on television, authors of books for adults can expect million-dollar advances and national book tours, not to mention appearance on *Charlie Rose* and other television shows. Children's books don't get quite so much attention, or at least they didn't until J. K. Rowling's *Harry Potter* books, each of which has sold millions of copies. Reading about them, it's tempting to see this as an opportunity. Because children aren't as discerning as adults, and their books aren't as long (again with the exception of Harry Potter, of course), it must be easier to write or illustrate for them. This must be a path to fame and fortune!

If that's what you're hoping, wake up and smell the hot chocolate. Like the 100-foot waves in the *Perfect Storm*, several factors came together to create the once-in-a-century *Harry Potter* phenomenon. No other book has ever sold as well. It may sound like I'm going out on a limb, but I believe that in the next 50 years, no other children's book, either on its own or in a series, will be as successful as the *Harry Potter* series.

> **Class Rules**
>
> Trends are a will-o'-the-wisp. Chase one, and by the time you've got a manuscript done and maybe even approved, a new trend has popped up. Stories based on current events go stale even faster. Because it takes two years to do a good job with a picture book, your hot item will have cooled off by the time it's on the market.

What's the harm of trying to emulate this kind of success, if it gets you motivated? The danger is that if a desire for fame and fortune is what drives you, you can end up chasing the trends and the "hot" areas of the market. A few years ago, for example, you might have tried to write a scary/funny series à la the *Goosebumps* series—but by the time you finished it, the market had moved on. Or it might lead you into developing a "commercial" illustration style, to the detriment of the quality of your work. Ask any published authors or illustrators, and they'll tell you that it's better to do what you like to do, or you won't be able to stick to it.

It's a Living

It's also true that in a more modest way, money *can* motivate you, if only to keep you at your work. Writing or illustrating can be a full-time job. This takes dedication, the ability to juggle multiple projects, and not least the will to face down the fear that sometime soon—tomorrow, next week, next year—you will run out of inspiration and out of income. Jennifer Armstrong, a successful full-time writer of fiction and nonfiction, comments:

> I don't know that I believe in inspiration, frankly. Either you want to write or you don't, but there won't be a beam of light coming through the window and into your ear.

> I always have multiple projects underway, so there's always something that has to be done. Deadlines are powerful motivators, as are mortgage payments and other bills. I've seldom known that whip not to work. I may be among a small group of writers for children and young adults who actually do make a living at this. I have to get my work done. That's all there is to it.

She has arrived at this point after several years of work, of course, and many successful writers and illustrators never do make their work a full-time job, but it is a possibility, with persistence and discipline. So appearing on *Charlie Rose* may be out of reach, but if you want to write or illustrate, you may eventually earn a living at it.

What kind of a living can you earn, you ask? There's no simple answer to that question. There's J. K. Rowling, of course, but let's be more realistic. There are a handful, perhaps a few handfuls, of people who may be making hundreds of thousands if not millions of dollars annually, largely because their books have been turned into TV series or movies: Marc Brown, creator of the popular *Arthur* books, is one such person. Many more people, like Jennifer Armstrong, make a full-time job out of writing or illustrating, perhaps combining it with school appearances or a similar related sideline. They have a solid middle-class income, but no more. And for the vast majority, working in children's books is what they do in the time they can find outside of their "real" job and their family life. Unfortunately, there's no telling which group you'll end up in, so I advise not making your income a key measure of success.

Vocabulary List

A story in which the moral or message the author wants to convey overwhelms the plot is called **pedantic** by editors. It's a story that teaches, but in a narrow way.

I Want to Be the Teacher

You love the way that children ask questions. Or maybe you are disturbed by the way in which children are raised today, or by the influence of the media. You feel that you have something to teach children. This is a worthy motive, but how will it affect your writing? Your desire to teach can powerfully affect your writing (or your illustrations, for that matter), whether it's fiction or nonfiction.

Writing fiction, in picture book or novel form, is one way to teach. If something bad happens to a child who acts in a certain way, the author hopes that this will teach the reader a lesson. This can be done effectively, and not so effectively. When a story is overwhelmed by its message, editors dismiss it as *pedantic*, and reject it immediately. Here's an example of a pedantic story.

Mary Who Didn't Listen

by P. Dan "Tick" Underdown

Once upon a time there was a little girl named Mary. She was like most little girls her age, which was six. She liked ice cream, she liked to play, and she liked to take care of her kitty. But in one way, Mary was not like other little girls. She never listened to her parents.

One day, Mary was playing *Treasure Chase* on the Zinblendo console for the TV. A fire truck went past, blowing its siren and making a big racket. Mary's kitty was scared and hid under the sofa. But Mary didn't hear the siren, she was so caught up in getting the next Gold Treasure. Mary played for hours. She was a very inattentive little girl. When her mother called her to supper, she didn't hear her. Her mother called her again, and still Mary didn't hear. Mary's supper was getting cold, and her father had to come upstairs and unplug the TV to get Mary to pay attention. Her mother and father were angry and said to her, "You are becoming Mary Who Doesn't Listen!"

The next day in school, Mary was drawing a picture of her kitty in her notebook when her teacher called on her. But Mary didn't hear her. Mrs. Maestra had to walk to her desk and close Mary's notebook before Mary would look up. Mrs. Maestra said, "You are Mary Who Doesn't Listen!"

And so it went on. Mary was so lost in her own little world that she never heard what anyone said to her, and she truly was Mary Who Didn't Listen.

But one day, Mary and all her friends were going to go to Playland, look at the kitties and puppies in the pet shop next door, and then have ice cream, to celebrate the end of school. While she waited for her friends to come, Mary started playing her favorite game on the Zinblendo upstairs.

When Sally's mother called for Mary to come get in the van, Mary didn't hear her. Sally and her mother and all Sally's friends called, but Mary didn't hear them. Mary's mother and father did, but they didn't say anything because they knew that their little girl needed to learn a lesson. Soon Sally's mother gave up, and she drove all the girls to Playland, leaving Mary behind.

Much later, Mary felt tired and stopped playing her game. Then she looked up. It was starting to get dark, and she realized that she had missed the trip to Playland. She was very upset, and she ran downstairs and said to her parents, "I'm going to listen from now on so I don't miss anything ever again!"

And do you know what? She did just that. She became Mary Who Did Listen, and she was a much happier little girl. So if you don't listen, watch out, because you might miss something.

What's wrong with this story? We know nothing about Mary beyond her problem, which is that she doesn't listen, and nothing happens to her but an experience that teaches a lesson. Even worse, P. Dan "Tick" keeps hitting us over the head with the "bad" behavior the child has. There is no humor and little dialogue. Imagine the illustrations that would carry the same message—literal and unimaginative, they would focus narrowly on Mary's bad behavior and its consequences. Put the text and illustrations together, and you'd get a book few children would want to read again, or even to finish.

If you want to teach children, don't despair. There are ways you can do it and be effective. In fiction, use humor and exaggeration, as in the classic *Struwwelpeter* stories. These classic stories, originally published in Germany in 1848, each feature a child whose outrageously bad behavior leads to a rather gruesome end—one is eaten by a lion, one starves to death, and so on. Children old enough to recognize them as fantasies find them extremely funny, and take them no more seriously than the violence they see all the time in cartoons. At the same time, they get the point.

Today, we take a gentler approach, but the humor of bad examples and the lesson they teach is exactly what Nancy Carlson plays on in *How to Lose All Your Friends*. David Wisniewski pokes fun at grown-ups while finding new reasons for the "rules" they enforce in *The Secret Knowledge of Grown-Ups*. You get the idea: A story in which a child who doesn't clean up his bedroom ends up being trapped inside could have a similar effect.

For older children, dramatizing a situation instead of talking about rules, even humorously, can work. Do you want to teach children about the dangers of drugs? Consider a novel in which one of the characters has a bad experience with drugs—but the author must let the experience develop naturally and refrain from commenting on it even through the mouth of another character. Trust your ability as a storyteller. If the story tells itself, and the consequences of a particular action are clear, the reader will get the point with no need to underline it during the story or repeat it at the end. Vicarious experience puts your message across.

On the other hand, you could teach through nonfiction. Again, your mission could overwhelm your writing. Even nonfiction—particularly nonfiction!—must be interesting. A list of facts or an essay that reads like an entry from an encyclopedia is a good solid piece of factual material. But it's also writing that has been overwhelmed by the author focusing too much on what she wanted to say, and not enough on how to say it.

Instead, present your material simply and clearly, with a narrative if possible. Consider a book like Eve Bunting's *Ducky*, about a load of plastic toys washed off a freighter that ultimately became an opportunity for scientists to learn about the currents of the Pacific Ocean. The story and illustrations bring this event to life through the "eyes" of one plastic duck; compare this to newspaper stories from the time to gain some insight into one way in which events or information can be transformed. For older children, Laurence Pringle's *An Extraordinary Life* (which I worked on when I was at Orchard Books) follows the life and migration of a Monarch butterfly, in story format. Again, there is plenty of information presented here, but it's woven skillfully into the story.

Does nonfiction have to be presented in a fictional form to be effective? No, but don't forget to make an effective presentation, and to use narrative form if it works, as Patricia Lauber does in *Volcano!* and Susan Campbell Bartoletti does in *Growing Up in Coal Country*.

So if you want to teach, you can, but don't lose track of the fact that you are a storyteller first of all.

I Get to Be the Mommy

You like taking care of children. Maybe you are a parent. You want to write stories that will help children feel happy and especially happy with themselves. This, too, is a worthy motive, but if it leads to you removing all conflict and difficulty from a story, it's gone too far.

In my work at Charlesbridge and other publishers, I saw many manuscripts submitted in which the author had worked very hard to remove anything painful or dangerous from the story. The following story shows this impulse in action.

The Happy Child

by Syrup E. Underdown

Billy was a happy child. He lived in a big house with his mommy, his daddy, his dog Spot, and his sisters and brothers. Every day when he woke up he smiled, because he knew he was going to have fun! He didn't care if it was a school day or a weekend day. He knew he would enjoy it.

One day, he woke up and smiled even wider than usual, because he was going fishing with his Grandpop. He got dressed and washed up. Then he went downstairs singing "I'm going fishing!" When he got downstairs he said, like he always did, "Good morning, Mom!" and, "Good morning, Dad!" He felt it truly was a good morning.

They smiled and said, "Good morning, Billy!"

Billy said, "Guess what? I'm going fishing with Grandpop! We're going to take Spot, and we're going to have lots of fun."

"I know, Billy, I'm sure you'll have lots of fun," said his mom.

Billy sat down at the table, unfolded his napkin, and ate his cereal. Just when he had finished, the doorbell rang. Billy jumped up and ran to the door. Just as he had hoped, it was his Grandpop! Billy called out, "Hi, Grandpop! I can hardly wait to go fishing."

"Hi, Billy, I'm sure we're going to have lots of fun," replied his Grandpop, smiling. When Grandpop smiled, Billy thought he smiled even more than most people because all the wrinkles on his cheerful face smiled, too.

As soon as Grandpop had said hi to Billy's dad and Billy's mom (who was also Grandpop's daughter) and all of Billy's brothers and sisters, they grabbed the fishing tackle from the back porch, got Spot from the backyard, and drove off to the fishing hole.

They were sure they were going to have a great time. And they were right! Billy caught lots of fish and had a grand time with his Grandpop. He was one happy boy when he fell asleep that night, and dreamed of going fishing again ….

The End

What's the problem with this story? To start with, it isn't a story. Nothing happens. Billy accomplishes nothing, because there is no tension or problem. Syrup E. has worked so hard to make the writing safe and reassuring that it has lost the feel of real life. Saccharine-sweet illustrations would accompany this one-dimensional narrative.

What to do? It is more truly and deeply reassuring to a child to see a character realistically overcome a difficulty than to read a story about a world in which there are no difficulties, because, much as we would like to believe otherwise, children know quite well that life is about difficulties and overcoming them. How could they not? They are in the middle of the process of growing from being helpless infants to resourceful, self-confident adults (or so we hope), and as they do they experience many triumphs (and failures). You do them no favors if you sugarcoat the world for them, and your writing suffers.

Published authors know this, and you can find many wonderful examples of books that give true comfort to a child by showing a child dealing realistically with a real problem. For a child confronting death, for example, you can find picture books, such as Judith Viorst's *The Tenth Good Thing About Barney*, nonfiction, such as Janet Bode's *Death Is Hard to Live With*, or novels, such as Katherine Paterson's *Bridge to Terabithia*. Parents are there to take care of children, but for you as a writer the challenge is to tell the story.

Having an Impact

You might have intuited this idea already from "I Want to Be the Teacher" and "I Get to Be the Mommy," but in case you didn't: One of the joys of writing and illustrating for children is that you *do* have a real impact on children's lives. Published authors hear all the time from children who have been affected by their work. Children will learn from, be comforted by, be challenged by, and be amused by your work, often in ways you can't anticipate.

Ironically, this is most likely to happen when you've successfully curbed an impulse to lecture or muted a desire to give a reader a verbal hug. Words and pictures that speak directly to children help them make sense of their world and their feelings, and have the biggest impact.

The next section explores how some creators approach their work, so that they can have that kind of impact.

Look What I Did!

An enduring motive for writers and illustrators is self-expression, finding satisfaction through the use of words or pictures to get across their feelings and experiences. This approach is the one that is most likely to keep you going if you aren't published yet, or you are published but can't land a new contract. Your own satisfaction with the way you put images or words together needs no outside validation.

The danger of self-expression is that you can get so caught up in your own pursuit that you lose track of your audience, and so create work pleasing to you, but to no one else. So develop a thick skin, but don't close your ears completely to what people—critique group members, your editor, a reviewer, a thoughtful child reader—say about your work. And don't lose track of your ultimate goal, which is producing a book that forms a coherent and satisfying whole. Self-expression can mean different things.

Personal Passions

Is there some area of knowledge about which you care deeply? In your passion for the subject, you'll find the motivation to get it across clearly, with the dramatic and exciting aspects of it that grab you right "there" to grab your reader.

Writing or illustrating can lead you to learning even more about a subject that intrigues you, and from there to other things about which you want to learn. For example, illustrator Michael Rothman did wonderful work for Sneed Collard's *The Forest in the Clouds*, showing the world of the Costa Rican "cloud forest." He already had considerable experience with rain forests, but this book gave him the opportunity to learn more, and he put what he learned into his illustrations. I talked with the noted nonfiction writer James Cross Giblin about his recent biography of Adolf Hitler. Jim told me that he got interested in this grimly fascinating subject while writing his biography of Charles Lindbergh, the flawed American hero—his flaws most apparent in his open sympathy for the Nazis. So follow your desire for understanding, and pass on what you've learned.

Open to Inspiration

When asked what inspires him, published poet and picture book author Charles Ghigna replied:

> Nature, kids, animals, sports, travel, the weather, daily celebrations of life, and my own childhood memories. My son, Chip, and my wife, Debra, also inspire many of my poems, as do my editors, neighbors, and friends. I often receive inspiration from reading newspapers, magazines and books. I guess one might say that everything inspires me!

Can You Keep a Secret?

No motive will carry you further than your own internal motive of a desire to express yourself. Your own innate drive to learn, to be moved, and to find fresh language to express your passions is what will keep you going when dreams of fame or fortune don't succeed.

A writer or illustrator with this attitude—one that you can cultivate—will always be motivated, and always have fresh ideas. Give yourself time to notice what is around you, and time to think about where it could lead you.

The Inner Child

Jan Wahl, an experienced picture-book author with more than 100 books to his credit, has this to say about writing for children:

> I don't try to write for editors or for librarians or for teachers—and, especially, I don't write for reviewers. I don't try to write for any specific child. I feel that's a big mistake.

Jan is not concerned with how people are going to react, and he doesn't even feel that a child he knows, or a classroom of children, can give him a clue as to whether or not he is succeeding. To him, writing for children means something else:

> It means enjoying afresh, each day, those insights and glimpses of the universe I had as a child. A writer can't ask anything more than this—what is it? That everything seems new.

However you do it—by following your own interests, by keeping yourself open, or by listening to your inner child—express yourself. No one else has exactly your point of view or your way of putting things. Expressing oneself, and getting better and better at doing so, is a powerful motive. Hold onto it, develop it, and you'll find satisfaction, even if you never get published.

The Chance of Getting There

No matter what your motives, you want to know what chance you have of getting published. The odds don't look good when you consider that there are usually thousands of manuscripts going through the doors of a typical publisher in a year, only a few of which are accepted for publication; publishers are similarly flooded with samples from illustrators. But consider that maybe 90 percent of those submissions and samples are just not very good, or are completely wrong for that publisher. Those who keep working at their craft, and who find the right publishers, have a chance of getting there. They'll still have to compete with the others who have what it takes, but with the help of this book you can get into that group.

And Stephen Mooser, president of the Society of Children's Book Writers and Illustrators (SCBWI), says this about the path to success:

> In my years with the SCBWI I have seen hundreds of people sell their first book. None of these books, however, came easy. They studied the market, they studied published children's books, they wrote and rewrote and wrote again.

They were persistent and they succeeded, even if it took 10 years. There is a lot of competition and you have to give it your best. I've published 60 books, but probably had that many rejected.

> **Playground Stories**
>
> Sneed Collard, a well-known writer of nonfiction for children, says: "Writing is a *long* road. I've been writing for 18 years now and only in the last 5 have I begun to understand what I'm doing. If you're not willing to put in the years and continue to grow, this field isn't for you. If you are willing to keep learning and growing, however, children's book writing can be an enormously satisfying ride."

I Got a Star

And real success is possible, though it can take many years. What does success mean? What "success" is varies from one person to another, but you may be surprised to hear that for most, it's not fame, or money (though a steady income is a good thing) that matters.

An author I know, Miriam Bat-Ami, won a prestigious award for *Two Suns*, an historical fiction book about a detention camp for European refugees in upstate New York during World War II. Her success did not come out of nowhere: in the early 1990s, I had published a picture book and a short novel of hers. A few years later, with another publisher, she published a novel. *Two Suns* came from a third publisher, six years after her first book. She tells us she needed that time, not only to work on the book but also to find the right publisher and the right editor for it. What does she most appreciate about her success? You might be surprised to hear:

> Success is fun because I get to see a plus figure on my royalty statement. Seeing a negative one is very depressing, as is seeing negative reviews.

> But there are things you can see with books that may not be the "successful" ones and those you remember. I do like seeing a teenager at a table next to mine reading my book and seeming so concentrated on it … Success is having someone come up to my son and say she wants to borrow another copy of my book to lend a friend. "Hey," I think, "she can buy it, but, hey, she likes it enough to ask for another copy." So I lend it out. But real success has to do with self-respect, and successfully working with an editor to tell the story I want to tell, and those are connected to my sense of myself as a writer.

There aren't any guarantees. You'll need persistence (possibly years of it), some talent, and a little luck, luck that you may be able to create, to have a chance of getting there. Do you have those prerequisites? You won't know until you try, so get to it.

The Least You Need to Know

- You probably won't become rich or famous in children's books, but you might be able to make a full-time job out of it.

- If you want to teach, find ways to dramatize your lessons or to present information in a narrative or other engaging form.

- To help children feel better about themselves, show children living in the real world and triumphing, not cocooned in a safe fantasy.

- One of the joys of working on children's books is the impact you can have on children's lives.

- Self-expression as a motive can lead to self-indulgence, but it's also an ever-expanding reason to keep working.

- Success is not assured, but the journey is worth it if you find the craft itself satisfying.

Chapter 5

The Piggy Bank and the Notebook

In This Chapter

- ◆ Supplies you'll need
- ◆ Organizational tips
- ◆ What files you may need
- ◆ A checklist to use before you sit down to write
- ◆ Great reference books to have handy
- ◆ Time-management tips
- ◆ The truth about income

Now we're getting to the nitty-gritty of the business of being a writer; if you're an illustrator, much of what is covered here will be relevant to you, too. (Turn to Chapter 6 for more details.) Although it may seem romantic to say to others at a cocktail party over canapés and Chardonnay, "Well, I'm a writer of children's books," hard work and organizational skills go with this title. So buck up and learn what you'll need to get started and compete in this "playground" of publishing.

This chapter covers the tools—both technological and traditional—that you'll need to succeed in writing (especially after you earn a book contract) and also some organizational and time-management tips. Moreover, we'll go over the truth about money.

School Supplies

Remember when the teacher sent you home on the first day of school with a list of required supplies? Today, as you embark upon a career as a children's book author, you'll also need certain tools and supplies.

So what do you really need—at minimum—to get started? Actually, not too much. In fact, you probably already possess many of the items in the following list:

- **A telephone.** This is a business, after all. You will find that you use the telephone often and for long periods as a writer—even as a writer of children's books. You'll make calls to colleagues, editors, contacts, and sources for research.

- **A computer with word processing capabilities and a printer.** An editor won't accept your manuscript scribbled out in pencil. If you can afford to own a computer, buy one. Otherwise, you can type up your final drafts at a friend's house or rent time on a computer at stores such as Kinko's.

- **Backup hardware capabilities.** If you have a computer, make sure you also have a way to back up your files—by saving them to a disk or a backup tape, burning a CD-ROM, or sending them to sites on the Internet—so that if something goes wrong with your computer you won't have to retype all your work.

Playground Stories

Nowadays, just about everyone writes on computers using word processing programs that do the duty of typewriters and more. If you're on a budget, and you're using a computer for writing only, you don't have to have the latest PC or Mac computer equipped with the latest version of Word. When I was freelancing a few years back, a three-year-old computer and a word processor called Word Express did everything I needed. You don't need to buy new. A 2-year-old, refurbished computer from a local store for less than $500 will suit you just fine.

- **Internet access.** You need Internet access either from home or by the hour at a public library or a retail store that rents computers. You may be thinking, "I'm going to write a children's book. I just need my imagination! Why do I need the Internet?" First, you can do a lot of research online. Second, you'll find fabulous and helpful information for writers there.

◆ **Electronic mail, known more familiarly as e-mail.** Nowadays, you can't communicate with an editor without e-mail. It's also a great way to stay in touch with writing and illustrating buddies.

◆ **Standard desk supplies.** Think paper (for the printer, notes, outlines, scratch), pens, pencils, files, a stapler, paper clips, and anything else you use to keep life organized.

◆ **A filing cabinet.** You'll learn about organizing it and what types of files you'll find yourself making a little later in this chapter.

◆ **Access to a fax machine.** You probably don't need to own a fax machine, but do need to know where you can fax from in your neighborhood. If you have a modem on your computer, in many cases you'll be able to set it up to fax directly from your word processing program.

That's it! Given these items, you can compete and do business in the world of publishing.

Can You Keep a Secret? _____

Here are three of the many useful World Wide Websites you can find:

◆ Harold Underdown's web location at www.underdown.org for articles and useful links

◆ Aaron Shepard's personal site at www.aaronshep.com/index.html, to see what one author has done with his website

◆ The Society of Children's Book Writers and Illustrators at www.scbwi.org

Really Cool Toys

I just gave you the basic tools to get going on your writing endeavors. But a few other items may prove useful as your career develops, including the following:

◆ **Camera.** Who knows when inspiration will strike? A picture may indeed be worth a thousand words.

◆ **Dedicated phone line (second phone line).** When you spend time researching online, you won't miss calls if you have a dedicated line. Moreover, you can run your business of writing through this line and keep work and home separate.

◆ **Laptop computer.** Co-author of the first edition Lynne swears by this item. "We had a fire in our home while I was in the midst of writing several articles and a book. Luckily, I had a laptop because my desktop was destroyed." Within one day, Lynne was back online in a hotel room, plugged into her editors by e-mail, and she could continue to write and meet her deadlines.

◆ **Business cards.** Establish yourself as a writer. Don't invest in anything fancy, but do print up cards (perhaps on your own computer) with your name, phone, fax, home office address, and e-mail address. You'll be glad you have them when you can pull one out to pass to another writer, an editor, or anyone else you make as a contact in the publishing world.

A Place for Everything

It's all about a system, really. You need to find the system that works best for you. But regardless, don't delude yourself into thinking that disorganization is your system. Everything put neatly away in filing cabinets and desk drawers isn't necessary if you can find what you want in the umpteen stacks scattered around your workspace. And when you are writing, you don't need to have an empty desk. But to thrive as a writer, you'll need to take your supplies and set them up before you begin writing.

Many writers also can't break the momentum after they begin. If they stop writing, for example, to find a sharpened pencil—yikes!—they can't get back to it for hours, days, or months. So it really is best to consider several organizational ideas before writing. Just like a pilot observes a preflight checklist, you should observe a "prewrite" checklist to be sure you have the items you need. Have reference books, computer supplies, sharpened pencils, your notes, your files, extra paper, candy, or anything else you might need at hand, so that you don't have to break the flow.

Here a Book, There a Book, Everywhere a Book, Book!

You can't avoid it. You'll need to fill a shelf in your writing area with reference books. Reference books every writer should possess include the following:

◆ **Dictionary.** Get a comprehensive one. Don't pick up the 200-pager at the 99¢ clearance center or even a pocket paperback edition. We highly recommend a quality, sturdy, hardbound, heavy dictionary: *Webster's Third New International* (the reference book copyeditors and proofreaders turn to) or the more portable *Webster's Collegiate*.

◆ *Chicago Manual of Style.* This is the bible of editors and publishers everywhere. There's (almost) too much information. But then again, you never know when you'll need to know when to capitalize something or how a book is laid out, right?

- *Roget's Thesaurus.* Invest in a good, hardbound *Roget's* today and never fumble for a synonym, antonym, or perfect word choice again.

- **This book,** of course.

- Strunk and White's *The Elements of Style.*

Now, do you have your reference books handy? If so, check this item off.

Printing Your Proofs and Backing Up Your Work

Do you have …

- Paper for your printer?

- Ink or toner in the cartridge of your printer?

- A disk on which to save your work?

Even in our technological age where paper seems obsolete when we move documents via e-mail, you just may want to proof your work the old-fashioned way—on paper. Without any in the printer, you won't have the option. And even if you do have the paper, if you don't have ink in the printer cartridge, you can't print. Finally, make sure you own plenty of whatever you will use to back up your writing. Writer after writer can recall horror stories of entire works disappearing in the twitch of a computer. As mentioned before, it's always best to save all your work not only on the computer's hard drive but also on something you can take out of your work area as a backup. If you can sound off an affirmative for the above three items, check 'em off.

> **Class Rules** _____
>
> Do you need everything listed here to succeed? No. You'll know what you need and what you don't. But don't sabotage yourself. There is a minimum. You need writing tools, a quiet, distraction-free (and that means child-free) space in which to work, a work surface you don't have to clear off every time you want to use it, and a schedule your family and friends respect.

Red Rover, Red Rover, Send Research Right Over

Are your research, notes, and any other documents necessary for your writing present and within reach? You'll hate yourself if you sit down to write and can't find important facts pertinent to your story line. If they're handy, then good. Check it off the list and move on.

The Secret Files Garden

Part of maintaining your research is, of course, your file system. But how do you know what topics need their own files? You don't. You'll probably determine how to file things as you go along, but here are a few examples right now on some obvious (and not so obvious) choices.

Keep separate files for …

- ◆ **Book ideas.** As one idea develops after another, it's easy to forget new ones. Note down your ideas so you can come back to them. Use a notebook if that's easier.

- ◆ **Research of topics.** Make a folder for every book that's gone beyond the idea stage. Whenever you come across related information or find yourself musing about a character, stuff the results into that folder. Then when you're ready to work on that piece, just pull the file.

- ◆ **People.** You might choose to use experts in your writing or need to call upon experts for a project. Many writers keep files on people involved in a particular topic.

- ◆ **Contracts.** After you sign them for a book deal, keep them.

- ◆ **Submission letters and proposals.** Keep track of the submissions and proposals you've sent out. Maintain a separate file, perhaps even organized by months, with printed copies of your correspondence.

- ◆ **Business expenses.** Writing is a form of self-employment, so keep a file for expenses such as telephone calls, printer cartridges, and any other item you may be able to write off if you have proof you used it in the course of your business.

There's a Time and a Space for Everything

Many years ago, Virginia Woolf wrote about the importance of having a room of one's own. She pointed out that in Britain, women had problems finding a space to call their own in which to write and the time to do it. Women weren't perceived as potential writers. Times change, but the situation for writers of children's books in North America today is not much different from what Woolf described.

Most of you are women, and if you're not, hey, you're a guy in a profession that is devalued partly because it's mostly an occupation of women. You probably have a hard time getting people to take you seriously—possibly even the people in your own family. And as a result, you have a hard time getting the space and time to write.

But you know what? You need that space. You need a desk, and good light, and room for the books you may need to refer to, and hours of time during which you don't need to worry about being interrupted or needed.

Playground Stories

Don't have time to write? Make time. Susan Campbell Bartoletti wrote and published several books while teaching full-time: "In order to make time to write, I woke at 4 A.M. to write before school. (My dog wouldn't even get up with me!) With my sixth book contract, I left teaching to write full-time.

"The morning hours still work best for me, and I have my best writing days when I'm at the computer by 4. I enjoy the early morning hours, while it's still dark outside. Ideas grow in the dark. It's the perfect time for creating, for taking that which is without form and void and separating darkness and light. I always feel as though I'm working toward the light."

After you have that time and space—and if you don't insist on it, you won't get it!—you need to cultivate the discipline you must have if you are going to stick with writing for the long haul. You've got to have that "butt-in-chair" time if you are going to write in your journal, try some writing exercises, plan out a project, and actually write it. So as mentioned before, give yourself a schedule, too. Maybe you can't get up every morning at 4 A.M. to write. How about two hours three nights a week while the rest of the family is watching television? Throw in Saturday afternoon and you've got 10 hours a week of solid writing time. You can get a lot done. Just do your best to resist the temptation to do laundry, or wash the dishes, or do any of those things that suddenly seem so tempting when a blank page is staring up at you.

Jack and the Bean Stock: Income

So with all this writing, you'll soon be rolling in the big bucks, right? Well, wrong. Most writers for children do not work full-time at writing. Some hold down unrelated jobs. Others bring in money through related work we'll go into in Chapter 33. Those who do write full-time have reached this blissful state after what amounts to an apprenticeship of 5 to 10 years of learning. Please don't quit your day job yet!

Sad to say, you may never pay the bills with the royalties and advances from your book writing—even with several books on the market. Even if one or more books does well, income from book writing—any writing really—is sporadic. We hate to burst your bubble, but how many rich and famous children's book writers do you know or know of? Yes, there are a few. But don't count on getting rich from children's books.

The Least You Need to Know

◆ A writer today needs certain tools to compete in the publishing world and write. These are a computer, a phone, fax access, and online capabilities including e-mail.

◆ You'll want to organize your writing area and have necessary supplies, reference materials, and research readily available to you before you sit down to write.

◆ Set up a filing system now to keep all the tidbits of information and ideas easily accessible to you.

◆ No writer should be without a good dictionary and thesaurus.

◆ Self-starters succeed as writers; schedule time to write and stick to it.

◆ Don't think that you'll earn riches by writing children's books. In fact, keep your day job.

Chapter 6

I Like to Draw

In This Chapter

- ◆ The difference between illustration and fine art
- ◆ Why you need to go to school
- ◆ How to get set up to work
- ◆ How to tell if you're ready to start contacting publishers

So far, I've introduced you to the world of children's literature and to getting started as a writer. In this chapter, I'll look at the first steps you need to take if your focus is on illustration.

Why Illustrate?

Perhaps you like to paint or draw, and are now considering pursuing work in illustration. Why would you want to do that? And specifically, why would you want to illustrate for children's books?

I'll start by drawing a couple basic distinctions. If your calling is fine art, you create works from out of your head, with no limitation in subject or approach. If you are to make a living as a fine artist, you need to please only one other person, the person who purchases what you have created.

To *illustrate*, in contrast, you must start with someone else's text. Depending on the kind of illustration you are doing, your interpretation may have to be literal, or you may be able to bring considerable creative license to your work. But in either case, you must start from the text. Your audience is also very different; to succeed, you must ultimately please thousands of book purchasers—customers in book stores, librarians in charge of ordering books, teachers finding books to use in their classrooms.

Vocabulary List

To **illustrate,** if you look at the Latin roots of the word, means "to make bright," implying that the illustrator interacts with and adds to a text. At its best, illustration is not merely decorative (though it may be beautiful), and it does not create its own artistic world, ignoring the mood and setting of a text—it develops from and meshes with a text to create a new, coherent whole.

If the challenges of illustration engage your interest, then why illustrate for children? Not, I hope, because you've tried other fields and think that you might make some money here. You won't get rich as a children's book illustrator. And not, I hope, because you "love children." As I tried to demonstrate in Chapter 4, your feelings about children can have some unfortunate side effects on writing and illustrating for them. Instead, as any practicing illustrator will tell you, it's a love of this craft that will keep you going: the challenge of developing your own, unique style, rather than imitating what seems to be successful; the challenge of putting a picture book together, so that it functions as one single piece of art, not a series of disconnected illustrations; the challenge of showing character, interaction, and setting in a single piece for a jacket or textbook.

Does that sound good to you? Then let's get started.

Getting Started

Much of what you need to do now overlaps with what a writer needs to do. You need to have an understanding of what kinds of books are published for children, how to find the best ones, what the different parts of a book are called and what they do, and so on. So go ahead and read the rest of Parts 1 and 2, and then come back here. I'll be waiting.

You've read Parts 1 and 2? Great. Now it's time to move on.

Going to School (Again)

Though a lot of what writers and illustrators need to know and do is similar, there's one big difference. It's very hard, if not quite impossible, to succeed as a self-taught illustrator. Many writers pick up writing well after they leave college, perhaps when they have children, are able to hone their craft through writing and rewriting, and, eventually, get published. They don't need to go into a specialized writing program (though some do) because much of their education was built around reading and writing. Anyone who's graduated from a liberal arts college has spent years getting general training in dealing with words.

You can't do what a writer does! A typical college graduate does not have an equivalent amount of what you could call "visual literacy." Let's face it: Our schools do not spend much time teaching us how to draw and paint, or how to interpret images, or how to present ideas visually. Just as someone who left school after the third grade is going to have a hard time writing novels, even the most dedicated self-taught illustrator may lack the specific skills needed to illustrate effectively. Drawing human beings, for example, can be a big challenge, because our figures and faces are so complex—and because people are so intuitively familiar with them.

Does that mean you need to go back to school for two years and get a degree in illustration? Not necessarily—some coursework may be all you need. Art schools like the Rhode Island School of Design, which has a well-known illustration program, have set up Continuing Education programs for people needing some specific training. Check an art school near you, and see what's available.

Can You Keep a Secret?

While most authors pick up their pens some years after they leave college, most illustrators go to art school at some point. Publishers won't ask to see your resumé and diploma, but realistically, it's difficult to reach professional standards without some schooling.

Class Rules

In addition to going back to school, and as a reference you are likely to turn to over and over again, get your hands on Uri Shulevitz's book, *Writing with Pictures*. Shulevitz is a Caldecott Medal–winning illustrator with a career spanning 40 years. His book explains picture-book illustration with many examples and contains a detailed start-to-finish guide to creating one. Though written at a time when black-and-white and pre-separated art were the norm in children's books, the principles he reveals are still very relevant to today's full-color illustrations.

Get Set Up!

If you are going to illustrate well, you need a work area. In a pinch, a writer can just work on the family computer, with a shelf or two set aside for supplies and reference books, but you need more space. You don't need a huge studio, but you do need a room apart from family hubbub, where you can work in quiet and leave pieces to dry, or pin up a sequence of illustrations, and not worry that they will be disturbed. This could be the guest bedroom, or a nook up in the attic, so long as it's your space. Get a drawing table, so that you can adjust the angle and height of your workspace, as soon as you can afford it.

Here are some other things you might want in your workspace:

- ◆ Supplies! Have *ample* quantities of your favorite paper, brushes, pencils, or whatever you use. You don't want to have to go get more while you're in the middle of a picture.

- ◆ A big piece of corkboard or something similar, so you can pin up sketches or a sequence of drawings.

- ◆ Visual reference materials: art books, files of pictures you've clipped, photo books.

- ◆ No distractions! Unless you work on a computer, don't have one in the room. No TV, of course, though a radio is okay if you like to listen to music while working.

Make your own list, based on what you want in your space, and make your space what you want it to be.

Get Some Books

Illustrators need a reference shelf. Start with Uri Shulevitz's *Writing with Pictures*, and consider getting some of the following, which will provide guidance in technique, book design, type, and other basics:

- ◆ *Picture This! How Pictures Work*

- ◆ *Words into Type*

- ◆ *Encyclopedia of Illustration Techniques*

- ◆ *The Graphic Artists Guild Handbook: Pricing and Ethical Guidelines*

- ◆ *Words About Pictures: The Narrative Art of Children's Picture Books*

For brief descriptions of these books, see Appendix B.

Are You Ready?

So you've gone to art school, or taken some classes, and started building up a stack of samples. Is your work good enough for you to put together a portfolio, a process I'll describe in Chapter 14? Are you ready to start contacting publishers? How can you know? Well, sometimes you can show your art to a published illustrator or an art director at a conference for children's books writers and illustrators and get his feedback (this usually costs a small fee, although it might also be free).

If you can't get a professional's feedback, try self-assessment. Choose a publisher that you feel could be a good match for your book. Research the company's most recently published books, following the procedures outlined in Chapter 20. Choose three books that have illustrations that are similar in style and medium (such as paint or pastels) to yours, and get your hands on the illustrations through your local library system or bookstore. Look through all of them carefully. Check how the artists show characters in different situations, how they choose to use or not use different perspectives. See if you can get a sense of their pacing and how they create excitement. Look closely at how the illustrators depict movement and facial expressions. Whether or not they are showing animals or people, and regardless of whether the style is realistic or cartoonlike, evaluate how lively and real the characters seem.

Then turn to your own work. Are your characters as lively as those you see in the published books, or do they seem stiff or clumsy? Are your illustrations as varied and interesting? Does your book have pacing like theirs? Does it build to a climax? In short, can you confidently say that your work is at least as accomplished as that which you see in these published books? If you can't, then don't start marketing yourself yet. You won't get hired, and you'll just waste time and money that would be better spent on classes or self-directed illustration exercises.

> **CAUTION**
>
> **Class Rules**
>
> Sending out mailings and doing all the other things you need to do to make connections to a publisher are costly. Don't even think about doing them if you aren't ready. Take some more classes, set yourself projects like creating a picture-book version of a folktale, and keep striving to improve.

The Least You Need to Know

- Illustration requires the illustrator to work with the text, not just create a nice picture.

- Unlike writing, illustrating requires some specialized training.

- You need a workspace and some reference books to work on illustrating.

- Assess your work carefully before jumping into marketing yourself to publishers.

It's a BIG World

In This Chapter

- ◆ How the children's publishing industry has changed in the past 40 years
- ◆ Why there are more and more paperbacks
- ◆ How buyouts and mergers have created a small group of very large publishers
- ◆ Who buys children's books now and why
- ◆ How children's books are selling
- ◆ How the Internet is changing children's publishing

Once upon a time, children's book publishing was a genteel industry run by white-gloved ladies with backgrounds as librarians. Today, everything is different. Or so the story is usually told.

That genteel business may be something of a myth, but there's no denying that the business *has* changed. In this chapter, you'll find out how. You'll learn about the decline of the library market and the rise of the consumer market, the growth of paperbacks, and the buyouts that have hit publishing just as much as other industries. You'll also get an assessment of just how much the Internet has affected the business, so far.

And why do you need to know this? Because you need to know who's buying the books. The business is not what it was.

The Golden Age

Publishers have been making books for children for about as long as there have been printing presses. Right through the nineteenth century, however, these were sidelines to their main business of publishing books for adults. In the United States, the first companies to create their own children's book divisions, with their own staff, did so after the First World War.

In the 1920s and 1930s, other publishers followed suit, hiring librarians to run their children's divisions. Why librarians? Because children's books were mostly sold to libraries back then, so if a company wanted to make sure that a book would appeal to the library market, it made sense to let someone with library training decide what books to publish. Librarians knew what they wanted. Solid informational books like Hendrik Willem Van Loon's *The History of the World*, which won the first Newbery Medal, and folktale collections with Arthur Rackham–style illustrations were in demand.

This was a fairly cozy little business, but a profitable one. More than one company had its literary but money-losing adult division kept alive by the steady sales of its children's books. In the 1940s, following pioneering research into what appealed to children, books got livelier: The bright colors in *Goodnight Moon* don't look exceptional today, but it was a groundbreaking book when it was first published—and not much of a success at first, either. Influential librarians didn't like it.

Looking back, these times seem like a golden age. "Commercial" considerations didn't rule the business. Publishing quality books that conformed to a librarian's judgment of what was right for children was what publishers tried to do. This started to change as early as the 1950s, when *Sputnik* spurred investment in science education in the schools and in funding for nonfiction books for libraries.

Paperbacks: Fun and Cheap

The business really changed in the 1960s. Federal money from Lyndon Johnson's "Great Society" programs sparked a minor boom in children's publishing. All of a sudden, there were federal funds for schools and libraries to use to purchase books. Many more picture books, with more and more creative art, could be published. And publishers realized that Americans were not all white, and books that reflected our multiracial, multiethnic, multicultural society started to come out in increasing numbers. Ezra Jack Keats's *A Snowy Day*, a prize-winning book in 1963, was an early sign of the changes.

This attractive and still popular book was one of the very first to matter-of-factly feature an African American child, a boy named Peter, as he enjoyed a snowy day in his urban neighborhood.

The rise of the paperback, which began in the 1960s and continues to this day, was possibly a more significant if less known change. Until that time, quality publishers, the ones focusing on the library market, published only in hardcovers. Hardcover books were expensive, and so few families could buy them. But when books like *Charlotte's Web* and *Stuart Little* came out in an attractive, large paperback format, more individuals bought them.

And the bookstore market began to change. Back then, there were no children's-only bookstores, and few large bookstores. Cheap, popular books like those published by Golden Books could be found in department stores and the like, but there were no inexpensive editions of the quality books sold to libraries. Those children's books took up a small section in most bookstores, and the booksellers expected to sell most of their children's books as gifts. When the "good" books started to be available in paperback, larger children's sections and children's-only bookstores started to appear, and gradually, bookstore sales became a larger part of the children's market.

Playground Stories

Until 1967, if a parent or a teacher wanted to buy a children's book, it had to be a hardcover or a low-quality paperback. But in that year, George Nicholson launched Dell Yearling, a trade paperback program. The first two titles, *Charlotte's Web* and *Stuart Little,* for which Dell paid Harper and Row an enormous advance for the time ($35,000), were not only huge successes, they also didn't hurt Harper's hardcover sales. Harper was willing to say so in writing, other publishers made deals with Dell, and the rest is history. Paperbacks, including books published as originals, not reprints of books first published in hardcover, are becoming a larger and larger part of the children's book market.

Starting in 1975, Random House published its new inexpensive "pictureback" line of original picture-book paperbacks, serious competition to Golden Books's inexpensive hardcover books. They sold well in bookstores. Improving technology also made paperback versions of hardcover picture books possible. At the same size, and same quality paper, but one half to one third of the price of a hardcover book, paperback picture books became more and more available. Today, almost every publisher publishes hardcovers and paperbacks, the paperback editions coming out a year or two after the hardcover, or less often at the same time. No longer do children's book publishers publish solely for the library market.

The Big Get Even Bigger

Other changes were taking place, too. In the 1970s, children's publishing was hit by the end of the federal funding that had supported its growth a decade earlier. Publishers laid off staff and hunkered down for hard times. Noted nonfiction writer and editor Jim Giblin points out that the photo-essay, a nonfiction picture book illustrated with photographs, goes back to this time. With library-oriented nonfiction not selling as well, publishers found that the photo-essay, which was more attractive, sold in bookstores.

Times got better in the 1980s. Though shortsighted tax revolts had further cut funding that libraries could use to buy books, the economy was good, and many parents had money to spend at the bookstores. And if they wanted to have books for their children, they had to spend money on them, because they could no longer count on finding them in the library. The business boomed—until the early 1990s, when sales went down and the buyouts, closures, and mergers began.

Class Rules

It's hard to keep track of the constant change in publishing, but you need to try. Don't rely on out-of-date information. Use a guide such as *Children's Writer's and Illustrator's Market*, and buy a new one every year. Contact publishers to confirm addresses. Don't send submissions to "Harper & Row" or to "Macmillan Children's Books." Those names no longer exist.

The story of publishing since then is a story of big fish swallowing big fish, big fish swallowing medium-size fish, and even a few cases of smaller fish somehow swallowing larger fish. Some of the biggest deals were the merger of Penguin and Putnam, the purchase of Macmillan by Simon & Schuster, the merger of Random House and Bertelsmann's Bantam Double-day Dell, the more recent purchase of the bankrupt Golden Books by Random House, HarperCollins's purchase of William Morrow, and Scholastic's acquisition of Grolier (Franklin Watts, Children's Press, and Orchard). The largest children's publishers today are part of media conglomerates, many of them owned by multinational corporations. We've come a long way from white-gloved library publishing.

Looking at the latest information available, from 2002, five big companies make over half of the approximately $2 billion in annual sales in children's publishing:

◆ Random House

◆ Penguin

◆ Scholastic

◆ HarperCollins

◆ Simon & Schuster

If you leave off Scholastic, which only publishes for children, the four remaining companies are also the ones that are publishing most of the best-selling books for adults. Truly, these companies are publishing giants, with thousands of employees, and are often part of even larger companies also owning cable channels, television stations, newspapers, and the like.

Who's Buying?

Because libraries no longer are the primary market for children's books, individual consumers increasingly are the buyers publishers must reach, and large companies dominate the landscape, children's books just aren't what they used to be. That ain't necessarily a bad thing! There are books available now reflecting the experiences of all Americans, though not as many as there might be. There are books available in a dazzling array of art styles and techniques. There are many more affordable, but high-quality books available. It's a different and bigger world. Children's publishing, in a way, has grown up. It's more like publishing for adults, for better or worse. What does that mean?

Eye-Catching Books

Time was, thoughtful reviews in respected journals helped libraries choose which books to buy. They still do. But consumers are also buying those books now. And partly in an effort to get their attention, the art in children's picture books, and on the cover of children's novels and nonfiction, has become ever more eye-catching.

Some children's picture books have art that seems to have appeal primarily for adults, which makes sense—adults are the ones buying the books. Some of the more sophisticated novels for children are read by adults, too. The trade association of children's books publishers, the Children's Book Council, even publishes a booklet highlighting children's books for adults, under the title *NOT Just for Children Anymore!* with the hope of inspiring booksellers to carry them and promote them in this way.

Can You Keep a Secret?

Publishers actively market their children's books, even picture books, to adults. We've seen ads in the *New Yorker* for *When Everybody Wore a Hat* (HarperCollins, 2003), free post-cards in coffee bar racks for *Dr. Pompo's Nose* (Scholastic, 2000), and blurbs on the back cover of *Olivia* (Atheneum, 2000), by David Hockney and Mikhail Baryshnikov. Those aren't aimed at children.

TV, Movies, and Candy

If a consumer knows the name of an author, illustrator, or movie, he or she is more likely to buy a book with that name on it. So the byword of the past decade was "brand"—a name that is known and respected and therefore likely to help sell a book and its associated merchandise, too. Brand names may be those of a book or author, or be brought into a book from the outside. Do not be quick to exclaim in horror at this phenomenon! Licensing of this kind is not an entirely new phenomenon; Lewis Carroll of *Alice in Wonderland* fame licensed such products as a *Through the Looking Glass* biscuit tin.

Some publishers have been able to create children's book brand names:

♦ *Dr. Seuss* became a brand name because his books were so consistently good *and* easily recognizable.

♦ *Arthur* has become a brand name after the success of the TV series based on the book.

♦ *The Little House on the Prairie* has quite deliberately been developed into a brand by HarperCollins. You can buy Little House picture books and Little House paper dolls, among other things.

♦ Celebrities from Shaquille O'Neal to Madonna may write or lend their name to children's books.

♦ Houghton Mifflin has hired writers and illustrators to create new *Curious George* books, to extend another "classic" brand name.

Publishers may also *license* a brand from another company. Licensing characters and the right to create books tied in to a movie (such as *Star Wars* or *Pocahontas*) or TV series has long been a way to associate a book with an already familiar brand name.

Vocabulary List

A **license** gives you the right to do something. In publishing, it gives you the right to publish a book or books, or to use a character or name or story created by someone else in a book (or some other product—a lunchbox manufacturer might license the right to make a Pokémon lunch box).

Licensing is part of a wider strategy publishers have of moving into the consumer market to replace lost library sales. At the same time that publishers have cut back on books intended for libraries, they have opened or expanded divisions that do brand-name publishing. As one example, look at Simon & Schuster, a large children's publisher owned by Viacom. Viacom also owns Nickelodeon, and Simon & Schuster has successfully published a large number of Nickelodeon-derived books. Other publishers are doing the same.

Our Friend Harry Potter

Good old Harry! He's shown the world something that we already knew—that a good children's book is a good book for children *and* adults. He's reminded us of the power of the imagination—the first four books came out long before any movie or licensed product, leaving his millions of fans free to imagine him as they liked. He's reminded us of the power of word of mouth—the first book became a hit in England because children told their friends about it, and they told their friends, and so on.

But will Harry have a lasting impact? Publishers do seem more open to publishing fantasy, and publishing books more than 200 pages in length, than used to be the case. Children's books seem a little more in the minds of the media than they used to be, meaning that it's not just the annual Newbery and Caldecott winners that get coverage. We can hope that older children will keep reading. (Until Harry, only a small minority of older children read books other than school books.) And we can hope that after swallowing the heftier price tag on a *Harry Potter* book, adults will now be more willing to pay more than $16.95 for a children's book, allowing publishers to make longer, larger, or otherwise more expensive books. Will these changes persist? It's too soon to say.

The Bottom Line

The bottom line, of course, is how much is being spent on children's books. Are sales going up, down, or staying about the same? Overall, the Association of American Publishers (AAP) says, children's books sales in dollar terms peaked in 2000 at about $2 billion, and have since dropped back a few percent, as the economy has weakened.

That overarching trend conceals bigger moves by different segments of the market. I already noted that paperback sales have gone up. Let's put some numbers on that: as recently as 1992, the AAP says paperback sales were $326 million, and hardcover sales were $850 million; by 2002, paperback sales had more than doubled, to $875 million, but hardcover sales had gone up only to $957 million. That's a big shift, and a shift that has grown through good times and bad, again largely due to the fact that relatively more books are now sold to consumers, and relatively fewer to libraries.

A second big trend is a demographic one. In the mid-1990s, there was a bulge of children in the age group for picture books, making this a growth category for publishers. Now those children are older, and chapter books are the growing area. Does that mean that you should write for older children? Not necessarily—this is a change of a few percentage points, so it's still possible to succeed as an author of picture books. As always, do what you feel you do best.

You can get a sense of trends, too. Try to get your hands every year on the issue of *Publishers Weekly* that looks at the previous year's bestsellers. It's usually out in March. In the most recent one I've seen, for books published in 2002, it's striking how many of the top hardcover titles are novels, and not just Harry Potter. There are also a couple celebrity books (by Lynne Cheney and Jamie Lee Curtis), but there are far fewer licensed (movie- or cartoon-related) titles than used to be the case. That's a promising development.

It's an Electronic World

The hype has died down from what it was, but the "new media"—the new electronic ways to publish or present material, from CD-ROMs to *e-books* and more—are a definite factor in publishing. None of the wilder predictions of the late 1990s have come close to coming true so far. This is a change to the business that's still mostly in the future.

Vocabulary List

A book that must be read in an electronic format instead of on paper is an **e-book**. These books can be set up for reading on personal computers or on special readers.

Several years ago, some saw CD-ROMs as a real threat to traditional books, and even to illustrated books. Many companies invested in CD-ROM publishing, only to discover how difficult it is to make money in this area. Today, reference is the only area of publishing in which CD-ROMS have had a big impact. That's not surprising. A CD-ROM is for many people an improvement over a multivolume encyclopedia set. Publishers have yet to convince the ordinary consumer that an e-book is preferable to a paper one.

Can You Keep a Secret?

It's not just you! It's hard to stay up-to-date with electronic publishing—even if you understand how it works. To help with both, I've put together a web page that explains what an e-book is in detail, gives examples of some popular e-book formats, discusses my experiences at children's e-book publisher ipicture-books, and provides a snapshot of the current state of affairs in children's e-book publishing. Go to www.underdown.org/childrense-books.htm.

Print-on-demand publishing (POD), in which single titles of books are printed when needed, is actually a kind of electronic publishing. It relies on electronic files of books and their use to create speedy printings of one book (or more) when needed. Academic and specialty publishers can use it to sell copies of their books in bookstores that can't otherwise carry them. Some companies are providing POD as a service directly to writers; you get books, but you have to pay for them. This technology could also enable publishers to keep a novel or black-and-white nonfiction title technically "in print" indefinitely, even if not selling lots of copies. So far, this doesn't work for books with color, and prices per copy tend to be high.

Developments will keep coming. For now, most publishers see electronic publishing as an opportunity to sell a book in another format, much like audiotapes or paperbacks, and not as a replacement for books themselves. For authors and illustrators, that means that e-books are not an area in which you have many opportunities to sell original work. But your publisher might well produce or license an e-book edition in addition to a print edition.

It's a brave new world in children's books, but also a big and diverse one. It's not the world we knew as children, but it's still a world in which dedicated and creative writers— and that means you—can find a place.

The Least You Need to Know

- ◆ Children's books used to be published mostly for sale to libraries, but that's not true anymore.

- ◆ Paperbacks are an increasingly common way to publish a children's book.

- ◆ Publishing companies are getting bigger and bigger and often are part of multi-national corporations.

- ◆ Publishers are trying to sell more books to consumers, and so make them attractive to adults; they also license movies, TV shows, and products to make their books instantly familiar.

- ◆ Children's book sales are down recently—but there are still plenty being published, and it's a cyclical business.

- ◆ Electronic publishing hasn't had a big effect on children's books yet.

Chapter 8

What's in a Book? A Guided Tour

In This Chapter

- ◆ What goes on the cover, jacket, and spine
- ◆ All the items listed in the front of the book
- ◆ The differences between dedications, forewords, and introductions, and where you find them in the book
- ◆ What you'll find in the body of a picture book, a chapter book, and other types of books
- ◆ The material in the back of the book

A book, any book, is made of many parts, with names you need to know. This chapter navigates you from cover to cover through the components of a children's book. You'll learn where everything from the copyright information to the glossary goes. Along the way, you'll also learn definitions used in the publishing world for specific areas of the book. Get ready because here comes your crash course in "the anatomy of a book."

It's a Cover-Up! The Cover, Jacket, and Spine

When you walk into any bookstore and pull a book from a shelf, you immediately see the cover—the front of the book, most likely covered by a jacket. You may have heard "don't judge a book by its cover," but most people do, or at least identify a particular book by its cover. To the publisher, the cover consists of three parts—the front, the back, and the spine. More about each part in a second. But first let's check out the whole cover.

The book's cover may either be hard (called *hardcover*) or pliable (called *softcover* or paperback). What gets printed on the front cover depends on whether the book is a hardcover or softcover.

Traditionally, hardcover books didn't have anything on the front and back covers, with the possible exception of a decorative design stamped on. Identifying elements are found, instead, on the *spine* of the book—the last and first name of the author, the publisher, and the title of the book.

Vocabulary List _____

When a book is produced with a hard, stiff outer cover, it is called a **hardcover** book. The covers are usually made of cardboard, over which is stretched cloth, treated paper, vinyl, or some other plastic.

When the cover of a book is pliable, the book is then called **softcover**. Pliable covers are usually made of thick but flexible paper or light cardboard coated with varnish or a synthetic resin or laminate.

But hardcovers come with jackets. According to *The Chicago Manual of Style, 14th Edition*, book jackets—nowadays glossy paper, as a protective wrapping for the hardcover—entered the publishing arena in the twentieth century. On the book jacket, you'll find identifying elements—the title, the author, the illustrator, the publisher, the *ISBN* (International Standard Book Number), the price, and on the flaps of the jacket, promotional blurbs about the book. Increasingly, children's picture books may also have printed covers that duplicate the eye-catching design of the jacket.

A softcover or paperback book does not have a jacket. The information you see on the front and *spine* of the jacket of the hardcover book is printed on the cover itself. Typically, you'll find some promotional information on the back, but not as much as that on the flaps of a jacket. Some publishers are also choosing to print promotional copy on the inside of the cover.

Vocabulary List _____

ISBN is the acronym for International Standard Book Number. This number gives the book a unique ID for orders and distribution. The publisher assigns the ISBN based on procedures set up by the R. R. Bowker Company and the International Standards Organization. You'll find the ISBN of your book in the bar code on the back of the jacket for a hardcover, on the back of a paperback cover, and on the copyright page. The center panel of the binding of a book is called the **spine**. The spine hinges together the front and back cover to the pages and faces out when the book is shelved. The pages of the book all connect at the spine.

Let's take a look at the hardcover jacket and the paperback cover for *The Tombs of Atuan.* The design is different, which is typical for a novel, and if you look at the back you'll also see that the ISBN is different.

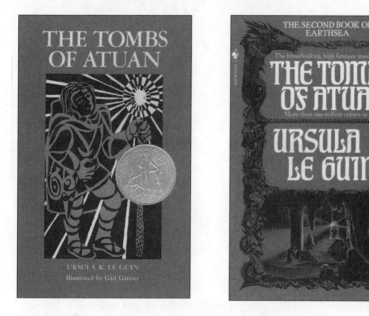

The hardcover jacket (left) and the paperback cover (right) of the same title may look different, though often for picture books they are the same.

Teacher Says, "Give It a Title"

When you first open a book, you see blank pages. These, including the one stuck down on the inside of the cover, are called endpapers. You can guess why! Publishers may gussy them up with maps or use fancy paper, but you don't need to worry much about them now.

Keep turning the pages. Soon, you should find the title page. The title page contains many things other than the full title. You'll find the author's full name (no initials unless the author goes by initials only), the illustrator, and the name and sometimes the location of the publisher. If the publisher has a logo, that appears here, too. The main point of this page, though, is the title.

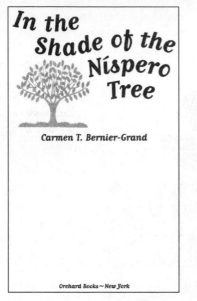

The title page in a novel usually has only the title, author's name, and publisher's name.

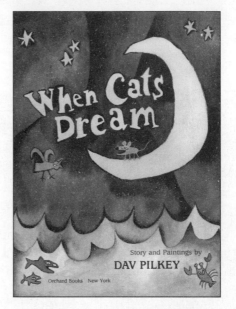

The title page of a picture book is usually more elaborate.

Legal and Other Details

The page directly after the title page is the copyright page and colophon (unless a publisher puts this material at the end of the book, for design reasons). Several kinds of information are printed here. Most important, the publisher states that it has copyrighted the text and illustrations in the names of the author and illustrator. (See Chapter 22 for more on copyright.)

Can You Keep a Secret? _____

Many of the elements of a book's design go back to the nineteenth century or earlier, and have been retained even though they may not be needed in a book. Title pages, for example, were much more necessary when books were published unbound, possibly in installments, to be bound and given covers by the purchaser. "Half title" pages, on which nothing more than the title of the book appears, occasionally appear before the title page as another one of these traditional elements.

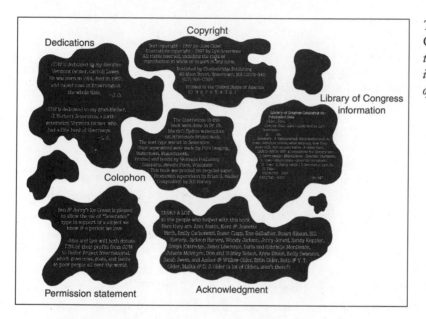

This copyright page, from Cow *by Jules Older, illustrated by Lyn Severance, includes many of the items often found in front matter.*

Other information besides the copyright appears here—see if you can find all of it in the illustration. You'll see the complete address of the publisher, how many printings the book has gone through, the Library of Congress Cataloging-in-Publication (CIP) data, the ISBN, and any acknowledgments of use of someone else's copyrighted material (though this can appear elsewhere). The CIP information helps get your book into the nation's libraries. The publisher submits the book to the *Library of Congress*, which assigns it its own number and creates basic cataloging information.

Picture books are reviving an old tradition in publishing—the *colophon*. The colophon provides information about the production of a book, such as the typefaces used, the names of the designer and typesetter, and the kinds of paint and paper the illustrator used. Often this appears on the copyright page, but if the information is lengthy the colophon may get its own page.

Vocabulary List _____

The **Library of Congress** is a federal agency charged with maintaining a collection of all books published in the United States, and with creating standardized cataloging information for libraries; most other countries have similar agencies. A **colophon** is an item in a book's front matter that gives information about how it was produced, from typefaces to the kind of paint an artist used.

The Stuff in the Front

Now that we've gotten through the business of the book, let's move on to other stuff you might find in the front of the book. Logically enough, all of this material is called the "front matter" by folks in publishing.

"For Me!" Dedications

As an author or illustrator, you may want to dedicate your creative efforts to someone. The publisher will place the dedication page after the copyright page, or, especially in picture books, on the copyright page as the first item.

Tables of Contents

Just after the copyright page and dedication, you sometimes find a table of contents. The average board book or picture book won't have one, of course. But plenty of other children's books—like anthologies, chapter books, or informational works—do include a table of contents. Sometimes the table of contents is simply called "Contents." The amount of detail a publisher goes into varies, but you'll certainly find the chapter number, chapter title if there is one, and the beginning page number of each. If the book has sections, they'll appear too, and sometimes subdivisions of chapters will be listed (as they are in the front of this book). Glossaries, indexes, and other material will also be listed.

Forewords and Introductions

After the table of contents, you may find either an introduction or a foreword—or perhaps both. Sometimes the foreword may be called a prologue. Generally speaking, a prominent expert or authority writes a foreword to a book. If you write a children's book based on astronomy, and John Glenn writes a few pages talking about your book and its merits, that's a foreword.

Typically an author writes an introduction to provide information integral to the understanding of the book or some background on the basis or making of the book. For a historical novel, for example, you may want to include an introduction to give your reader some background on the period of time in which your novel takes place.

Contents

This table of contents from The Forestwife *by Theresa Tomlinson shows chapter titles as well as chapter numbers.*

What's Between Your Head and Feet? Your Body!

It takes a while, but once you get past all the business and practical details, you get to the good stuff—the stories, the poems, the learning, the history—the content itself! Let's take a look at the *body* of the book. In a picture book, the body of the book is the story and the pictures that accompany it, in one straightforward narrative. For other kinds of books, the setup may be a little more complicated, and other elements appear.

Vocabulary List _____

In journalistic or creative writing of any kind, the "meat" of the story—or the story proper—is termed the **body.** Basically, the body of any work is the work itself without any extraneous information like the copyright page or the dedication or the index.

Chapter Books

The identifying factor of a chapter book—a novel for kids—is simply that the text is broken up into chapters. The chapters may or may not have illustrations. Seems easy enough, right? But you have choices. A chapter may just have a number, or it can have its own title. Look on your own shelves for examples. Get a sense of the length of chapters. Do they vary much? Are they longer in books for older children?

Alphabetical and Other Setups

Chapters aren't the only way the body of the book can be broken up. Authors can be as creative with the structure of their book just as they are with the content. Especially for picture books, the letters of the alphabet may break up and organize the body of the book. Jerry Pallotta, for example, introduces a variety of types of jets and explains how a jet engine works in his _Jet Alphabet Book._

A chronological structure works well in books set up as diaries. Lisa Rowe Fraustino's _Ash_, for example, is written as the journal of a boy dealing with the breakdown of his older brother, while Patricia McKissack's _A Picture of Freedom_ from the "Dear America" series follows the life of an enslaved girl on a Virginia plantation.

Other Elements

Chapters and other ways of putting the body of the book in order aren't all that can appear there.

You can also find …

♦ Pictures with captions and labels.

♦ Tables.

♦ Special elements like pop-ups.

♦ Running heads. (These go across the top of the page and help you know where you are in the book.)

♦ Headers, subheaders. (You'll see these throughout this book, as a way of breaking up the chapters.)

Go to the Back of the Line—Back Matter

Children's books often include what we in the industry call "back matter." Basically, back matter includes anything of informational purposes other than the text—a glossary, recommended reading lists, an index, information about the book, games to play based on the book, and other material. Much of this is written by the author, but some may be added by the publisher.

More About Bugs for Lunch

There are more insects in the world than any other kind of animal. More than 800,000 insects have been studied and named, but scientists believe that there are probably millions that nobody knows about yet. It's a good thing that insects are food for so many creatures, or the world might be overrun with them.

The *NUTHATCH* is called the upside-down bird because it walks headfirst down tree trunks as it searches for food. With its strong beak, it pries out insects, caterpillars, and insect eggs that are hidden in cracks in the bark.

SPIDERS catch insects in webs and traps made of silk. Each species of spider has a distinctive design for its web or trap. When they catch more than they can eat at one time, most spiders wrap the leftovers in silk to save for a later meal.

BATS fly from their roosts to look for food as the sun goes down. But even in total darkness, they can catch insects. Bats send out a constant stream of sounds that are pitched so high that people cannot hear them. As these sounds hit objects, they echo back to the bat. When an insect flies across this beam of sound, the bat can tell exactly where the bug is and can swoop down to catch it in flight.

A *GECKO* is a small lizard that lives in warm climates. Many people like to have geckos in their gardens and backyards. They know that geckos will come out of hiding at night to eat moths and other insects that people find pesky.

Back matter in a picture book may include additional information, as in this page from Bugs for Lunch *by Marge Facklam, and can include recommended books, sources, a glossary, or even an index.*

Are you a picture-book author who's thinking, "I can see that in a book for an older child or in a nonfiction book, but not a picture book"? But in many cases picture books have back matter, too, especially nonfiction picture books or books based on folktales. Just what is in the back matter varies enormously. In the back of the paperback edition of the novel *A Wrinkle in Time*, there isn't much. Yearling Books includes descriptions of four other books by Madeleine L'Engle as well as a short biography with her picture. For an example of more extensive back matter, check out *The 20th Century Children's Book Treasury*. In this anthology of picture books, the reader will find "Biographical Notes" about each author, a "Guide to Reading Ages," and an "Index of Titles, Authors, and Illustrators."

Back matter in a chapter book can be lengthy. This is the first page of the back matter in James Giblin's When Plague Strikes.

SOURCE NOTES AND BIBLIOGRAPHY

So many books, magazine articles, and newspaper reports were part of the research for *When Plague Strikes* that it would be virtually impossible to list them all. Here I'll single out those that contributed significantly to the planning and writing of the book.

OVERALL

Four books stimulated my thinking when I was deciding how to treat the subject of plagues in history. They were:

Plagues and Peoples by William H. McNeill (New York: Doubleday, 1977). This fascinating book describes the decisive role that disease has played in the historical development of the human race. From it I gained a much clearer notion of how plagues like the Black Death could travel from one continent to another.

The Doctor in History by Howard W. Haggard (New York: Dorset Press, 1989). A history of medicine and its practitioners from prehistoric times to the early years of the twentieth

197

We urge you to browse books, specifically looking at the back matter. In fact, go out now. Pull several books from different age categories and just pore over the back pages. See what other authors and publishers have included. Think about whether or not you think it adds to the book. Do any of the books you examined seem to have something missing? Keep all of this in mind when working on your own book. A book can be put together from a large grab bag of components in many different ways, and you can be as creative with those components as you are with any other part of your writing.

Class Rules

Don't be afraid to mention your ideas for back matter in a proposal for a book. In fact, keep notes on all your ideas for any back matter and list those possibilities in the proposal with examples. You'll give the publisher a more complete vision of your work.

The Least You Need to Know

♦ A book contains many elements, each of which has a name and a purpose.

♦ Hardcover books have a jacket, which details specifics about the book, whereas softcover books must fit all the information on the cover.

♦ Business aspects of the book—copyrights, publisher information, and dedications—occur at the front of the book before the copy.

♦ The body of the book is your work—the book!

♦ Many books—even picture books—contain back matter. This back matter may include anything from a biography of the author, to suggested games to play, to an index or glossary.

Part 2

Finding Out
What's Possible

Now that you know the basics, there is much to learn if you want to reach
your destination. This part clues you in on the different formats and age
levels books get slotted into, and shows you some of the genres within
which you might be writing, from pure fantasy to the most straightforward nonfiction.

You'll also learn about various types of publishers, and the difference
between books for series and books that work best as individual titles.

Think you're ready to launch your manuscript into the world? First, read
up on how to get good feedback, and then proceed.

Chapter 9

Animal, Vegetable, or Mineral? Book Formats and Age Levels

In This Chapter

- ◆ A look at fiction and nonfiction
- ◆ Picture book vs. chapter book
- ◆ The lowdown on easy readers, story collections, and more
- ◆ The different kinds of books with chapters
- ◆ Who reads "children's books"—adults and teenagers, too

You know you want to illustrate or write for children, and you've explored the classics and the current titles. By now you're probably on a first-name basis with the librarians and booksellers in town. But what about the kind of book you might create? Do you know the difference yet between chapter books and picture books? How about board books and easy readers?

In this chapter, I'll give you an overview of different children's book formats, and how they more or less align with different age levels. I'll also explain why you may be writing not only for children, but for adults, too. In Chapter 10, I'll move on to some common subject areas.

The Main Categories

First, you need to know a couple basic distinctions: between fiction and nonfiction, and between picture books and books with chapters.

Tell the Truth, the Whole Truth

What you may know as *nonfiction* books from your school days are now often called *informational books*. This makes sense—why define a category by what it's not?

Playground Stories

Is nonfiction less creative than fiction? Not so, says nonfiction author Sneed Collard:

I actually began my writing as a self-indulgent and ignorant fiction writer. In fact, my first four children's sales were all fictional stories. The problem was, I was having so many interesting experiences as a biologist that I just couldn't help writing about them. Once I began writing nonfiction, I loved it. It provided me with a great excuse to learn more about biology *and* could be just as creative as fiction. I'd go a step further and say that a nonfiction book offers *more* opportunity for creativity than fiction. It's extremely rare to find a fiction picture book that truly breaks new ground. Nonfiction, on the other hand, has not even begun to peak as far as creative possibilities.

Many different approaches and subjects fit under the nonfiction tent. Here are just a few examples:

Vocabulary List

Also known as an **informational book, nonfiction** can include writing in which the author presents information, activities, or knowledge; recounts a historical event; or creates a biography.

- Books that present "just the facts" might introduce dinosaurs, such as *Dinosaurs! Strange and Wonderful*, by Laurence Pringle, or burial customs, as in Penny Colman's *Corpses, Coffins, and Crypts: A History of Burial*.

- Stories about real people, as long as they are based only on verifiable information, are biographies, a major type of nonfiction. Barbara Cooney's *Eleanor* is a picture-book example.

◆ Some companies specialize in how-to books for children. One is Klutz Press, publisher of *Coin Magic*, which tells how to perform 24 magic tricks.

If you like to do research and write or illustrate what you've learned, you can work on nonfiction.

Have Fun Lying

Fiction is what we make up, though it may have a basis in fact. As renowned writer Jane Yolen, author of novels, picture books, poetry, and much else, puts it, "Memory is just one more story. And sometimes not a very good one at that. It needs that sandpaper touchup, a bit of paint, a little lie here, and a bigger lie there—and so fiction is born." Although nonfiction can never be based on an entirely invented incident, fiction can find a basis in fact. Fiction is not truth, though it can hold truth within it, such as the truth of personal experience, or universal themes. As you delve deeper into these two wide categories, you'll find the boundaries between them are very blurry.

As with nonfiction, there are many types of fiction. You'll learn about these in more detail in this and the following chapter.

Vocabulary List

Fiction is writing from the imagination. Fiction is "made up," though good fiction does, paradoxically, seem real.

Playground Stories

Continuing her discussion of fiction writing, Jane Yolen offered a look at the evolution of her fictional works from actual experiences. She says:

> *Owl Moon* is a compilation of lots of owling trips that my husband took with our children. *The Girl Who Loved the Wind* is a fairy tale allegory of my life. The *Commander Toad* books are pun-filled romps with a serious message at the core. Yet they each started with something real—a memory of something actual—and then went on to make something "realer." Bad grammar, but a true statement nonetheless.

Pictures vs. Words

After you've taken in the fiction/nonfiction distinction and noted its fuzziness, move on to formats. Very generally, children's books may be dominated by pictures, in which case we call them picture books; or dominated by words, in which case we call them chapter books.

For the Little Ones: Picture Books

When people think of children's literature, picture books often come to mind. These are the books Mom and Dad read to you at bedtime, or the teacher read to you at story time. In a picture book, a line or two of text typically accompanies a page of illustration, though the amount of text can range from none at all to a paragraph or two.

Most picture books are pretty short, and not just because their audience—younger children—have pretty short attention spans. Most picture books are printed in full color, and that's expensive. Because books get printed on a sheet of paper that's printed on both sides, then folded and cut, picture books come in lengths of 16, 24, 32, 40, 48 pages or sometimes more; 32 pages is the most typical length.

For Big Kids: Chapter Books

When kids move from picture books to reading books themselves—with chapters even!— they've entered the realm of chapter books. Here, the words are dominant, though these books may also have illustrations. These range from easy-to-read novels with short chapters and limited vocabulary up to serious novels and nonfiction for teenagers, and from short books with illustrations, perhaps 48 or 64 pages long, to meaty 300-plus-page tomes with no illustrations at all. Think of the *Frog and Toad* books, *Island of the Blue Dolphins*, the *Nancy Drew* series, and *Bridge to Terabithia*. These are all chapter books of different types.

What's for Who? How to Tell

Underlying these basic distinctions, and the following categories, lies that basic truth that children are constantly changing and growing. This makes what works for a 3-year-old vastly different from what works for a 12-year-old. And that makes your work much more complicated than if you were creating books for adults. How can you know how to adjust? Although there are no hard-and-fast rules, you'll begin to learn some rules of thumb. Keep these in mind, and remember there are exceptions:

- **Length.** The shorter the text, the younger the child, usually. A notable exception: Beginning readers may start to read with books that are shorter and simpler than the picture books that were being read to them.

- **What you do with words.** Cumulative or predictable language, using the same familiar words over and over, or using rhyme and rhythm: All of these can make a text work better for younger children.

- **Complexity of sentence structure, vocabulary, plot, design, and illustration.** All these can become more complex for older children.

- **In fiction, the age of the main character.** Generally, children read about children at least as old as themselves. You won't find too many 11-year-olds savoring a story about a third-grader.

- **Subject matter.** Are the concerns addressed in the book the concerns of the intended audience?

Now, on to some more details about certain kinds of books.

You Can Throw 'Em

Any parent of an infant or toddler knows *board books*, the simplest kind of picture book. You'll know one especially well when an angry 18-month-old child hurls one from across the room and hits you in the forehead with it! Why is a baby book so sturdy—and dangerous? Well, these little titles are made literally from paperboard or cardboard, not paper, so they can stand up heavy use, and so that the pages are easier to grasp and turn.

Traditionally, board books consist of several thick, hard pages with one or two words of text and an illustration on each. There are usually no more than 16 pages. Repetition rules. One page may say, "Peek-a-boo, cat!" Turn the page, and you'll find "Peek-a-boo, dog!" These books are simple, direct, and brief, just right for babies to experience in the lap of a parent.

Lately publishers have been converting lengthier children's picture books into the board-book format. Early and successful examples of such conversions are the Margaret Wise Brown's titles of *Goodnight Moon* and *Runaway Bunny*. Now many other publishers of picture books are jumping on the baby-book bandwagon and producing board-book versions of popular picture books (sometimes, unfortunately, they cut pages or otherwise change the original). This trend has gone so far that most of the books you'll find in the board-book area of a bookstore didn't start out as board books.

Vocabulary List

Board books, a kind of picture book, are short, thick, square-shape (usually) simple books for infants and toddlers. They may tell a brief story or introduce basic concepts like colors or numbers.

This is not an area of great opportunity for writers. It's not just that most board books are converted from an existing picture book. Even the originals being made are often written "in-house" by a publisher, or developed by a publisher with an illustrator.

Writers and illustrators should both keep in mind that there are many more true picture books being published. No matter how much they interest you, the way into board books may be through picture books.

"Concept books," which you can find in both regular picture book and board-book format, are a special type of picture book. They explore a concept rather than tell a story. In a way, they are nonfiction for the very young. Ruth Krauss's *A Hole Is to Dig* was one of the first concept books. It's a classic well worth reading. For more recent examples see Tana Hoban's *Colors Everywhere* or Suse McDonald's *Peck, Slither, and Slide*. Though this isn't always true, concept books are often illustrator-created, because text is minimal.

> **Class Rules**
>
> You'll read a lot about word count and page length in this chapter. But use these numbers to help you figure out what a manuscript might be, not as rules for writing. As Jane Yolen says, "Should be, what an awful concept. A book should be as long as it needs to be, not some arbitrary length. I must remind myself that a story has a beginning and a middle and an end. Not a word count."

Read It Again: More on Picture Books

Picture books probably account for more books on the shelves in the children's department than those in any other format or for any other age level. Children beg for them, parents love them as a vehicle for literacy, and people buy them as gifts for children *and* adults all the time. They can be fiction or nonfiction, and because they are read by adults to children, and used in school, they vary in length from a few hundred words to as many as 2,000. This is a very flexible format, allowing for all kinds of subject matter and approaches.

Book people distinguish between two kinds of picture books. "True" picture books have stories that are carried at least as much by the pictures as by the words. Maurice Sendak's *Where the Wild Things Are* is a good example of this type. You couldn't follow the story without the pictures. Illustrated story books or picture storybooks, on the other hand, have a story that could be read on its own. The illustrations add to it but the story would make sense without them. Virginia Burton's *Mike Mulligan and His Steam Shovel* is a good example of this kind. Illustrated storybooks also often have more text, perhaps a full paragraph per page, or a chunk of text facing an illustration. Many classic children's books fit in this category; it is less common today.

I Can Read This: Easy Readers

Remember the thrill of reading your first book yourself? Children may start with those picture books that have fairly simple texts, but beginning readers soon crave more than books like those that relatives read to them. They want more. More words. More length. More to read. But be careful. You don't want to overwhelm this reading group. Because these books, under various names, aren't read by parents to children, they must have simpler vocabulary than picture books do, vocabulary that beginning readers can handle. Sentences must be short and simple, and stories can't be too long or too complicated. Illustrations, though still important, are subordinate to the words.

Can You Keep a Secret? _____

Author Larry Dane Brimner notes these basic distinctions among books for beginning readers:

- ◆ **Easy-reading picture book.** 32 pages: This is a picture book with easy-reader vocabulary and sentence structure.
- ◆ **Easy (or early) reader.** 48 to 64 pages.
- ◆ **Early chapter book.** 48 to 64 pages.

Lengths vary from several hundred words to 1,500 words.

The *Arthur* books by Marc Brown are a good example of the first easy readers kids pick up. You might also want to study an entire program, such as the Simon & Schuster *Ready-to-Read* books, and the careful gradations between the levels of its program. Easy-to-read books can be nonfiction, too, as in the Harper *Let's-Read-and-Find-Out Science* program, actually originated by the now-defunct Thomas Y. Crowell publishing company in 1960, and still going strong 40 years and a change of publisher later. The best thing you can do to focus your energies in this area is immerse yourself in the books.

As you browse, note that series dominate in this area, unlike picture books and novels. You can find single titles, but kids just starting to read want more of the books they like. So by publishing them in series, publishers make those books easier to find and more likely to be purchases. Note, too, that many of these series aren't being added to continually. And so if you want to write or illustrate early readers, you'll need to find the publishers interested in new titles. (Proposing an entire new series, for a beginner, is almost impossible.)

Vocabulary List

For more detailed information on writing early and easy readers, surf over to "Targeting the Emergent Reader," an excellent article by Joan Broerman that examines this tricky area: www.underdown.org/early_rd.htm.

In most kinds of books, you can just sit down and write a story, using your judgment about vocabulary. But easy readers are one of the types of books that often must be built around a carefully selected vocabulary list. When even *Make Way for Ducklings* proves too advanced, or when the audience delights in simple rhymes and sounds, then books like *One Fish, Two Fish, Red Fish, Blue Fish* appear on the shelves.

Mom, Can I Get This? Novels and Chapter Books

Children can move from early-reader books to true chapter books as early as second grade. Chapter books, especially those for middle-grade readers, are what we think of when we fondly remember classic novels for children—such books as E. B. White's *Charlotte's Web*, Laura Ingalls Wilder's *The Little House on the Prairie*, and Beverly Cleary's *Ramona the Pest.* For younger readers, these may have some illustrations, and be no more than 64 pages in length, but they range up to 200 pages or more. These books don't have controlled vocabularies, though writers must keep in mind their audience and not get too sophisticated (or too easy!).

Chapter books, which can be nonfiction as well, are simply books with chapters. I include a number of kinds of books with chapters in this category, but be warned: The term "chapter books" is used by some people only to mean books between early readers and true novels. Here is the range of all books with chapters:

- **Easy readers with chapters or "early chapter books."** 48 to 64 pages (approximately 6- to 8-year-olds).

- **Young middle-grade.** 48 to 80 pages, longer if nonfiction (7- to 9-year-olds).

- **True middle-grade.** 80 to 160 pages, occasionally more (8- to 12-year-olds).

- **Older middle-grade or transitional.** 128 to 200 pages or more (10- to 14-year-olds).

- **Young adult or YA.** Up to 250 pages (12 plus).

- *Harry Potter.* Several hundred pages (almost all ages). I'm only half-joking— *Harry Potter* books need an entry of their own because they break so many rules. Be careful not to assume that you can do the same.

It's difficult to make hard and fast distinctions between the different levels, so until you develop an intuitive sense of them, just write, and remember Jane Yolen's warning about word counts.

For the Backpack

Want to write something similar in form to books for middle-graders but more sophisticated in content? Don't forget the *young adult* audience. Loosely, that's teenagers.

The publishing business started to target teens separately from other children relatively recently. Authors such as S. E. Hinton, Walter Dean Myers, and Judy Blume started to write more challenging novels for teenagers in the late 1960s, and the young adult category was invented in response. As noted in the October 18, 1999, feature "Making the Teen Scene" in *Publishers Weekly*, the trade magazine for publishing: "From *The Outsiders* in 1967 to *Smack* in 1998, publishers have consistently released books by talented authors who speak directly to a teen audience about sophisticated, though teen-appropriate concerns."

Vocabulary List

Young adult (or YA) books are exactly as they sound. YA is the term used in library collections and by publishers to designate teens.

Teens are likely to be insulted to find their books near the board and picture books of younger children, of course. And so for years, publishers, librarians, and booksellers have struggled over where to shelve teen titles. Sometimes there's a separate YA section in the library, store, or catalogue. Sometimes there isn't. As a writer, don't concern yourself too much with this.

Class Rules

Don't censor your writing for a teen audience. Adults sometimes underestimate the sensitivity and self-awareness that teens possess. Long before there was an official "young adult" genre, authors who respected teens were reaching them. J. D. Salinger's coming-of-age novel *The Catcher in the Rye* caused controversy among adults when it was published in the 1950s, but is now considered a classic.

That's a Lot of Stories!

Cutting across the age categories we've looked at are collections. You can find a collection of just about anything, from picture books to literary young adult stories. Some are put together from existing books—publisher-compiled collections like the complete *Curious George*. But others are new and original works, and a type of book in which some authors do well.

Folktales and Fairy Tales

Do you remember the stories of Hansel and Gretel? Sleeping Beauty? Both are fairy tales, a form of writing that developed from folktales. *Fairy tales* and *folktales* are an important part of children's literature. The only difference between the way we pass on folktales today and the way it was done ages ago is the medium. We have books, while in years past the stories were passed on orally.

Vocabulary List

A **folktale** is a story that has been passed down orally and may appeal to both adults and children, while a **fairy tale,** though like a folktale in form, is told specifically for children and involves more literary elements or stylistic devices. Both usually feature supernatural beings, the use of magic, happiness for the good, and punishment for the bad.

You'll see plenty of such stories made into picture books, but many don't work well for an audience that young. What to do, if you love these? One approach is to put together a collection. Watch out for copyright infringement. (For guidance, see Chapter 22.) Virginia Hamilton's *The People Could Fly* and Howard Norman's *The Girl Who Dreamed Only Geese* are great examples of collections of retold folktales.

Short Stories and Poetry

You can also put together other kinds of collections. Short stories can be collected for book publication, though extremely few short story collections for children are published. Those that are tend to be for older readers, and to include works by several writers. Look at James Howe's *The Color of Absence: 12 Stories About Loss and Hope.* Howe wrote one of the stories and collected the others, meaning that he had to seek permission to use them. If you want to publish only your stories, stick to magazines, at least until you are famous enough to put together a collection like Roald Dahl's *The Umbrella Man and Other Stories.*

Poetry collections are a similarly tough sell, because the few publishers that do publish poetry look for an overall theme and a distinctive style. Ironically, that's not what publishers usually receive in the mail. Publishing companies receive a surprising number of big miscellaneous collections of poems from aspiring poets: Don't go there! Take a look instead at Paul Fleischman's *Joyful Noise: Poems for Two Voices*, which won the Newbery Medal in 1988. This collection not only focuses tightly on insects, it does so through the use of an innovative two-voice device.

As with short stories, if you love poetry you can also set out to create anthologies of the work of many poets, but again you'll have to handle permissions.

The Adults in the Way

We're less than halfway through our tour of the many varieties of children's books, and you already may be wondering if you have to know exactly what kind of book you've written to get it published. The short answer is "no." You don't need to be able to say to a publisher, "This is an early chapter book aimed at a 7-year-old reader." But you need to have some feel for what you are doing and how it fits into the established categories.

Why? Because you can write something wonderful and not get anywhere with it, if the "gatekeepers" don't know what to do with it. *Not only children read children's books.* Editors read them first. Then parents, grandparents, teachers, and librarians largely decide what their children read, though teenagers typically have some control over their own spending. These people are the gatekeepers, and it's a fact of life that you must get your book past them to the child you want to reach.

Sometimes, that can be a problem, especially if you want to write something that children will handle just fine but might not be approved by every adult. Still, the best children's books appeal to both children and adults. Always have, and always will. Some appeal more to adults than others do, as noted in Chapter 7. Should you, then, aim your writing at adults? No, because if you do, you may miss children altogether. Concentrate on children, and if you do your job really well, maybe you'll reach adults, too.

The Least You Need to Know

- Nonfiction writing aims to inform readers about real things, people, or events.

- Fiction writing may begin with a real experience but goes beyond it to tell about something that did not happen.

- Picture books are heavily illustrated with little text for the younger child. Someone other than the child reads the book to him.

- Chapter books have more text, and contain, of course, chapters. They get longer for older children. Other children's book formats include board books, easy readers, and collections.

- When you write, you will not only be writing for the child, but for adults, too.

10

Can I Write That? Subjects and Genres

In This Chapter

- ◆ The difference between literary fiction and popular fiction
- ◆ A look at the genres of children's books
- ◆ Examples of fantasy and science fiction for children
- ◆ The world of multicultural books
- ◆ Historical fiction and fiction in nonfiction books

The preceding chapter introduced some basic book formats and examined the kinds of books written for different age groups. This chapter delves into subject matter. Almost any subject or type of writing done for adults can also be done for children—*if* you take the right approach.

In addition to giving you an overview of some of the different genres, this chapter offers many titles for you to peruse at your leisure; reading some of them will deepen your understanding of each area.

Good Books (Literary Fiction)

Not all children's books are created equal. As with anything in this world, some books are seen as "better" than others. *Good* usually refers to the high end of any product; more carefully crafted, from better materials, the high-end products are also usually more expensive. Well, it works the same in children's literature. Some publishers aim for those who seek quality—libraries and the customers of independent bookstores, to drastically oversimplify—while other publishers use lower price, bells and whistles, and movie tie-ins to attract less "refined" tastes.

Let's look at a few examples of quality and literary picture books:

♦ *Mirette on the High Wire*, by Emily Arnold McCully

♦ *Zin! Zin! Zin! A Violin*, by Lloyd Moss

♦ *A Snowy Day*, by Ezra Jack Keats

♦ *A Bargain for Frances*, by Russell Hoban

♦ *This Land Is My Land*, by George Littlechild

If in your discovery of children's literature you haven't read one or more of the bulleted titles, you really should seek them out. Analyze them. Ask yourself, "What makes these books outstanding works of literature?"

Here are some examples of children's novels that are considered high-end, literary choices:

♦ *Tuck Everlasting*, by Natalie Babbitt

♦ *Catherine, Called Birdy*, by Karen Cushman

♦ *The Watsons Go to Birmingham*, by Chris Crutcher

♦ *A Wrinkle in Time*, by Madeleine L'Engle

♦ *Walk Two Moons*, by Sharon Creech

♦ *The Chocolate War*, by Robert Cormier (YA)

Again, if you haven't read the books on this list, go back and study them.

They're, Like, *Soooo* Popular: Popular Fiction

How many of you adults out there love a really great scare and pick up Stephen King night after night? Or how many romance novels sell directly off the racks in supermarkets, gobbled up by adoring fans of lovely heroines and muscle-ripped heroes? Now, now. Get your nose out of the air! Popular fiction appeals to just about everyone. And just as Mom and Dad may not always read Shakespeare, children don't always cuddle up to *The Secret Garden*. And why should they? You like Stephen King? They like *Goosebumps*. You like romance novels? They like *The Princess Diaries*.

Here are just a few examples of popular fiction for younger children:

- Any of the *Arthur* books by Marc Brown
- Any of the *Maisy* books by Lucy Cousins
- *The Magic School Bus* series

Here are just a few examples of popular fiction for the older reader:

- *Dear America* novels
- *Magic Tree House* series
- Matt Christopher's sport novels
- *Animorphs* series

Popular books and good books generally come from different publishers, or at least from different divisions within the same company. Depending on what approach you are taking, you'll need to seek out the right kind of publisher; you'll learn the differences in the next chapter.

Swords and Sorcerers and Talking Bunnies

What those good or popular publishers actually publish is another story, of course. Brace yourself, because if you feel like you're being hit over the head with a certain concept, sorry. But it bears repeating: Whatever adults like, children like. This goes for many of the common *genres* (types of writing): fantasy, mystery, historical fiction, and so on. Some areas, of course, are more popular with children than with adults, and vice versa. Mystery stories are an established genre for children, for example, but not as big as they are for adults. I'm not going to go into all of the children's genres, but instead introduce some of the most common ones.

Vocabulary List

While the format of a book refers to its physical appearance—picture book or chapters, soft- or hardcover—the **genre** of a book refers to the type of writing—fantasy, historical fiction, multicultural, or nonfiction.

Our first stop, *fantasy* and science fiction books, have been a mainstay of children's publishing for a long time. The kind of fantasy publishers want requires some study, however.

Let's take a look at some of the areas within fantasy and examples of some titles.

Science Fiction

Science fiction (SF) is a kind of fantasy for a simple reason: It gets shelved with it. Also, as in fantasy, things can happen in science fiction that can't happen in our world; faster-than-light travel in a way is just as fantastic as casting spells. There is more fantasy for children than SF, and almost no SF for younger children, but there are some wonderful books. For a couple of good examples, read two Newbery winners: Madeleine L'Engle's *A Wrinkle in Time* and Lois Lowry's *The Giver.*

If you want to write SF for children, just remember that you face a crucial challenge: making an unfamiliar world believable without overwhelming your reader with the details. That may be one reason why there is less SF than fantasy for children—children meet dragons and witches and magic in their earliest reading, but not laser guns, warp drives, and force fields. You've got a steeper hill to climb as a result.

Traditional Fantasy

One of the best-known traditional fantasy titles ever remains J. R. R. Tolkien's *The Hobbit*, and the movies of *The Lord of the Rings* have brought that weightier and more demanding work to a new generation of children. In addition to *The Hobbit*, other books you might check out to further explore traditional fantasy include Ursula Le Guin's *Earthsea* books or Susan Cooper's *The Dark Is Rising* series.

Fantasy may be even more common in picture books. For example, pick up any stories with witches and ghosts in the plot, or stories that involve imaginary friends, and you just picked up a child's fantasy title. Children know at an early age that these are fantasies, but they enjoy them. Moreover, fantasies can provide small children with a way of dealing with their own feelings and developmental problems. The monsters in Maurice Sendak's *Where the Wild Things Are*, for example, may be physical symbols of a child's own destructive impulses, or of their fear of some external threat.

Can You Keep a Secret? _____

For short histories of fantasy and science fiction in children's books, read the informative essays in Anita Silvey's *The Essential Guide to Children's Books*. For a current guide to the field, read Marnie Brook's article "Make the Impossible Possible," which is online at www.underdown.org/sffantasy.htm.

Mon Dieu! The Clock Is Alive! Personifications

Bringing inanimate objects to life and giving them human qualities—*personification*—is not common in mainstream publishing (the "good" publishers), though you'll find it is popular. *Budgy the Helicopter*, by Sarah Ferguson, the Duchess of York, is a typical effort in this area. A mainstream publisher published this book, but celebrities sell books regardless of the content. Your average author would not have been able to sell this same story to Fergy's publisher.

You are not a celebrity, so personification is an area you want to avoid. Publishers that actually take manuscripts from the outside don't want this kind of story, and they wouldn't even spend much time looking at it because they would assume it's from a real beginner. Many beginners gravitate toward turning an inanimate object, like a clock or a car, into something with human qualities. Now that you've been warned, don't do the same.

Class Rules _____

Stay away from alliterative animal names—like Sammy Squirrel or Rocky Raccoon. "Ugh!" will immediately exit the mouth of an editor. Alliteration as a stylistic tool in prose is one thing, but when matched with an animal character, it's downright trite. You'll show yourself to be an amateur if you do it.

Watership Down vs. Sammy Squirrel: Anthropomorphism

In Richard Adams's serious fantasy novel *Watership Down*, the bunnies do talk. Far more common in what you might call "animal fantasy" are picture-book stories in which animals stand in for people. They dress like people do, talk like people do, and get into difficulties like people do. This technique is known as *anthropomorphism*. Venture into this territory at your peril! Any book with talking beasts must quickly prove itself

Vocabulary List _____

Anthropomorphism and **personification** have much in common, but aren't the same thing. Anthropomophism involves giving human characteristics to animals. Personification is making characters out of ordinary nonliving objects.

unique and original, or a publisher won't look twice. As for writing more substantial fantasies for a much older audience, like *Watership Down* and *Redwall*, keep in mind that your tone can't be cutesy and your world must be rich and believable.

Stories Dressed in Facts: Historical Fiction

Stories dressed in facts—this is an unusual way to describe *historical fiction*, but an accurate one. The most important thing to remember about this hybrid genre is this: They are stories, not fact. Though fact weaves itself into the tale—and oftentimes with incredible detail—the stories themselves are fiction, and get shelved in that section of the library or bookstore.

Classics that fall in the category of historical fiction include, of course, Scott O'Dell's masterpiece, *Island of the Blue Dolphins*, and the Colliers's *My Brother Sam Is Dead*. Fittingly, the award for historical fiction is named the Scott O'Dell Award. More recently, *Catherine, Called Birdy*, by Karen Cushman, set in the 1200s, and *The Beetle and Me: A Love Story*, by Karen Romano Young, set in 1984, suggest the range of time periods that are possible. The Newbery Medal winners for 2002, Linda Sue Park's *A Single Shard*, and for 2003, Avi's *Crispin: the Cross of Lead*, were both historical fiction. There's some great and popular writing being done in this area. See the *American Girls* books by the Pleasant Company, *Dear America* from Scholastic, and the *American Diaries* books by Simon & Schuster—proof positive that kids love historical fiction.

Vocabulary List

If you yearn to tell a story of a child caught up in a historical event, or just living in different times, you are writing **historical fiction**. In this type of writing, the main character and often many others are invented, while the setting and other details are based on careful research.

Neighbors Next Door and Far Away

One area of children's literature has developed only recently—multicultural literature. What is it? Most broadly defined, it's literature that simply takes into account the fact that we live in a multicultural and multiracial world. As recently as the 1960s, very few books were published in North America that had main characters who weren't white. In response to criticism and in an attempt to reach new markets, publishers have slowly brought African American, Hispanic, and Asian American authors and illustrators into the field.

Multicultural books aren't a genre so much as an approach. As a result, many types of books fall under this definition. Start with picture-book stories like the delightful *More*

More More Said the Baby: Three Love Stories by Vera B. William. Move on to novels that are based in a particular culture, such as Laurence Yep's *Dragon's Gate* or Christopher Paul Curtis's *The Watsons Go to Birmingham*. And don't forget nonfiction, such as *Black Diamond: The Story of the Negro Baseball Leagues* by Patricia McKissack, and *Talkin' About Bessie* by Nikki Grimes.

Just what it is and who can write what about whom is the subject of considerable and sometimes bitter debate. On one side are writers who believe that they can imagine anything without the benefit of personal experience, while on the other side are cultural guardians so concerned with authenticity they'd limit writers to writing only about their birth culture.

Realistically, there is a middle ground. Where is it? Well, how much experience of a culture do you need to be an insider? Visiting a country for three weeks is personal experience, but writing about it from anything other than a tourist's outsider perspective will be very difficult. Your imagination may be powerful, but it may invent details that conflict with actual reality. Working in an immigrant community as a social worker may give you personal contact with it, but only as a visitor and a caregiver, not someone part of it 24 hours a day, 7 days a week. But immersion works, as one can see in Paul Goble's illustrated retellings of Lakota legends. Originally from England, he's made this his life's work and has received the approval of tribal elders. If you want to write about a culture other than one you grew up in, choose one that you've truly lived in, not one to which you are an outsider.

Can You Keep a Secret?

This chapter can only begin to describe the field of multicultural books, but if you want to learn more, a great place to start is "Fifty Multicultural Books Every Child Should Know," found online at www.soemadison.wisc.edu/ccbc/50mult.htm.

The Facts Dressed in Lies: Fiction in Nonfiction

We've talked about taking facts and immersing them in fiction, but what about immersing story into truth to teach more vividly the concepts at hand? When you take a nonfiction concept—let's say the planets of the solar system—and, to teach about the planets, you weave a story line into the facts, then you're "dressing the facts in lies." You're also probably making the learning process much more accessible and interesting to a child. Let's take a look at the different ways authors use this vehicle to teach kids.

Telling a Story

The most tangible example of this area probably occurs with telling a story. The popular television program *The Magic School Bus* started life as a book series. It gives a great example of fiction being use as a medium for fact. In the series, the teacher, Miss Frizzle, leads her students—Arnold, Phoebe, Ralphie, and Tim, among others—on adventures in a school bus that transports them all over the world of science. The bus—and the kids—have traveled to the dawn of age, inside the human body, within the solar system, and beyond to learn. Essentially, the characters and the story remain ancillary to the lesson. But, no one can deny the powerful tool of the fiction incorporated into the lesson. *The Magic School Bus* books and videos fly off the shelf.

Playground Stories

You may be surprised at what you finally decide to write. Susan Campbell Bartoletti, author of *Growing Up in Coal Country* and *A Coal Miner's Bride*, confesses, "Given my interest in historical fiction and nonfiction, it's hard to believe that I was one of those kids that whined about history class. I didn't like class lectures. I didn't like taking notes, I hated the textbook. But I crave stories—all kinds of stories—and history just happens to be one of the places I look for stories."

Some other titles you might want to read to obtain a better idea of this genre include: *Minn of the Mississippi*, by Holling Clancy Holling; *Cathedral* and similar books, by David Macaulay; or more recently published, *An Extraordinary Life*, by Laurence Pringle; and *Prairie Town*, by the Geiserts.

Drama

Some nonfiction books in this category use the techniques more commonly found in fiction while sticking pretty closely to the facts.

Check out or buy the following books for good examples of factual books enlivened by dramatic writing:

- *The Great Fire*, by Jim Murphy
- Russell Freedman's books
- *The Tiger with Wings*, by Barbara Esbensen

Straight Nonfiction

As noted briefly in the previous chapter, there are a number of kinds of straight non-fiction, books in which the author (and illustrator, if there is one) strive to present just the facts.

These include how-to books: Just as this book is a how-to for you to write and publish for children, many how-to books exist for kids. We mentioned Klutz Press as one publisher that specializes in these books, but you'll also find such titles as *Passport on a Plate*, which presents recipes from around the world, and *Handtalk: An ABC of Finger Spelling and Sign Language*, by Remy Charlip and Mary Beth Miller. From cooking to card games, from hula dancing to sign language, kids want to know how to do it all!

Some books present information: Take a look at the *Everything Kids'* series in the cash wrap areas of bookstores. You'll find the *Everything Kids' Nature Book*, *Everything Kids' Money Book*, and *Everything Kids' Space Book*. In the book that covers money, there's everything a child might want to know about it—the history of money, all about banks, what goes into starting a business, information about investing, and a whole lot more. Informational books, such as Children's Press's *True Book* series, also belong in the library and in schools; this series has more than 150 books, all in the same 48-page format and targeted at early elementary-age children. These books cover topics from geography and history to earth science and even to trucks and tractors.

Some tell real people's life stories. Otherwise known as biographies, these make up a big part of the nonfiction section, from the highly respected *Lincoln: A Photobiography*, by Russell Freedman, to the popular *Britney Spears*, by Alix Strauss. Children enjoy real-life, nonfiction tales about other kids, too. A popular example of this idea is Rebecca Hazel's book, *The Barefoot Book of Heroic Children*, which brings together the stories of some of the most exceptional children in the history of the world.

Or you might tell a story from history. In this category, the author tells the story of events of the past. Patricia Lauber, for example, wrote the photo-illustrated *Volcano: The Eruption and Healing of Mount St. Helens* about the recent eruption. James Cross Giblin wrote *When Plague Strikes* about three of the great plagues: the Black Death, smallpox, and AIDS.

In short, there are many ways to write both fiction and nonfiction. Publishers will be more interested in some kinds than in others, so your challenge now is to keep reading and figure out which publishers are right for you.

The Least You Need to Know

◆ All children's books are not created equal. As with many products, there are popular books and books seen as having quality.

◆ Just as there are for adults, there are different genres and types of books for children.

◆ Significant areas in children's literature include fantasy of various kinds, science fiction, historical fiction, and multicultural literature.

◆ Nonfiction may be "just the facts" or may use some of the techniques of fiction in order to be more engaging.

Chapter 11

Apples and Oranges (and Bananas): Differences Among Publishers

In This Chapter

- ◆ The differences between mass-market, trade, and institutional publishers
- ◆ Series vs. single titles and other consequences
- ◆ Why these differences matter to you

You can tell a picture book from a novel at 20 paces. You know there's more to children's books than talking animals and the first day of school. But answer me this: are all publishers alike? You may already have the idea that they aren't—let's take that idea and run with it.

Different publishers have different needs, and those differences matter. Some publishers don't even want to hear from you. In this chapter, I'll show you the different kinds of children's publishers and the books they publish.

Pineapples and Oranges—and Bananas? Different Kinds of Books

Children's publishers don't all sell their books to the same customers. Different customers want different kinds of books, and that means that there are different kinds of publishers. The three basic kinds are trade, mass market, and institutional (sometimes called educational) publishers. You know the saying "That's comparing apples and oranges"? Well, comparing trade, mass-market, and institutional books is doing just that. These three types of publishers can be very different.

Pineapples—Trade Books

Trade books are our pineapples. When publishers come together and talk of "trade" books, they're talking about books of all kinds for general readership, usually of higher quality, usually of higher price, and usually to be sold in bookstores (the book trade), with some also going to schools and libraries. Trade publishers are the quality publishers who produce the literary fiction we discussed in the previous chapter. In contrast, mass-market publishers produce the popular books—the inexpensive books, the books based on movies and TV shows, and also the less expensive editions of the books that started out in the trade. Trade books can be either hardcover or paperback—the form of the book doesn't matter. Trade publishers strive to produce books that people will buy based on their quality.

So don't confuse trade paperbacks with mass-market paperbacks. Generally, trade paperback books have the higher quality of a trade hardcover. Also, trade books virtually always remain larger in format than a mass-market book. And while you may find mass-market books on racks at newsstands and in supermarkets, you won't find trade paperbacks there (*Harry Potter*, as usual, excepted).

What should you send to a trade publisher? Well, you'll need to study the books they publish to see just what genres and formats they publish, as we explain how to do in Chapter 16. But in general, the "good" books we mentioned earlier are the kinds of books trade publishers seek. And in general, they and the institutional publishers are the ones you want to contact. They need original work. Although they are quite successful, mass-market publishers don't need originality.

Oranges—for the Masses

To find out what mass-market publishers do need, look at the other end of the book-publishing spectrum. We've already mentioned that mass market refers to paperback books that you can find in supermarket or newsstand racks. Other places you may find mass-market books include budget retail establishments like Kmart and Target. The big difference between mass-market and trade is cost. Imagine you're in the supermarket checkout line. Suddenly you notice the latest Danielle Steel novel that you've been dying to read as a guilty pleasure you've hidden from friends and relatives. Wow! Instead of the $24.95 price tag on the hardcover at Barnes & Noble, this pocket-size paperback only costs $5.99! Welcome to the world of mass market. These books are low-end, high-volume titles. No frills. No fancy book jackets. Just text on inexpensive paper. They are oranges, in short, and are very different from those trade pineapples.

The Childish Masses

The premise of high-volume, lower-end quality of mass-market books runs pretty much the same in children's publishing—but not quite. According to a late 1990s article in *Publishers Weekly*, "The Children's Mass Market Business," by Sally Lodge, "Children's mass market publishing business" is a "license-driven game," and this is still true today. Mass-market publishers "license" the right to do a book (or, more likely, many books) based on a children's TV show or movie or even a famous children's book. Parents pick the books up because they recognize the name, and buy them because they're cheap.

Can You Keep a Secret?

Whereas a mass-market publisher of children's books may release more than 500 titles or more a year, some trade publishers of quality children's books won't even publish 50 titles in a year! Moreover, the quantities printed and sold of those 500 or more titles will probably exceed the print runs of most—if not all—of the trade-released titles several times over. That's mass-market!

Mass Appeal: What Publishers Want

This licensing approach isn't completely different from what the adult mass-market publishers are doing. Name recognition is everything, but for adults it's Danielle Steel, John Grisham, and Stephen King, while for children it's Disney characters, Teletubbies, and Barney. Eminent creators such as Eric Carle, Dr. Seuss, H. A. Rey, or Beatrix Potter are also becoming name brands in this area; however, you can't expect to do the same until you are well along in your career (or until you are dead). And of course, as with adult mass market, some children's mass-market books originally appeared as more expensive trade books.

Opportunities for creative types are limited in this area. Mass-market publishers do produce original books, especially novelty books, but they usually do the writing themselves. And whether they are putting together the latest series of stories based on a Nickelodeon hit or repackaging acclaimed hardcovers in inexpensive editions, these publishers don't want your original work. They may hire you to turn out a dozen stories featuring their characters. Illustrators might do better, although you may find you can only get work through an artist's rep and that your creativity is strictly limited. The companies controlling the characters being licensed usually have the power to approve how they are depicted, and they aren't going to let a character from Sesame Street, for example, look or act differently in print from the way he does on the screen.

Bananas? The Institutional Market

As if the pineapples and oranges of trade and mass-market publishing weren't complicated enough, you also need to take note of publishers that concentrate on schools and libraries, or the institutional market. They typically produce books that look much like trade books, but that sell almost exclusively to schools and libraries. Just to make things more complicated, you may occasionally find their books in bookstores, too. You'll find clues to a publisher's identity in their catalog, so be sure to study how to read one in Chapter 18.

What you might call hard-core institutional publishing are those series of biographies, country profiles, and the like, that children turn to for good, solid information. These are the books that are published by companies such as Franklin Watts or Enslow. Browse a library's children's nonfiction section and you'll find many examples.

As previously suggested, needs and interests vary among these three types of publishers. In later chapters, I'll show you how to learn more about those needs and interests. Before you can do that, though, you need to get a grasp of series and how publishers handle them.

Please Be Series: One Book vs. Many

Someone scanning the shelves in a bookstore or a library could easily conclude that most children's books are published in a series. That may explain why editors at trade publishers continue to receive letters and manuscripts from authors who have written 1 story, or perhaps who just have an idea for 1 story, and are proposing a 24-book series complete with accompanying dolls and coloring books. Editors are used to rejecting those proposals, because the author doesn't actually have a good idea for a series. Or more likely, the author sent the idea to a publisher that doesn't publish *any* series. So what can you do if you want to develop a series?

Class Rules _____

Editors at publishers such as Charlesbridge, where I used to work, don't like to see manuscripts proudly presented as the "first book in a series" because they primarily publish single titles. If a book is a phenomenal success, they might want to do another; however, at the beginning, such publishers prefer for authors to put their energy into 1 book instead of planning the first 12.

What's the Big Difference?

What's the difference between writing a single book and developing a *series?* Actually, that's like asking, "What's the difference between one baby and quintuplets?" With one baby, you possess a single, unique person who remains distinctly his or her own person, unattached in birth to any other human being. Quintuplets, however different or unique from each other, are also alike in genetic coding and shared space. Books in a series are no different. Each book contains new content, yet continues with the same "genetic code"—content, setting, theme, format, characters, or purpose. The books are linked much like multiples are linked.

Vocabulary List _____

Books linked in theme, purpose, characters, style, setting, or content can be part of a **series.** Each subsequent book in the series continues one or more of these elements. Often the series will also have a title, just as a book does.

Series or Single Title?

Every series begins with one book, right? But not every book is part of a series, nor can it be. In fact, the vast majority of titles published for children are single titles, and so they should remain. Many authors write only this kind of book, and many fine children's books started as one book and remained so. Consider such Caldecott Medal–winning titles as *Mirette on a High Wire*, by Emily Arnold McCully, Peggy Rathmann's *Officer Buckle and Gloria*, or Allen Say's *Grandfather's Journey*. All have compelling characters, but they were published as single titles and, in spite of their success, have not spawned a series.

Class Rules _____

Don't assume that a book with one or more sequels is part of a series. Although sequels may feature many of the same characters as the first book, a series goes on much longer. The five books in Lloyd Alexander's *Prydain Chronicles* are more of a set than a series. Think *Baby-Sitters Club, Animorphs,* and *American Girls* as examples of series.

Many authors are tempted to take a beloved character or an idea and build a series out of it. But it may not be a good idea, if only because the publisher who would be interested in a story that stands nicely on its own would not be interested in it as part of a series. For the most part, trade publishers publish single titles, and that's what you should write or illustrate for them. The other kinds of publishers, mass market and institutional, do produce series. So proposing a series to a publisher that doesn't want them is as fruitless (sorry) as submitting a manuscript for a single book to a publisher that only publishes series.

I Didn't Mean to Do That: The Unintended Series

What if you write a book and never even consider that it will evolve into a series? What if the one book you write becomes so "tickling" that kids yearn for more? What if the concept is so engaging that the public wants more? That's exactly what happened with Laura Numeroff's delightful picture book *If You Give a Mouse a Cookie*. Kids loved the idea of "if, then" that Numeroff explored. Finally, after many antics, the mouse comes full circle and returns to the beginning and the cookie. Children immediately embraced the simple concept and funny actions of the story's little mouse and child and wanted more. Numeroff responded with *If You Give a Moose a Muffin*, *If You Give a Pig a Pancake*, and *If You Give a Cat a Cupcake*. The author's single title resulted in a series of four. *Voilà!* The unintended series. Of course, this doesn't happen very often.

Let's Get Series Now

Mass-market fiction is home to one kind of series. For example, consider one of the most popular children's book series of all time: the *Nancy Drew* mysteries. In the series, our sleuthing teen unravels tales of the unknown and uncovers mysteries. Each story involves a different plot and scenario, but two common elements—Nancy and a mystery—remain throughout the series. Style, format, and length also do not vary.

Vocabulary List

A **packager** or **development house** is much like a publisher, except that its work stops with the completion of a manuscript, or in some cases with the printing of the books. A publisher puts its name on the books and handles the sales and marketing.

For lengthy series such as *Nancy Drew*, which are developed by independent companies called *packagers* or *development houses*, there might even be a "bible"— a notebook detailing all the character quirks, dress guidelines, history, and other information—to ensure consistency from book to book.

Other well-known fiction series such as *Goosebumps* or *Sweet Valley High* have similar characteristics. Mass-market is a very different world from the more prestigious trade-publishing world, and the kind of writing an author does for a series is different from the kind of writing done for single titles. Single-title books can stand on their own. Books written for a series, especially for a planned series, often can't stand alone. Or all the books are essentially the same, providing comforting and satisfying familiarity by rerunning the same plot, with minor variations, over and over again.

Are fiction series like the ones mentioned the only ones? No, there are others, as the following sections discuss.

School and Library Publishers

Not all series books fit into the fun category like the *Animorphs* or *The Boxcar Children* books. Some series books are downright bookish—or, rather, textbookish! We're talking about nonfiction series titles that publishers develop specifically for schools and libraries. These are the bread-and-butter of institutional publishers, sometimes confusingly called "educational" publishers, but they are not textbook publishers. As noted by Dorothy Hinshaw Patent in a *Horn Book Magazine* article, "As trade book publishers have cut down on the number of science books they publish, institutional publishers have rushed to fill the gaps, producing more books than ever. They have come out with every conceivable kind of series, especially in biology—life cycles of animals, habitats of the world, and so forth." Not surprisingly, some knowledge of school curriculums comes in very handy.

These series come in different forms. Some are short and focus on a specific subject area, such as 12 books on 12 different habitats. Others are identified by a specific design, length, and vocabulary level, such as the *True Books* of Children's Press. There are hundreds of titles within this series, grouped into series within the series, on subjects such as national parks, continents, and transportation. Or one subject area, such as biographies, will be the focus of an ongoing series that continues to add titles.

Series nonfiction generally doesn't pay well, but it can be a training ground. Noted writers like Seymour Simon started out writing series books for Franklin Watts, an institutional publisher. Now he publishes with top-level trade publishers.

The writing experience itself may also be different from writing for trade publishers. When asked whether he found writing for library publishers like Children's Press to be different from or similar to writing for trade publishers, Larry Brimner, the author of *Brave Mary, Dinosaurs Dance, E-Mail, A Migrant Family*, and many others, first pointed out a difference that is not as great as it used to be: "There was a time when one could look at books published by educational publishers and identify them by their appearance. They looked 'text-bookish,' as if they belonged in schools. Today, thankfully, this is largely no longer the case." However, he says that any manuscript that does not fit into an existing series or serve to launch a new one will be a very hard sell. Also, as noted in our story, the publisher's focus on the school market may limit what an author can do.

Playground Stories

Larry Dane Brimner notes one significant, and perhaps surprising difference between institutional and trade publishers:

> I've also found that because of their reliance on educational consultants, school and library publishers sometimes restrict a writer's artistic expression. A phrase that is artfully crafted and expressed may be rewritten because the consultant may not understand why an author has begun a sentence with a conjunction or used a fragmented sentence and doesn't understand how these departures from "school English" can be used as teaching points by teachers. This typically is not the case with trade publishers, where an author is much freer to express himself with language that is artistically crafted.

Writing for institutional publishers, then, can be different from working with trade publishers. If you know this from the beginning, you're less likely to be disappointed.

Getting Down on Your Knees

If you've concluded that you do indeed have a viable idea for a series, you next need to take care in getting it to a publisher. Choose the kind of publisher carefully, of course, by researching their program to make sure that they publish the types of books that you envision. For the more mass-market fiction series, such as *Goosebumps*, look to packagers rather than publishers. You'll find information about specific packagers and publishers in "market guides" such as *Children's Writer's and Illustrator's Market*.

If you're an unpublished author, you may not get anywhere, no matter how good your idea. You need credentials, so our final suggestion is that if you want to write a series, your best bet may be to develop your "chops" as a writer by writing other books first—perhaps single titles or contributing to existing series. Many packagers hire writers to actually write the books in a series after the series author outlines them. Many institutional publishers extend some of their series with new books from other authors. Look around and learn about the world of series before jumping into it, and you're more likely to succeed.

" " **Playground Stories** _____

Bruce Balan, author of the *Cyber.kdz* series, notes that there are always exceptions to the "rules":

> A fiction series requires a proposal that will sell your idea to an editor. As editors see thousands of these proposals, yours must stand out. So not only do you need a new or fresh idea for your series, but it is very helpful to find an interesting way to present it. I sold *Cyber.kdz* with a proposal that was written as a series of e-mail communications between myself and the fictional kids of the books …. *Cyber.kdz* taught me that you don't always have to follow the "rules." I was told repeatedly that it was impossible to sell a series without prior series-writing experience as well as middle-grade fiction experience (for a middle-grade series). I had neither. Remember, there is always the exception!

Double Vision! The Blurring of the Boundaries

You've got it all figured out, right? You know about institutional, trade, and mass-market publishers, and you know that you need to account for their very different needs when you deal with them. Don't hold on to those distinctions too rigidly! You also need to know that things are changing in publishing; we call this a blurring of the boundaries. Lately, publishers are producing "high-end" mass-market books, also known as "mass with class," which can just as easily sit in a Borders as in a Wal-Mart. These books, though still softcover, are made from high-quality materials. At the same time, trade publishers are creating inexpensive versions of their books, and reaching into the mass market. Perhaps not as inexpensive as a generic coloring book, but certainly less than the $15 price of a hardcover, these books run the gamut from classics like *Goodnight Moon*, priced reasonably at about $6, to *Blue's Costume Party*, a $4 stapled softcover based on the popular Nickelodeon character.

As a result, it's not as easy as it used to be to get a sense of what a publisher is doing because they may be doing a lot of things at once. You need to work harder to find out where the right home for your manuscript is.

The Least You Need to Know

- ◆ Books may be published as a trade title, an institutional title, or a mass-market book.

- ◆ Series are usually published by mass market and institutional publishers, not by trade publishers.

- ◆ You have to approach different kinds of publishers differently.

- ◆ Lately, the lines are blurring between trade and mass-market.

Chapter 12

Is It Ready to Hand In?

In This Chapter

- ◆ Find ways to ensure your manuscript is ready to send to a publisher
- ◆ Learn why the opinions of your friends may not tell you much about your manuscript
- ◆ Get the skinny on critique groups
- ◆ Discover the best ways to receive a good critique of your work
- ◆ Learn about children's writing programs and classes

You've learned about children's books and the publishing business, and you think you're ready to send your manuscript to a publisher. Are you? Okay, you've heard fabulous things about your writing abilities, but you need more than your neighbor's sister's opinion. You need to learn how to obtain useful criticism that will help you improve your manuscript and make it publisher-ready. We'll give you several options for improving your writing and discovering just when the time is right to hand in your manuscript.

Rabbit's Friends and Relations

You may remember that Rabbit, in the *Winnie the Pooh* stories, had a horde of friends of relations, none of whom were much help in getting

Pooh unstuck from his hole. Like Rabbit, you might tell your closest and dearest friends and relations about your aspirations to write a children's book. And, of course, they will support you and your creative side. Show them your first effort, and they'll invariably exclaim, "Fabulous!" "We loved it!" "It'll sell a million copies!" This sounds encouraging, doesn't it?

In reality, your relatives and friends—though well meaning—aren't the best choice if you seek an honest and educated response to your work. It's wonderful to have the support of your mom or your hubby, but in most cases, they don't possess the skills and experience needed to evaluate your manuscript. So go to them for support, but to others—experts—to provide you with criticism. Ugh! Criticism. It seems like such an ugly word. In truth, criticism helps you become a better writer. Let's begin the process.

Reading Aloud

I know many writers who use the simple but powerful feedback tool of reading their work aloud. When you do this, you hear things that you won't notice when reading a manuscript over silently. An awkward construction jumps out at you. A missing transition reveals itself. Try it for yourself, and you'll see.

One Is the Loneliest Number

The first person to whom you should read your book aloud is none other than you! Stand up, pick up your clean, typed (or printed) sheets of creative genius, and begin to read out loud. Although you may feel funny at first, you'll soon become comfortable with the sound of your own voice and begin to perceive and hear where changes need to be made. If you hate being alone, pull the dog into the room and read to your pet.

Guided Responses

After you've listened to your own words and made any changes from your review, pull in an audience to hear your words. Now is the time to gather sisters, brothers, uncles, neighbors, and co-workers together. But don't ask them to listen and tell you what they think. Instead, give them specific tasks. Ask them to tell you how the story sounds and if they can catch any problems, such as an awkward word or a confusing phrase. You may even want to give your audience a *response sheet*.

Here are some examples of the types of questions you can include on a response sheet. You may even choose to let the parties read your story silently first and then respond after your reading.

1. What is your gut reaction to the story? Did you feel any emotions while reading it/listening to it? If so, what did you feel?

2. Please read the story aloud. Are there any awkward breaks in the text? If so, where are they?

3. Please note any word choices that you think are wrong or not precise. Is there a different word I could have used? What?

Vocabulary List

In the writing process, often a writer relies upon a peer editor to improve the manuscript. For writers or peers with little editing experience, sometimes a **response sheet** is useful. On the sheet, the writer lists certain ideas, devices, or grammatical points for listeners to consider. Then the person listening or reading the manuscript need only go through the response sheet to help clarify the writer's problems or strengths.

4. What age group do you think would most enjoy this book?

5. Who is my audience?

6. Please mark egregious grammatical errors and correct them, including the following:

   ◆ Comma splices

   ◆ Misplaced modifiers

   ◆ Misspelled words

   ◆ Change in verb tense

   ◆ Punctuation errors

   ◆ Run-on sentences

   ◆ Sentence fragments

7. Finally, what do you like best about this story? What don't you like about this story? How might I improve upon this story?

The Director's Chair

This may sound strange, but another way to get a different perspective on your writing is to have someone else read it to you. You'll hear it afresh, and because that person won't be familiar with it, you'll notice problems more easily than if you were reading it yourself. When you read the story, you can juice it up with drama and fix its rhythm, but someone coming to it cold won't be able to do that. Sit with a copy of the text and make notes as your mouthpiece reads.

Apples of Your Writing Eye: Children

You've read solo, and you've coerced your friends and family into listening to your work. Now comes the true test of your skills: reading to children. After all, you want to write for them. Children may not provide you with expert grammar advice, but what they do provide is even more valuable. Children offer you a direct emotional response to your story. Because children love being read to, though, don't take an enthusiastic response as a sign that your book is ready to go. (And above all, don't offer it as a sign of the quality of your work when you write to a publisher. Any writer sending a manuscript to a publisher can claim that kids love it.) So if you want to use children as critics, you have to learn to interpret their responses and even guide them.

Class Rules

Be careful while you are reading to a room of kids. You'll want to read expressively—but not with over-the-top dramatics. Kids naturally gravitate toward drama. You may con them into loving your book when, in actuality, they loved the way you read your book. Choose short selections from your work and from two published books. Watch their reactions. To which were they most attentive? Where did they react spontaneously to the action?

Start with children who don't know you. Your own children or your neighbor's children are hopelessly biased, and you wouldn't want it otherwise. Instead, gather a junior focus group. How do you go about wrangling together a group of kids to listen to your work and provide unbiased feedback?

You go to where the kids are. Depending on the age your book targets, seek an audience either through a day-care center/preschool, elementary school, or middle/high school.

Set up your reading group as thoughtfully as you can. It should be fun for the children, but also useful to you, a market researcher. Find two published books with stories of the same type and of similar lengths. Type them out like yours. Practice reading all of them so that you can spend as much time as possible with your eyes on the children. Watch their reaction. What is their body language? Listen for spontaneous *aahs* and *oohs*. Listen for whispering and other signs that you've lost their interest. How they react may tell you more than what they say afterward, but do ask them questions when you are done reading. Ask them if they had a favorite part and why, or ask questions to help the children draw comparisons. Don't "coach" them with hints about what you expect them to like.

Of course, you can't just step into a local school and start reading. You need to follow procedure. If you know a teacher who happens to teach the same grade or skill level of kids to which you're targeting your book, ask her to host you for a class reading. Then you don't need to gain permission through the office, which may involve filling out forms and having a background check done. If you don't know an educator (which is more likely the case), you can approach your local schools and explain that you are a children's book writer hoping to gain some feedback on your book from kids. You may have to let the principal, teacher, and parents read your manuscript first before they will give you permission to use the classroom. Unfortunately, due to the dangers of our world, schools act as the children's protector as well as the their educators. Expect them to be wary of you.

Know-It-Alls: A Critique Group

Every writer—from the novice to the expert—knows the merits of joining a writer's group and receiving critiques on her work. We highly recommend that you seek out a local writer's organization or club and join. If you can't find one, then create one. And if there aren't enough writers in your area to sustain one, look into exchanging critiques by e-mail with people you've met at conferences and classes.

You'll find the experience and keen eyes of other writers a tremendous asset to your own writing. You, in turn, will also provide an invaluable service to your fellow club mates: your keen observations about their work. Generally, club members will all bring their work "to the table" where a read-around occurs. Each member reads another member's work and responds to it. Sometimes, copies of your work are required for all members who then take them, read them, and report back at the next meeting on your story.

Beyond the great instructional feedback you'll receive, the camaraderie between members extends beyond the meetings and the critiques. It's comforting to know that there are others with aspirations like yours, learning the ropes, writing, hoping one day to publish their book. The group can serve to keep you focused toward your goal and intent on retaining your dream.

Critique groups can be tremendously helpful, but they can also err in two very different ways. If the group is too supportive, with most comments being along the lines of "What a wonderful story," everyone will feel great about his writing, but won't be pushed to improve it. On the other hand, if the group nitpicks every line, or is never satisfied with anything, its members won't know where they stand. Strive for balance in your group.

Playground Stories

Lisa Rowe Fraustino says: "A successful and lasting critique group is like a family, with all its commensurate joys and foibles. Commitment and caring are its lifeblood. We are very vulnerable to each other as we lay our writing open for criticism. Through it we strengthen our manuscripts and our own characters. But the very best aspect of being in a strong critique group isn't, to me, the critiques, but the camaraderie and support involved. Once a month we are not alone with the page." Her group has produced several published writers.

Can You Keep a Secret?

Several major universities offer specialized programs in writing for children. One of the best programs, an MFA in Writing for Children and Young Adults, comes through Vermont College. For more information, go online to www.tui.edu/vermontcollege/templates/grad.php?article_id=10. Others offer summer institutes—there's probably one near you.

Another valuable aspect of critique groups is that information of the right kind seems to naturally gravitate toward them. One person in the club may know where to find that information you need about moose behavior. Another member may tell of a writer coming to town and orchestrate a meeting. A third may have news of changes to a publisher's editorial staff. The "brain trust" within these groups is wonderful. It's like having several personal trainers for your creative spirit. So what are you waiting for? Grab your manuscript and join a writers group.

Writing Classes

Here's something you'll hear over and over from experienced writers. You should never, never stop learning. Being a writer, or for that matter an illustrator, means always trying new things and trying to improve on what came before. Writing classes, seminars, conferences—all improve your writing and help hone your craft. Each year, all over the United States, writers meet for workshops and classes, usually taught by experienced authors. These are great settings in which to learn and to get objective and often skilled feedback on your writing.

Beyond the workshops and classes, you can find specialized programs in writing and even writing children's literature. And if a college degree in writing isn't what you envision or want, local colleges, universities, and extension campuses typically showcase a host of composition, writing, and English classes for those who just want to improve their writing skills. See what's available in your area—and when considering teachers, apply the criteria we suggest for writing consultants later in this chapter.

Playground Stories

Not all authors favor the group approach. Says Charles Ghigna:

> Stop attending workshops. Read other writers if you must, but for heaven sakes save your soul and stay away from how-to workshops and conferences. At worst, they'll drain you of your creativity. At best, they'll have you writing like everyone else. Keep what little originality you have left from childhood. Protect it. Nurture it. Let it run wild. That's all you have. That's all you need. The only way to learn to write is to write. There is no other way. Workshops and conferences can only take you away from the real work—the real world of writing.

The perspective works for Ghigna, who has authored more than 25 books, including *Tickle Day: Poems from Father Goose.*

Critiques by Professionals

What about critiques from professionals, such as freelance editors or published writers? Well, your writing group may include a few professionals who already are offering you advice without charging you. So why pay a fee? Or if you've got money to spend, why not use it on a class? Certainly, if you take a class, you should receive some good input. But good writing consultants can provide you with the insight and detailed criticism that will most improve your writing. If you work with a good consultant, it can be like working with a good editor. The trick is finding the good ones who are out there.

Good Guys and Bad Guys

Your challenge is to find the good professional and not just some fraud who poses as a professional and charges a fee to make money. Believe me, there are frauds out there. They prey on writers wanting to succeed—even at great expense. Most real writers—professionals—consider their work an art form. Though they do charge for the classes and critiques they give (if they have time for them at all), writers usually like to offer sage wisdom to fledglings and nurture their success. After all, we were all in the same place at one time. Be particularly wary of those people who call themselves "agents" and want to charge you a "reading fee" to evaluate your work. You are not likely to get useful feedback for that fee—or any help finding a publisher. So how do you go about finding an honest and learned writing consultant? You act like a detective and do your research. As you come across possible candidates, ask yourself—or them—questions like the following:

- Who recommended this person? How did I come across him or her? If someone you respect—such as another writer in your writing group—highly recommends the consultant, that's a good sign. If, on the other hand, someone who no one has ever heard of approaches you, be wary.

- Has the person actually published any writing, or worked for a publisher as an editor? Ask for books the person wrote or edited. Look for someone with a track record of publishing with a publisher—not self-publishing. And check out the books and make your own judgment on the author's writing.

- Ask for references. Who else has the consultant helped? If the list includes a few established and respected writers and *you can verify* that the consultant actually helped the writer, you're in good shape. But if the consultant can't provide references, run.

- Ask for a resumé. Where did the consultant previously work? Other publishers? As an editor? At a fast-food chain? You get the idea. The more experienced the consultant or agent is, the better your chances of receiving a helpful critique.

- Finally, don't automatically run from a substantial fee. Many good professional writers must charge a fee to weed out the less serious and to allow themselves time for their own work.

The key to finding a professional is asking questions. Just as all law-enforcement agencies run background checks on future cops, you need to run your own background check on anyone who charges to look at your work. If you don't want to do this, you're better off working with people you know—the people in your local children's writers group, the staff at the local college, and even your own friends and relations—with some guidance provided by you, of course.

The Least You Need to Know

◆ Although well meaning, relatives and friends may not prove the best choices for critiquing your work. For one, they are biased. You need to seek out unbiased parties to look at your work.

◆ Start with yourself. Read your work aloud and listen to the language, words, and beats to begin the editing process. Have someone read it to you.

◆ Join a writers club, take a class or two, and seek out professional perspectives of your work.

◆ Don't forget that kids want the straight scoop about your story. Observe their reactions to your work carefully.

◆ When seeking the help of a professional, thoroughly investigate the individual's credentials.

Part 3

Out into the World

When your manuscript is ready to go, you need to know just how to send it. Or if you want to get work as an illustrator, how do you do that? Feeling unsure and thinking some name-dropping might help? This part tells you just how it might help, and how it might not help.

This part gives you the guidance you need by looking at some publishers and their catalogs, and then looking beyond them to some parts of the children's market that aren't so fully explored. Finally, this part explains just how important you are to publishers, and how you can best contact them and start to work with them, once that first precious personal letter comes.

Know the Rules, If You're Playing

In This Chapter

◆ How to prepare your manuscript

◆ What you must, and must not, include in a submission to a publisher

◆ What a cover letter is and how to write one

◆ How not to put a manuscript reader to sleep

So you've finished your manuscript and you're ready to send a copy to dozens of publishers to see how many of them are interested. If that's your plan (or something like it), stop—you're already breaking two of the basic rules. Following the rules won't guarantee that you get published, but it may save you some time, spare you some grief, and help you come across as a professional.

In this chapter, you'll learn how to prepare your manuscript and a letter to go with it, untangle the mysteries of unsolicited manuscripts and multiple submissions, tips on writing cover and query letters, and some alternative ways to get in the door at companies that have closed theirs.

The Basics

It's hard not to obsess over the treasured story or nonfiction work you're about to send off into the world. You want it to be just right. Should you type it double- or single-spaced? Should you write a letter to go with it? What else do you need to send? Fortunately, what you need to do is pretty simple.

Sew a Label on It

Getting your manuscript ready to go is straightforward. First of all, type it, using double-spaced lines. Editors don't bother to read handwritten stories. On the first page, either upper right or upper left, put your name and full address. That's important, in case the manuscript gets separated from your letter and envelope. Skip a few lines, and put the title. Skip a few more and start the story. You can skip straight to a second page and start the story there, but that's not necessary.

Make sure the manuscript is easy to read. Type it using both capitals and lowercase letters; ALL CAPITAL LETTERS MAKE A STORY MORE DIFFICULT TO READ. Though *the fancy typefaces that come ready to use with word processing programs are tempting, don't use one of them either;* good old Times Roman or Courier is just fine. A book might use a fancier typeface, but right now, your goal is to make your manuscript as easy on the eyes as possible. And that means that white—not pink, neon yellow, or textured—paper is your choice.

Break the manuscript up into paragraphs. Start a new page only when you come to the end of another one. Don't try to type it out as if in book form. That's particularly important if you've written a picture book; 32 pages, each with one line on them, can be frustrating to read. Editors are used to imagining how a book would be laid out, so we prefer a standard format, whether that means the manuscript is 1 page or 200 pages long. If you want to, you can put a double line break wherever you imagine a new page, but that's not necessary.

After the manuscript is ready, make a copy of it. Never send out your original and only copy.

Send a SASE, Don't Be Lazy!

If a publisher doesn't like your manuscript, you'd rather not know about it. But to keep track of who has seen it and who hasn't, you need to enclose a *SASE* (pronounced *say*-zee). Always, always include a **s**elf-**a**ddressed **s**tamped **e**nvelope for the publisher's response and the return of the manuscript. This can be expensive, especially if a novel is involved, but don't take a shortcut and include an envelope "for response only," as some writers have started to do. This sends a message that you don't care enough about your work to get it back. Sure, you kept a copy, but can you bear to imagine your work being thrown out or recycled? Maybe you can, but don't let a publisher think so.

Vocabulary List

The envelope a rejected manuscript gets returned in is a **SASE**, which stands for self-addressed stamped envelope. It carries your complete address in the space where the address belongs, and it must be large enough and accommodate enough postage for your manuscript.

Be Properly Addressed

You may not know the individual to whom you are sending your manuscript, or even his name, but experienced writers always include a brief cover letter. You'll learn what you need to write in it later in this chapter, and some samples are provided in the back of the book.

Put your manuscript, SASE, and cover letter in an envelope. If the manuscript is only a few pages, you can fold it neatly and put it in a standard business-size envelope. Don't jam it into something smaller. If the manuscript is longer and you need to send it unfolded, use a plain manila envelope. You don't need to bind or cover it. Type up or neatly write an address label and send it all by the good old U.S. mail.

And Then You Wait

You'll also need patience, but don't send that with your manuscript. Hold onto it. Most publishers these days need a minimum of three months to read through their submissions, and some take much longer than that. If you want some assurance that the publisher received your manuscript, use the inexpensive "Delivery Confirmation" option from the U.S. Postal Service, or include a stamped, self-addressed postcard and request that it be returned to you when your package is opened. But don't be surprised if that postcard doesn't come back to you right away—some publishers don't even open manuscript submissions until they read them.

That's it. Letter, manuscript, SASE, envelope, and patience are all you need to make an unsolicited submission to a publisher.

What's an Unsolicited Submission, Anyway?

Some many thousands of manuscripts a typical publisher receives each year come from authors who are already working with that publisher. But many manuscripts are *unsolicited*, meaning that the publisher did not request them. Some publishers still read these, in the hopes of finding the next Margaret Wise Brown or J. K. Rowling. Maybe that's you.

Though the odds are long, the unsolicited manuscript is your foot in the door. You'll have to find out which publishers read them (you'll learn how to do that in Chapter 18), because not all do. Thanks to this policy, children's books are one area of publishing in which you don't need an agent or a friend in the business, because if you follow the rules and have chosen the right kind of publisher, you've got a chance of finding a home for your work.

Vocabulary List

An **unsolicited manuscript** or **unsolicited submission** is the same thing—a manuscript that a publisher did not solicit, or ask for, from an author. You send solicited or requested manuscripts in response to a letter or phone call from a publisher, and if you are doing so, you should write that on the envelope.

Vocabulary List

The **slush pile** consists of all the manuscripts that a publisher has received from writers the publisher doesn't know. They will be read, eventually.

When your manuscript arrives at a publisher, the envelope is opened, probably by an intern or an editorial assistant. She may then read it herself or leave it for a junior editor to read. What a cruel fate! You had hoped it would be read by Mr. Olympian Bigshot or Ms. Children's Publishing Wonder. Don't be discouraged. Mr. Bigshot and Ms. Wonder are so busy with the authors and illustrators they have in their stable that even if they read your manuscript and loved it, it's unlikely they'd publish it anytime soon. Editors at their level see many more "publishable" manuscripts over the course of a year than they can actually publish.

Fortunately, the junior editors and assistants reading the unsolicited manuscripts are exactly the people you want to reach. They don't already have well-known writers to publish. They can rise up in their company by discovering writers with promise. So they spend as little time as they can filing and typing letters, and as much time as they can mining the *slush pile*.

Some publishers, of course, don't accept unsolicited submissions. If you aren't a published author or don't have an agent, they won't read your manuscript. This seems terribly unfair, and your natural response might be to try to find a way in through a back door. There *are* ways to do that, and you'll hear about some of them later in this chapter and in Chapter 17, but it may not be worth the effort. The companies that have closed their doors just don't need to find new authors. You can spend a lot of energy and time making contact with editors at one of those companies only to discover that they don't "have room on their list"—they've already got enough books signed up for the next few years. Instead, consider spending that time finding out about companies that really want your work.

I've Been Waiting Forever

Why bother to find the right company to send your manuscript to? After all, your acquaintance, Savvy Writer, tells you that it can take six months or longer to hear back from a publisher. Even the "fast" ones don't promise a response in less than three. You know that the first editor to read your work may not fall in love with it. It could be years before you get it to the right person. But Savvy suggests a solution. Why not send your manuscript to a bunch of publishers at the same time, say 20 or 30?

It's tempting to resort to *multiple submissions* and send copies of your manuscript to several publishers at once. You'll keep track of whom you sent it to, and if one of them offers to publish it, you'll let the others know. Think twice before you do this. You may be helping to kill the goose that lays the golden egg by overloading the publishers that still read the slush pile, causing more of them to close their doors. You may be wasting paper and postage on mailing 37 copies of your manuscript when further research would have helped you target 3 or 4. And some publishers are keeping their doors open by only reading manuscripts that are clearly identified as *exclusive submissions* to that publisher.

Vocabulary List

An **exclusive submission** is a manuscript sent to only one publisher. A **multiple submission** is a manuscript sent to two or more publishers at the same time. A simultaneous submission is the same as a multiple submission.

Can You Keep a Secret?

You've sent your manuscript to a publisher that receives 6,000 manuscripts every year, and publishes only 60 books, most by its current authors. The odds against someone even reading your manuscript look very long. But many of those submissions will disqualify themselves; they're badly written or have been sent to the wrong publisher. Yours might be one of only a few hundred, or a few dozen, truly worthwhile manuscripts.

Whether you choose to submit your manuscript exclusively or to a short, targeted list, is up to your own sense of ethics, but do not resort to scatter-shot multiple submissions to dozens of publishers. No week goes by at Charlesbridge, the publishing company where I used to work, without the need to open and return a novel, sometimes even a novel for adults. This is a waste of time for both staff and authors, because Charlesbridge doesn't publish novels, and never has. What's the problem, you ask? Writers sending out manuscripts multiply and indiscriminately further overload the publishing staffs who read the manuscripts, and contribute to publishers' decisions to close their doors.

Dear Somebody

After you've got your sense of ethics settled, you are ready to launch your manuscript into a sea of many other manuscripts. With your name and address on your manuscript, no publishing credits to cite, and no specific person to write to, why should you bother to write a letter to accompany the manuscript? Why not just put the manuscript in the envelope and send it off? Because a letter is the polite and professional thing to do, even though the envelope says "Submissions Editor" and your letter's salutation is "Dear Editor."

Vocabulary List

A **cover letter** is the letter that accompanies your manuscript.

Class Rules

We've heard some authors say that a Post-It note with a brief greeting is all that you need to send with a submission. We don't agree. If you know the editor, that's fine; otherwise you're assuming a degree of acquaintance by being so informal. Write that letter, and let your professionalism and personality shine.

Covering a Cover Letter

Check Appendix C for some sample *cover letters*. The absolutely necessary elements of a cover letter are few:

◆ Your name and address

◆ The publisher's name and address

◆ The date

◆ The salutation: "Dear Editor"

◆ The title of your manuscript

◆ The type of manuscript it is

◆ A brief and tempting description of your manuscript

◆ Your signature

What Not to Include

The list of what *not* to put in a cover letter (or include with it) is much longer, but the most important items not to include are as follows:

- ◆ Your resumé

- ◆ A marketing plan

- ◆ Endorsements

- ◆ The statement that your children loved it (of course, they did)

- ◆ Apologies for your lack of experience

- ◆ A lengthy plot summary

A good cover letter is simple and businesslike. It contains the necessary information, and no more, and it does not distract the editor from the business at hand, which is reading your manuscript.

Why Can't I E-Mail Them?

I can hear people whispering in the back of the room, "Why is he telling us about the right kind of paper, the envelope, and SASEs? I'm just going to e-mail my manuscript to the publisher!" It would be nice if it worked that way, but so far, it mostly doesn't. Publishers are slow to change, and making their submissions process electronic is not a high priority.

Be sure to research what a company expects you to do. Some companies do accept queries by e-mail, but few accept submissions that way, with the exception of web publishers (and that's a whole other ball game). They're more difficult to read onscreen, you can't stuff them in your briefcase to read on the subway, or perhaps editors just prefer to have all submissions come in one stream. For whatever reason, don't expect to be able to e-mail your manuscript. Stick to snail mail, and cultivate your patience.

"Query First": Letters About Manuscripts

Sometimes you'll find another hurdle to simply sending off your manuscript to a publisher. Some publishers, particularly for novels or longer works of nonfiction, require a *query letter*, in which you ask them if they want to see your manuscript or not. This procedure has advantages and disadvantages for you. On the one hand, it may save you postage and copying costs. It's also completely acceptable to send out several query

Vocabulary List

A **query letter** is a letter you send to a publisher to ask, or query, if it is interested in seeing the manuscript.

Can You Keep a Secret?

Editor and writer Jackie Ogburn has written a thoughtful and funny guide to cover letters and query letters, complete with sample letters showing what to do and not do. You can read it online at www.underdown.org/covlettr.htm.

letters for the same manuscript simultaneously. On the other hand, it gives the publisher the opportunity to say no before even seeing your manuscript.

If a publisher does not require a query first, and your manuscript is short, it's usually better to just send the manuscript. That saves you the time you would have spent waiting for a response to your query, and it lets you put your best foot forward—your manuscript.

If you must query, or choose to do so to avoid sending out your 500-page fantasy epic, remember that your letter is meant to intrigue the reader, so that he will want to read your manuscript. If your manuscript is fiction, including a paragraph or two from it can be effective. Choose a passage that displays your style to good advantage. If you have a nonfiction piece, think about what it is that makes your subject interesting. And be sure to include sample chapters or an outline if the publisher's guidelines request them.

That's a No-No!

The quality of your writing will get noticed, in the end, but be sure to avoid the common mistakes that might mean that no one actually bothers to read your manuscript, or dismisses it quickly when he does.

Neatness and Spelling Count

You thought you could stop worrying about spelling and punctuation when you left school, right? You were wrong; presentation counts in publishing, and you will lose points for spelling mistakes, bad grammar, and even bad style. An editor is learning about *you* as she reads your cover letter and manuscript. If you come across as a sloppy typist or a careless speller, she may expect that to continue if she were to work with you.

Class Rules

Do your best to write a decent cover or query letter, but don't obsess over it. The letter doesn't have to be perfect for someone to read the manuscript accompanying it or request the manuscript it describes.

I've seen amazing things in cover letters, starting with authors who get the name of the publisher wrong, or get my name wrong. And I've seen plenty of bad grammar, poor style, and even almost illegible photocopies. It's not that publishers discriminate against the spelling- or grammar-challenged. But we do assume that the appearance of your submission says something about how much you care about your manuscript. If you care enough to ask your friend who knows grammar and spelling (and we all know someone like that, if we ask around) to check over your cover letter and manuscript, then you're the kind of author with whom many children's book editors want to work.

Pink Envelopes and Other Horrors

Feverish visions of the swaying heaps of manuscripts that make up the slush pile understandably drive many to desperate measures in an attempt to make theirs stand out from the rest. "If they read mine first, maybe they'll appreciate it better." Actually, you're more likely to come across as naive, so avoid the following ploys and variations on them:

- Express delivery of any kind—your wait will be just as long after the manuscript arrives.

- Pink, neon yellow, or decorated envelopes—editors evaluate your writing, not your taste.

- Fancy covers, folders, or binding.

- Enclosures of food, stuffed animals, or toys—they won't fit in the files.

- Faxing your manuscript—you can't send a SASE and it's harder to read.

A plain envelope, white paper, the right postage, and a SASE are all you need.

More Than I Need to Know

What would you think of a building contractor who put more time and energy into a sign announcing the work he was doing than he did into the simple ground-level patio he was constructing for you? You'd wonder about his sense of priorities and worry that the effort he put into the sign took time away from his work on the patio.

That's how editors react when someone sends a five-page marketing plan to go with a three-page picture book manuscript. The marketing department can take care of that, if they publish the book. Editors feel the same when they see a plan for a lengthy series, if they work for a publisher that prefers to sign up single titles. And they react the same way when someone tells them about his life at great length, or encloses a detailed resumé, when nothing in his experience relates to the piece he has written.

These kinds of things happen too often. When I was an editorial assistant at a large company, a group of us assistants developed an irreverent rule of thumb: "The quality of a manuscript decreases as the amount of other material enclosed increases." Put your effort into your manuscript. An editor cares about that, and nothing else.

The Wrong Kind of Bedtime Book

The time-honored tradition of parents putting their children to sleep by reading them a book should not extend to your reader's reaction to your manuscript. Any editor or other reader of manuscripts sees hundreds of manuscripts a year, and will be put to sleep quickly by certain kinds of submissions. Though you'll find exceptions, most editors at trade publishers, the ones you'll be targeting, become very sleepy when they encounter the following:

- Cute, fluffy animals

- Writers imitating a popular author and claiming they are the next (fill in the blank)

- Stories that contain thinly disguised moral lessons

- Memories of someone's childhood

I could give other examples, but you will need to find from your own experience what gets a reaction (even if it's just a personal rejection letter) and what doesn't. Imagine that poor assistant, slumped in front of a stack of 100 manuscripts to read by 5 P.M. Then imagine her jumping up and running into her boss's office, and saying, "Hey, this one's got something different about it." That's the reaction that you want to invoke. In fact, an unusual, unconventional, difficult-to-publish, but wildly creative manuscript is more likely to get a response than one that plays it safe, follows the rules, and just isn't that different from anything else.

So go for it! Write your best, not what you think someone wants to see, and send it the right way.

The Least You Need to Know

- Manuscripts need to be typed, double-spaced, on plain paper, with your name and address on the first page.

- A submission to a publisher needs a short cover letter, the manuscript, a SASE, and a stamp.

- Multiple submissions are multiple copies of the same manuscript sent out to more than one publisher; avoid them if you can.

- A good cover letter is short and doesn't get in the way of a manuscript, while a good query letter makes an editor want to ask to see a manuscript.

- Avoid certain kinds of submissions, unless you want to put a manuscript reader to sleep.

Chapter 14

The Rules for Illustrators

In This Chapter

- What a portfolio is and what you need to put in it
- How to put a "dummy" together
- The kinds of work you can get from publishers
- Different ways to market yourself

So you're ready to start marketing yourself as an illustrator? In this chapter, I'll explain what a portfolio is and what to put in it, what else you'll need to prepare to show people, and how to start contacting publishers.

Take a Peek in My Portfolio

You might think that a portfolio is just a big carrying case with a zipper, into which you can stuff art that you want to carry from one place to another. In publishing terms, a *portfolio* has a more specific meaning. It's a thoughtful selection of no more than 15 samples of your best work, aimed at the needs of a particular publisher, and possibly carried in an actual portfolio. So if you are approaching a publisher of novels, choose individual pieces that grab the eye, because they need jacket illustrations. For a publisher of picture books, be sure to show a few sequences of illustrations, since a picture book is much more than a collection of individual illustrations. You need to have your portfolio ready to take or mail in when a publisher expresses interest in you; it may lead to your being offered a contract, if it confirms that you can do the job the publisher has.

Vocabulary List

A **portfolio** is a large, sturdy folder-type case, usually with handles, ideally with pockets inside the covers, and some means of closing it. A portfolio is also a careful selection of illustration samples in that case, chosen for the specific publisher who will see it and possibly including a dummy book as well as individual tear sheet. **Tear sheets** originally were work an illustrator (or writer) had done that had been torn out of a magazine or other source. Now a tear sheet can also be a photocopy of such a sample. A **dummy** is a manuscript laid out in book form, with sketches of all the illustrations and at least two or three finished pieces.

The samples should not only show your best work, but be of good quality. Do not include original art, but do include *tear sheets* or good-quality color copies. Do not use smudgy printouts from your color printer. Do not send slides. Do not send black-and-white copies unless your work is done in black and white.

Can You Keep a Secret?

Artist's representative Christine Tugeau notes some essentials in samples for children's publishers: "character development, interaction, real space, and a narrative feeling." Find out what she means by each of these items online at www.underdown.org/cat_advice.htm, and see also "Getting Out of the Art File" at www.underdown.org/artfile.htm.

What should the samples show? At a minimum, as Christine Tugeau reported of a conversation with an art director, you need "good drawing, good composition, good color." Good drawing: Do the figures, objects, and structures look real? Good composition: Do the different parts of it work together? Good color: Are the colors you use compatible and appealing? Keep in mind that you are showing what you would do with an illustration assignment. You do not want to include your wonderful fine art work, for example, if those pieces do not function well as illustrations.

For work on picture books, one of the most important areas in children's publishing, you will help your cause greatly if you can also include a *dummy*. This is a stand-in for an actual book, and a necessary stage in creating a picture book. To prepare a dummy, break up the text as you would in a book, remembering to leave a title page, a copyright page, and any other necessary pages outside of the main text. Reread Chapter 8 if you aren't sure what to include in a book. Tape or glue the pieces of text onto separate pages, and generally set up the book as if it were a full-size finished book, with a title page, copyright page, and so on. Put sketches where you intend to have illustrations—you don't have to complete all the illustrations. Do two or three finished pieces. Then make color copies of them so it won't be the end of the world if anything gets lost, and put the color copies in place in the dummy.

Tuck your dummy into your front pocket, along with a letter and resumé. Tuck some samples for your viewer's files and a SASE (self-addressed stamped envelope) into the back pocket, and you're done. Of course, you'll have to redo it every time you send it out or show it to a different publisher.

Can You Keep a Secret?

Theresa Brandon has created a fantastic online resource for aspiring illustrators at www.theresabrandon.com. From her home page, click through to "The Drawing Board for Illustrators," where you will find a FAQ file, articles, pricing information, and more.

Where the Work Is—and What It's Like

Where should you look for illustration work? At the publishers discussed in this book you'll find a wide variety of work. A guide like *Children's Writer's and Illustrator's Market* will help you with the details of who to contact and how to contact them. The following sections explain what to expect from different publishers.

Trade Publishers

If you contact trade publishers, you'll be looking for work on picture books and jackets mostly. Some chapter books have interior illustrations, and an illustrator might be hired to do the jacket and a dozen black-and-white illustrations for the interior, but these assignments are less common than they used to be. When you work with a trade publisher, you'll typically be paid a royalty for picture books and a flat fee for a jacket. You'll have considerable artistic license, and you'll usually have plenty of time to work.

The Other Guys

Mass-market and educational publishing are big markets for illustrators. Lots of individual illustrations are needed for textbooks, on tight deadlines. This work can by cyclical, as textbook publishers only do new programs every three years or so. Mass-market publishers also need illustrators, often for ongoing picture-book series based on popular characters, or for workbooks, activity books, and many other kinds of products.

I put these two publishers together because both expect illustrators to work to their schedule and specifications, and both usually pay fees, rather than royalties. Many illustrators make a living from their work in educational publishing, and so you should not ignore these areas if you want to illustrate full-time.

Be aware that it's difficult to get work in these areas unless you have an artist's representative. And watch out for the dangers of "work-for-hire" contracts. It can be okay to be paid a fee, but if the fee gives the publisher the right to keep your original art and to re-use it indefinitely, put your foot down. You deserve to get your art back, and ideally you want to give the publisher "single use" only. Failing that, push for limits on what the publisher can do with your work, such as restricting them to a particular market. I'll say more about both these issues in Chapter 17.

Contacting Publishers

Getting work as an illustrator requires you to spend a good bit of time marketing yourself. It's not enough to find a dozen publishers you like, to send them each a sample of your work, and then sit back and wait for the assignments to come in.

Nor will having a good portfolio help you if you don't first get publishers interested enough to ask to see it. There are some settings in which you can show a portfolio cold, but mostly you need to have it to show to people after you've contacted them in some other way.

What do you need to do? Let's look at how most publishers keep track of illustrators. To start with, there's a favored group of illustrators who the art director or an editor already work with regularly, and who they will always turn to first when a manuscript needs an illustrator. They may also have a small file of people they would like to work with in the future. If the right manuscript comes in, they'll contact one of them. Then there's the samples that came in recently and are still sitting on their desk. After that they may browse through some catalogs, or look at the files they have from artists' reps they like. They are likely to turn to the art sample files, which are probably overflowing and badly organized, only as a last resort. If you are in the art files, you may never get out.

Consider any or all of the strategies discussed in the following sections to enhance your chances of being both liked and remembered.

Playing Well Together with Others

Before you even think about the specific strategies you are going to use to market your abilities to publishers, think a bit about your personal style. This time, I don't mean your art style. I mean how you relate to others.

Are you shy? Are you thoughtful? Are you assertive? Whatever your style is, don't let it become a liability. If you know that you get quiet when meeting new people, and you have to meet with a publishing staffer in person, plan some questions you want to ask ahead of time (not asking questions can be interpreted as not being interested). Make some of the questions personal, but not too personal: Ask them what their most recent project was, or what their favorite childhood books were. Don't go to the other extreme, and become a pest like the person described in the box.

Class Rules

Your personality and approach to your work are as important as the work itself. A colleague who read a draft of this section wanted me to be sure to mention, "The person who was so overly aggressive in seeking work (calling more than once a day and having me paged out of a meeting). Those people got none of my attention, as I thought that if they were going to annoy me that much without work, they would certainly annoy me if I gave them work."

You need to do this self-evaluation because when you contact an art director, designer, or editor, they do not just evaluate your illustration ability. They evaluate, perhaps sub-consciously, how you would be to work with. Don't come across as someone who does great work but would be a constant energy drain—someone who resists making any changes, or responds slavishly but unimaginatively to suggestions, or who needs constant and unreasonable amounts of encouragement. Strive to be the positive, problem-solving person with whom anyone would like to work. Publishing is still a personal business, so remember you are marketing yourself.

Mailings

The previous chapter went into some detail about how a writer can contact a publisher. As an illustrator, much of what you should do is similar. You should send away for guidelines, or find them on the company's website, before contacting a publisher: Make sure you get the illustrator guidelines. When you send a publisher samples (a small selection of color samples), you should include a cover letter and an SASE if you want them returned (but don't expect them to be—illustration samples, typically, are either filed or discarded), and you should take some care to get them to the right companies.

Illustrators do some things differently:

◆ Send samples to the art director, not the editor. If you don't have a name, that title, or the words "Art Department," should get you to the right place.

♦ Contact as many companies as you want to at the same time, because you are hoping to be put on file for future projects, not to get a job right away.

♦ Send color postcards as reminders to publishers who you've contacted before. Include your address and phone number (and e-mail) so that a publisher can request more samples if interested.

Realize that mailings are often just a first step, but they can be a very useful one. If you do a mailing to 30 publishers, and 2 art directors contact you and ask to see more, you've done well.

The Portfolio by Mail

Before children's publishing got to be big business, most illustrators lived in the New York City area, and could come in and leave a portfolio with a publisher. Some publishers still have "drop-off days," but the industry is more scattered now, and so it's often possible to send in your portfolio by mail. If you're asked for your portfolio by mail, do not send in a full-size portfolio with large samples. You need to have something ready that you can send in a small package, such as a ring binder with your tear sheets in clear plastic pockets.

Personal Contact

If you can arrange a meeting with an editor or art director, great, but look also for portfolio showcases in which dozens of artists show off their work to browsing publishing staff. I've been to such showcases, organized by local chapters of such groups as the Graphic Artist's Guild or the SCBW-I, in both New York and Boston, and I believe that they happen in other parts of the country. People do get discovered at such events, so if there's one in your town, consider taking part.

Directories

If you've ever visited a publisher of any kind, you might have noticed the bookcase with the big heavy illustrator directories, also known as sourcebooks. In these annual tomes, you can find hundreds of illustrators, all seeking work in some area of publishing. At children's publishers, with one exception, these books gather dust and are consulted only in desperation, because 95 percent of the illustrators and photographers in them are seeking work from magazines and the like, and don't work in a style that suits children's books.

Fortunately, there is an exception. *Picturebook*, a relative newcomer, was started by some children's illustrators, and it caters specifically to them. It has gotten considerably thicker and is now the directory of choice for people looking for illustrators. Buying a page in it also costs considerably less than the other, general-purpose directories, and you get 1,000 reprints of your page to use in mailings, and space in their online portfolio.

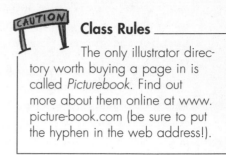

Class Rules

The only illustrator directory worth buying a page in is called *Picturebook*. Find out more about them online at www. picture-book.com (be sure to put the hyphen in the web address!).

Think carefully before buying a page in a directory. Every year, I see some pages in *Picturebook* with work that just isn't good enough, or which is presented in an amateurish way. Those illustrators have wasted their money. Wait until you have a few publishing credits—a sample from a magazine will be looked at more carefully than an unpublished presentation piece. When you do jump into a directory, build the rest of your marketing around it by mentioning it in every mailing you send out and using the tearsheets they gave you.

Do's and Don'ts of Websites

On first glance, a website might seem to be the ideal way to market yourself as an illustrator. Web space is cheap, your website is accessible to all, and you can put up some scans of your best work. Then you wait for the assignments to come. It's not so simple. Just because you have a website, you can't be sure that anyone is coming to it. Imagine putting up a huge billboard in your driveway. It's impressive, but you are the only person driving past it. To get visitors to your site, you have to register with search engines, contact directories of illustrator sites, and generally make sure that people looking for sites like yours will find yours listed in the places where they start their search. Even with this effort, you might not get many art directors coming to your site.

Can You Keep a Secret?

I've put up a brief list of some personal author and illustrator websites at www.underdown. org/topsites.htm. The sites listed will give you an idea of what's possible in a personal site and may provide inspiration as you build your own.

You are more likely to get them to come another way. Ironically, a website can be most useful to you as a supplement to more traditional marketing. Include the URL in all your samples and mailings, and then if someone wants to see more of your work, he can just go to the website, instead of waiting for you to send it. That convenience factor could help you land an assignment from an art director facing a looming deadline. Even for a less urgent project, the easy availability of more samples is a plus.

If you do build a website, put up a variety of work, and include at least a few samples that will display at a large size on a monitor, at higher resolution, to really show off your work. The files will be larger, but most publishers have high-capacity Internet connections, so this won't be a problem. Try to develop a special feature that will help people remember you, such as a series of pages showing the process you go through from rough sketch to finished piece. As with all your marketing efforts, your website should reflect who you are as a person, so put some thought into the overall presentation and design.

However you decide to market yourself, remember that it can take years to break in, so keep at it. Try different things, follow up contacts, and don't give up.

The Least You Need to Know

- A portfolio is a careful selection of your best samples, aimed at a particular publisher's needs.

- Individual illustration samples aren't enough; you may also need to create a complete book dummy to send out.

- Different publishers have different kinds of work available to illustrators.

- Mailings, directories, personal contact, and websites can all be part of your campaign to market yourself as an illustrator.

Chapter 15

Who Draws the Pictures?

In This Chapter

- ◆ Who is responsible for illustrations, and why?
- ◆ What instructions a writer can expect to give to an illustrator
- ◆ Notes on photo research—the only area in which authors have to work on illustrations
- ◆ Writers can relax and enjoy the magic of illustration

Children's books have better illustrations than ever before, printed to exacting standards, in a wide variety of styles. Visual riches can be found in any decent children's bookstore or library. This treasure trove can be daunting—and sometimes misleading. Books are published as a package of writing and illustration, which can give beginning writers the idea that they are somehow responsible for all of it.

We're here to tell writers to relax. Whether writers like it or not—and some people don't like it at all—publishers almost always put themselves in charge of choosing and overseeing illustrators. Writers are best off sitting back and letting it happen. Often enough, the results are magic.

But I Can't Draw

Looking at the end of the publishing process and seeing a gorgeous picture book, it's easy to assume that the beginning of the process must be more than just a manuscript. You obviously also need the illustrations that go with it. And so many aspiring authors apologize for not including illustrations with their manuscript, send sketches or computer art as a substitute, or even get a complete set of illustrations done by someone the author knows.

Can You Keep a Secret?

Just because you've written a picture book does not mean you need to create the pictures. Check a publisher's guidelines just to be sure, but you'll find that, in almost all cases, all an author has to do is write.

In fact, in just about every case, a publisher does not want or expect an author to include illustrations when sending a manuscript. Why should a writer be responsible for illustrating a story, after all? A writer's skills are in working with words, not paint or pastels.

My Brother-in-Law Can

Sometimes editors will open a package and find a manuscript accompanied by a carefully rendered set of illustrations, all done by the author's brother-in-law, or daughter, or neighbor, or best friend from college, or—you get the picture. As I said before, these aren't needed, but sometimes authors want to include illustrations for good and personal reasons. One reason might be that the author likes the illustrator and enjoys working with him, for example.

This can get sticky for both writer and illustrator. Here's the scenario: A writer knows and likes an artist and thinks that this person is just the right match for a story. The artist completes some illustrations, you make careful color photocopies of some of them and send them along with the manuscript, and you are confident that the two of you are doing the right thing. Unfortunately, you aren't.

Publishers almost always choose the illustrators for their illustrated books—picture books, chapter books with illustrations, or other types of titles. They hire and pay the illustrator. And let's face it, they know more illustrators than any individual writer does, and they have experience matching texts with artists. Therefore, the publisher most likely won't like the illustrator. As a result, you might reduce the chances of their responding to the manuscript the way you want them to. Those illustrations might not show the manuscript to its best advantage. Or the publisher might not like being told what to do.

Playground Stories

Published illustrator and occasional author Megan Halsey says: "I believe there are two types of storytellers in the children's book field .... A writer tells their story using words. An illustrator tells their story using pictures. There are some people who do both successfully but that is a *rare* occurrence." She goes on to say that especially when you are getting started, it's best to stay with the one thing you are good at.

Here's a simple rule of thumb to follow: If you're a writer, don't include illustrations done by someone you know, unless that person is Maurice Sendak. And if you're an illustrator, don't agree to do illustrations for a friend's manuscript unless your friend is Jane Yolen. To rephrase a popular bumper sticker: Friends don't ask friends to illustrate their stories.

I Hired Someone

It doesn't happen too often, but there's another scenario worth mentioning, to head you off in case you are considering it. Sometimes writers go out and hire an illustrator in the hope that this will increase the chance that they will get a story published, or perhaps so that they can have more control over how it is illustrated. (As explained later in this chapter, publishers normally don't let an author have too much to say about how a story is illustrated.)

If you're an independently wealthy writer, can afford to hire a designer, editor, and a copyeditor, and to pay to have a book printed and distributed, this could be an effective strategy. For submissions to publishers, though, this strategy is no more likely to succeed than is hiring your brother-in-law. In such circumstances, any good illustrator will (and should!) charge a writer thousands of dollars to do the work. He or she will want this money up front, because there's no guarantee the book will ever end up being published. And even if a writer does find a good illustrator, there's also no guarantee that a publisher will have the same aesthetic tastes. If you are the illustrator in a scenario like this, don't even consider it unless you are compensated in advance, you can use the work as a way to build your portfolio, and you have a written contract that grants ownership of the art to you. In other words, in almost all cases, don't do this. Traveling to a national children's book conference or taking a class would be a better use of time and money for both of you.

Why Don't You Get Dave Caldecott?

So you've accepted that you can't hire your brother-in-law, but you'd still like some say in how your book looks. Maybe you've heard that a beginning writer is better off if her story is matched with a famous illustrator. Well, if you are offered a contract, there's no harm making suggestions to your editor or even including them in the letter you write to accompany your manuscript.

Just don't get too attached to your preferences. Illustrators whom a writer is likely to know—unless you're a children's librarian or reading teacher and spend your days immersed in the latest children's books (lucky you)—are the top-of-the-heap people, the Caldecott winners, the professionals who've been around for a long time. Even if a publisher agrees that a particular illustrator would be a wonderful choice, these well-known artists are just the ones who are least likely to be available.

The Publisher's Job

Simply put, the publisher chooses and hires the illustrator. For the writer, this is a blessing and a curse. The writer isn't responsible for finding an illustrator, but also can't insist on a particular illustrator. Many writers see the story as theirs, and want the book to follow their vision. If that describes you, try to step back a little. Yes, the story is yours, but turning it into a book is a true team effort, and one that's coordinated by the publisher. In addition to the illustrator, perhaps a dozen or more people will be involved in taking what could start out as a 2-page typed manuscript and turning it into a sturdily bound 32-page full-color book. You'll learn more about some of those people in Chapters 21 and 22. For now, understand that with so much of the time and expense that works that magic being the responsibility of the publisher, it's no wonder that the publisher wants to be the one deciding who illustrates a book. And after all, they've probably got more experience than you do in making that kind of decision.

But I Want to Illustrate

Some of you still have an objection, right? Forget about brothers-in-law and famous illustrators—you want to illustrate your book yourself. You've always had some talent, and you don't see why you should split the money you'll be paid with someone else.

For Professionals Only

If you are a professionally trained illustrator, or an unusually adept self-taught one who has taken some classes, then you can realistically hope to be considered as the illustrator of your own manuscript. Take one of a few different approaches.

The simplest one is to include samples of your work with the manuscript, and mention in your cover letter that you would like to illustrate the manuscript. These samples could be related to the story or not, but in any case should be color photocopies or printed samples, sometimes called *tear sheets*. Don't send slides, which are a hassle to deal with, and *never* send original art.

To push even harder for consideration as an illustrator, the best way to show your abilities is to send a *dummy*. Both tear sheets and dummies are defined in more detail in the previous chapter, so refer to Chapter 14 if these options interest you.

> **Class Rules**
>
> If your illustration abilities aren't up to professional standards, do yourself a favor and don't include them in a submission to a publisher. While reading submissions at the various publishers I've worked for, nothing made me reach for a form rejection letter faster than amateurish illustrations—be they watercolor, crayon, or computer clip art.

Doing all the art for the book won't do more to convince an editor that you are the right person for it. After all, editors usually choose an illustrator before any art for a particular book is done. Doing all the art will just take you extra time, time that could be wasted if another illustrator does the book. Even if you are chosen, you may find that after you start working with the professionals at your publishing company, you have to take a new approach and jettison some or all of the work that you already did. In this and all these other scenarios, be prepared to be flexible.

Best Foot Forward

If you're an illustrator and a writer, as far as a publisher is concerned you're really two different people. One of you might be the author of a book, and the other might be the illustrator. You might end up working on the same book, but you might not. In this situation, you've got to put your best foot forward, or it might end up firmly in your mouth.

Often the best way to do that is to have the publisher consider your ability as an illustrator separately from your ability as a writer. This book gives you guidance for putting your best foot forward as either a writer or an illustrator. With the exception noted previously, if you want to write and illustrate, you should follow separate paths when contacting publishers.

Instructions to the Illustrator?

Okay, you're a writer who accepts that you're not an illustrator, and that your job is to write. But you have some instructions you'd like to pass along to the illustrator, or you'd really like to see what he's doing and make sure that it fits in with your vision for the book. Be prepared for a shock. Though policies vary from company to company, many publishers do not allow the author to have contact with the illustrator while he or she is at work. If you're an illustrator, you're probably relieved to hear this. You like the freedom to develop your own vision. So what can both of you expect? Some publishers may show the writer the illustrator's sketches, but some won't even do that. How can a writer expect to have an influence? There are a few different paths.

Not in the Manuscript

Many authors, particularly those who have written a book with very little text and proportionally more reliance on illustrations, want to include guidance for the illustrator for the manuscript. This can range from general instructions as to how the characters "should" look to page-by-page advice on what to illustrate, where to have page breaks, and so on. Including this attempted guidance in a manuscript is a bad idea, however.

Editors and illustrators alike are experienced at reading unadorned manuscripts and envisioning how they would turn into picture books. Experienced authors know this, and happily cede control of this area to them. So if an editor sees notes to the illustrator in a manuscript, he or she may assume the author is inexperienced, or would struggle with letting the illustrator do his or her job. The editor is likely to remove such notes, and is less likely to put the writer into contact with the illustrator.

What's Okay—and What's Not

The writer's voice is heard. A writer's advice may not be followed, of course, but it will be heard. Writers must simply provide their guidance in an appropriate manner.

For example, if your story relies on surprise elements in the illustrations, or a page turn at a specific point, you have justification for saying so in a cover letter when you submit it. But if you just have ideas about the color of someone's hair, or how a house should look, keep these to yourself until your book is underway, and even then, be prepared to accept that your editor or illustrator may have different ideas. Offer your ideas in a letter or phone call, but don't expect them to be followed.

Be Flexible

Therefore, writers need to be flexible. If your story is based on childhood memories, offer snapshots as reference materials, but don't expect every detail to be kept the same. The illustrator needs to find an independent vision. If your story calls for characters with different hair colors, and you see one as blond, one as brunette, and one black, don't be surprised if the illustrator makes different choices.

Both writer and illustrator must understand that they each bring unique talents to a book's creation. Just as an illustrator cannot expect a writer to revise a manuscript to suit the illustrator, a writer cannot expect an illustrator to revise his or her work. These kinds of revisions do happen, of course, but not routinely. As you obtain more and more experience, you may have opportunities to work with your counterpart—but don't expect it. At least at the beginning of your career, you'll work separately and the editor will mediate. Your common goal is to produce the best possible book.

Laying Out the Book

Sometimes it can be useful for the author to lay out the book as it would appear in print. You can get a sense of whether you've provided what's needed—sort of the reverse of the exercise of typing up a published picture book text into manuscript form. In this case, you're looking to see if you've created enough different scenes, some of which can be set in the same place, as long as something new happens.

Cut up a copy of the manuscript and see what happens when you spread it out across 28 pages, which are the usable pages in a picture book. In some places, you might put text on every page, while in other places you might put text only on one page of a two-page spread. Is there enough? Too much? What happens when a page turns? Does the story just continue, or is there a new direction or a surprise? Compare it in your mind to books you've read.

You'll find that you get a better sense of how your manuscript might work in book form. Do not, however, send this to an editor as part of a submission. She won't want to see it. Use it, learn from it, but keep it to yourself.

Photo Research: The Exception

In one notable area, publishers not only allow the author to contribute to the illustration process—they sometimes insist upon it. This is when the book being created is photo-illustrated. This type of book spans the age ranges, from the photo essay, a nonfiction picture book with minimal to a considerable amount of text, to the photo-illustrated book for middle school or high school children.

When making a submission of a book that is to be photo-illustrated, either because that's the only kind of book the publisher does, or because that's the way you want to see it published, and you know that this publisher is open to it, it's okay to include samples and lists of possible sources. You may be required to do the photo research, so the publisher wants to see that you are ready to do the job.

> **" "** **Playground Stories**
>
> Nonfiction writer Ginger Wadsworth advises that researching photographs can be just as important as researching information. Find out who controls the right to reproduce a photograph you'd like to use in your book; it could be a private photo agency, a government agency, a historical museum, or an individual. Have a tentative budget ready for the photographs you suggest using, and in many cases publishers will pay the fees, or help you pay them. If you're clever, even high fees can be okay, she notes: "Do you want to spend $300 on a picture [the price for the black-and-white cover photo of my book *Rachel Carson, Voice for the Earth*]? My publisher said yes after I had obtained the right to use several family photos for free."

Magic Happens!

Can you imagine *Goodnight Moon* without its familiar and charming bunny family? Of course not. And yet it didn't have to turn out that way—in the early stages of the book's development, the characters were to be humans. The idea of them being bunnies developed later. Almost all books go through changes, of course. But it's the illustrations that can really transform a story and make it much more than it was when it was just a manuscript.

Noted picture-book author Tony Johnston was pleasantly surprised when G. Brian Karas showed the characters in *Three Little Bikers* as sheep. She hadn't imagined them that way, but they were fun. So relax. Work on your writing and let that magic happen when it's the illustrator's turn to work.

The Least You Need to Know

♦ Writers can heave a sigh of relief—they don't have to provide illustrations to go with their picture-book manuscripts.

♦ If you want to illustrate, make sure you measure up to professional standards before sending your work to a publisher.

♦ Writers don't need to send all kinds of suggestions and information to an illustrator.

♦ The only kind of book for which an author has to work on the illustrations is a photo-illustrated book.

♦ Illustrators add unexpected and magical things to a writer's words.

I Know Somebody Who Knows Somebody ...

In This Chapter

- ◆ Find out why calling editors or otherwise trying to make personal contact can be a bad idea
- ◆ How to use names you know, and how not to use them
- ◆ The value of conferences for making contacts, and how not to blow it
- ◆ Contests as a way to a contract

Many children's publishing companies, particularly the larger and better-known ones, have closed their doors to unsolicited submissions. They might accept samples from illustrators, but just not turn to them very often. In both cases, they are working primarily with people they know. After spending years honing your skills, reading the latest books, and learning about publishing companies, you are frustrated.

Maybe you think you've got a solution to this problem. Knowing someone is *the* only reliable way to get someone to look at a manuscript or peruse a portfolio, and that's all you need, right? After he does, he'll recognize your brilliance. Or maybe you've come to believe that your work doesn't even have to be brilliant to be published, as long as you have a friend in the business.

As is usually the case when dealing with a nugget floating in the pool of common knowledge, there is some truth to all this, but the truth is a little more complicated than you might think. This chapter sorts through the various strategies people have used to finagle their way into the inner sanctum, and shows you what might work for you, and what won't.

Closed Doors: How to Pick the Lock

If a publishing company won't read an unsolicited manuscript, then it's reasonable to think that the way to get someone to read it is to get someone else to ask for it. If you don't know anyone with connections, what better way to do that than by making a phone call and asking for an editor? Or if you're an illustrator, why not call the art director?

Sounds good, but most editors and art directors just don't like getting calls from people who are eager to sell themselves. These calls are time-consuming, and so many companies instruct receptionists, company operators, and assistants to do everything they can to avoid putting through calls from writers and illustrators they don't know.

Such calls are no better liked at companies that open their doors a bit wider. I always advise writers at conferences not to call to get my okay to send something. "If someone calls, it's just another opportunity to say no, and since it's impossible to evaluate a manuscript on the phone, and good manuscripts may not sound good in a phone call, I'd rather just get a letter and a manuscript. That's what I need to see anyway." And keep in mind that even if you do "get to yes" and have an editor's request for a manuscript, that probably won't affect how the editor views it when she finally does read it, days or weeks later. The editor might not even remember your conversation. The same thing goes for an art director and an art sample or portfolio. The person from the art department might not remember you.

You may be wondering if a personal visit to a publishing company might be more effective than a phone call. Put that out of your mind right away. Although there are instances when people with dynamic, persuasive, charismatic phone personalities and deep pockets for their phone expenses occasionally get to talk to an editor or art director, paying a personal visit just won't work. If you show up at a publishing company without an appointment, you won't get past the receptionist. Want to visit *with* an appointment? You'll have to call to make one, and even if you get through to someone, she won't want to take the time to meet with you unless she's already working with you.

Can You Keep a Secret?

Read a funny and footnoted version of an imagined phone call to an editor in Wendy McClure's "Let The Mail Prevail! A Guide to Etiquette, Status Calls, and More." Find it on-line at www.underdown.org/etiquet.htm.

No, cold calling and knocking on doors, which are tough as a technique in just about any sales job, are not at all effective in children's publishing. Some other ways of making personal contact can be, however, so read on.

A Friend in the Business

Maybe you are one of the lucky folks who knows someone in the business—another author or illustrator, or, best of all, someone who works at a publishing company. Understandably, you want her help, and if you believe in your manuscript as much as I hope you do, you probably believe that she will be happy to give it. As your friend, she may feel obliged to pass your work on to someone she knows, or perhaps let you mention her name in a cover letter. That may not mean that she likes your work! In other words, she probably really cannot help you get published. You will be more likely to get a personal response if you write with a more detailed or enthusiastic personal endorsement from someone the editor or art director knows, but she will still evaluate your work just as stringently.

Go ahead and use a contact like this if you have one. But don't be a pest to your friend, and realize that she is more likely to be useful to you if you ask her about her experiences. She'll enjoy talking about herself (who doesn't?) and you'll get to increase your knowledge.

Class Rules _____

When you mention someone in a letter who suggested that you contact an editor or art director, make sure it's someone she actually knows, or at least that she will recognize the name. I've often been amused to receive letters proclaiming "so-and-so suggested that I send you the enclosed manuscript. He thinks it would be just right for your list," but I had no idea who that so-and-so was.

A Name on the Envelope

If you don't have an agent (this is discussed in Chapter 17), it helps to send your manuscript to a specific person, have someone like your lawyer send it out on your behalf, or proclaim your affiliation with a professional organization. The following sections give you the lowdown on these scenarios.

To a Particular Person

Does it help to have an editor's name on an envelope? Some people believe so, and will go to the effort of calling publishers to get the names of editors if they haven't been able to find them out in other ways. (*Literary Market Place*, among other books, lists staff by name, but becomes out of date and doesn't include everyone.) But if the editor doesn't know you, the manuscript is likely to be shunted to the slush pile anyway. If you do put a name on an envelope, make sure that you've spelled it correctly. Make sure that editor still works there—don't rely on three-year-old writer's guides. And don't put a letter to one publisher into an envelope that is addressed to another. (I've seen it happen.)

Some folks take what looks like a creative approach and contact the head of a division or company, or even someone in the marketing department. In the first case, the hope is that the big boss will pass the letter on, and that because the letter comes from him or her, it will then be treated with more care. Sorry, but those manuscripts and samples are treated like everything else and sometimes sit around for weeks in the head honcho's office. In the second case, you might be trying to excite someone in the marketing department who will then send it along with an endorsement. This is not a good idea. People in marketing have their own jobs to do, and these too just get passed along—if they aren't simply thrown out. In addition, there is a great risk when sending material to someone whose job description does not include handling them. If your materials are so badly misdirected, the person who receives them might think you are clueless and not pass them on intentionally.

Can You Keep a Secret?

Who reads their own mail? Who needs to find exciting new authors so that they can move up? Assistant and associate editors, that's who. If you have the name of someone at this level, because it was mentioned in a newsletter or at a conference or someone you know knows the person, use it. The less-established editors want to hear from you.

From Your Lawyer

Writers without agents sometimes ask their personal lawyer to send in manuscripts on their behalf. The letterhead is usually impressive, and you may feel confident that with your lawyer involved from the beginning, a company won't mess around with you. Unfortunately, most lawyers know nothing about publishing or how to write to a publisher. One lawyer, for example, contacted me after a trade show. I hadn't attended the show, but the lawyer must have picked up my card at the company booth. So the lawyer opened his letter by mentioning having met at the show, a meeting that could not have happened, and then proceeded to briefly introduce three different clients, one of whom didn't even write children's books. I was not impressed. If you don't have an agent, keep it simple and write on your own behalf, because it's with you the publisher will be working.

I'm a Member of ...

Some writers and illustrators mention their membership in professional organizations, and may even note them on their envelopes. This tactic can work, particularly if you belong to the Society of Children's Book Writers and Illustrators (SCBWI) in the United States or the Canadian Society of Children's Authors, Illustrators, and Performers (CANSCAIP) in Canada, the two national children's writers and illustrators organizations. A few publishers with closed doors actually open them to members of these organizations, on the reasonable assumption that someone who belongs to one of them has been working on his writing and learning about the market for a little while, and so is more likely to be sending something interesting and well targeted. See Appendix B for information on how to join. If you belong to another, less-relevant organization, such as the National Writer's Union or the Graphic Artist's Guild, it may not hurt to mention it, but it won't earn you any credibility.

Conferences and Schmoozing

Perhaps the best way to make contact with an editor (and less frequently, an art director) is to go to a conference like those sponsored by the SCBWI and other organizations, and actually meet someone.

Playground Stories

Marilyn Singer's first three books were signed up and published in quick succession. Her fourth, *It Can't Hurt Forever,* was not. She picks up the story: "If there's one thing a writer must have, it's perseverance. And luck. And *contacts.* I went to my first SCBWI conference and met Liz Gordon, then an editor at Harper & Row (later to become HarperCollins). I introduced myself and asked if I could send her some stuff. She said yes, and off went the novels. Back came a note. Was I was willing to do extensive revisions on *It Can't Hurt Forever?* ... I revised my novel and Harper published it."

As Marilyn Singer's story illustrates, meeting editors at conferences really can work for you. But there are ways to do this, and ways not to do this. Understand from the beginning that editors are normal human beings who do not enjoy being besieged by eager authors. They do expect to meet people at conferences, but they don't respond well to pitches or to manuscripts thrust in their hands (or slid under the door of their bathroom stall, as has happened). They particularly do not like it when someone relentlessly promotes herself, badgers them for advice about her 300-page story about her puppy, or plunks down next to them at lunch and attempts to lock everyone else out of the conversation.

There are always one or two people like that at conferences, and they may succeed in getting the editor's attention, but not her respect. Like Marilyn, be polite, and don't expect someone to take your work home with her; write to her after the conference.

Remember, too, that a conference is not an opportunity for a one-time smash-and-grab raid. In the long run, you'll do even better to get involved with the organization sponsoring the conference. You'll get to know more editors if you help plan a conference than if you only attend one, and you're more likely to impress them with your professionalism, too. Most editors have published writers they met at conferences, but they are usually the folks who've been in it for the long haul, not the ones who show up at just one conference.

Editors also may attend trade shows at which publishers show off their books to booksellers, librarians, or other organizations of people interested in children's books. These shows are a great place to go to find all the latest children's books under one roof, all organized by publisher. They are *not* a great place to go to meet editors, with the possible exception of the American Library Association (ALA). That's the only show editors attend in numbers: Most of the people staffing publishers' booths are marketing and sales people. Even at the ALA convention, editors may be looking after their published authors or attending meetings, and though they may be polite and listen to a pitch if they aren't busy, they'll have forgotten it by the time they leave for the day. Above all, don't try to share your manuscript or art samples with people in the booth. They are very busy dealing with customers, and even if they do accept your materials, they are likely to be lost or discarded when the show closes. Take catalogs and guidelines, if available, and use the show to find out about publishers you didn't know, but a show is not a place to sell a manuscript or leave an art sample.

Faking a Contact

I mention the option of faking a contact—claiming you met an editor when you didn't, pretending to have been referred by a famous writer, or some other ruse—in a cover letter only to urge you *not* to do this. If you're found out, you can forget about working with that publisher, or, if you are found out later, you'll destroy the trust that had built up. Even if you're not found out, you'll be worried that you will be, and you'll never be entirely comfortable. And of course, making up things like this is just wrong.

Win a Prize!

Some companies sponsor contests. For example, the small but respected multicultural publisher Lee and Low sponsors a "New Voices Award" for picture-book fiction. Delacorte offers a similar prize at the other end of the age spectrum: the Delacorte

Press Prize for a First Young Adult Novel. This award allowed Christopher Paul Curtis, winner of the 2000 Newbery Medal, to get his foot in the door. Even if you don't win in a contest like this, your manuscript will be read, and you may hear from someone.

In addition to publishers' contests, organizations like the SCBWI offer grants, some of which unpublished authors can win and use as a credential in a submission.

Useful but Not Essential

In the end, all of these ways to find or create or make use of a contact can be useful, but you can get yourself discovered without a contact, too. To some extent, the way you choose to submit your manuscripts or sample illustrations should suit your personality.

Do you think that there's a right way to do things, that there's one right publisher for you? Can you be stubborn in going after that? After you find that one right publisher and start to correspond, keep at it. That's what Bruce Balan did with a submission to Green Tiger Press (a small company now gone in a merger). It took him a year and a half, but Green Tiger Press eventually accepted a manuscript that he was convinced was right for them.

Are you a people person? Do you enjoy meeting and getting to know people? Then spend some time going to writer's conferences and other events. Don't try to hand a manuscript to every publishing insider you meet. Talk to them and find out what they do. Keep in touch with them. Later, when you have the right kind of manuscript for them, you can send it to them. Or if it's not right for them, maybe they can tell you who is. We know several authors who got published this way.

Are you systematic? Then do your research. Set up lists of publishers to contact and go down the list. Keep at it until you make a contact or decide you need a new system.

There are as many ways of getting published as there are people. Just stick with it, and don't be discouraged by initial rejections.

The Least You Need to Know

- ◆ Phone calls and office visits don't help you make contact with an editor or art director.

- ◆ Putting a name on the envelope or in your cover letter is only useful in certain circumstances.

- ◆ Conferences and contests are good ways to make contacts.

- ◆ Faking a contact or going out of your way to create a contact isn't worth your while. It's possible to be published without knowing someone.

I Need an Agent!

In This Chapter

- ◆ What literary agents and artist's representatives do
- ◆ How to tell if you need and are ready for an agent or rep
- ◆ Why it's difficult to get an agent or a rep
- ◆ How and where to find agents and reps

At some point in the careers of many authors and illustrators, having an agent in your corner can look like a very good thing. In this chapter, I'll show you what agents do, and help you decide whether or not you really need one, and how to find one if you do.

Secret Agents

Not too long ago, children's book agents were only a little more common than ivory-billed woodpeckers. I'm talking about the 1960s, when authors and illustrators generally represented themselves. Those children's book agents who did exist typically worked for a larger agency and may have handled clients in other areas too. There just wasn't enough money being paid to children's book illustrators and writers to support more than a few agents. Times have changed. Publishers have grown busier, our genteel little business has become more profitable, and now people can make a living specializing in agenting children's book manuscripts or representing illustrators.

On hearing about all the closed doors in children's publishing, in fact, many authors and illustrators decide they need to get a *literary agent* or an *artist's representative*. After all, they reason, publishers with rules against unsolicited submissions do not apply them to agents. Provided that the agent is someone a publisher knows, which isn't always the case because anyone can call himself an agent, submissions from an agent will be treated with respect.

Vocabulary List

A **literary agent** acts on your behalf, selecting and writing to publishers with your manuscript, negotiating with the publisher, and generally going to bat for you. Some also work with you to help you develop your career. An **artist's representative**, also called an artist's rep, gets your samples out to publishers and otherwise acts much like an agent.

What's in It for You

Of course, an agent doesn't just help you get your foot in the door. What does an agent do? Agent Jennie Dunham of Dunham Literary notes three main functions:

- ◆ **Submit material to publishers.** Agents can submit manuscripts to any publisher and know who to submit to from their full-time, firsthand experience.

- ◆ **Negotiate contracts.** Agents understand the terms and may have the clout to get a better deal than an individual author can.

- ◆ **Collect monies and distribute them.** Agents handle payments from multiple publishers and check royalty statements.

Artist's reps do similar work. They typically make sure that the right publishers see your work with several sample mailings per year, and personal visits once a year with art directors and editors. When asked, they follow up with more print samples and books, or suggest possible artists for a manuscript or program need. They also negotiate your contracts and handle invoicing and payments from publishers. An agent may withhold some of the rights associated with a manuscript, as explained in Chapter 21, but rights to illustrations are more likely to stay with the publisher because they can't easily be sold independently of the text.

What's in It for Them

For this work, an agent or a rep gets a commission from you. Agents typically charge 15 percent, though a few still charge what used to be the standard 10 percent. Artist's reps receive higher commissions of 25 or 30 percent because their expenses are higher. (They share in the cost of buying directory pages, and pay for printing and postage on mailings.)

With the exception of the commission, all this sounds great, doesn't it? The question is, should you take time out from sending manuscripts and samples to publishers to send them to agents, so that you will have someone who will be sending your work to publishers for you?

To Agent or Not to Agent?

Indeed, agents open doors. But first you must open theirs, and that's a challenge, too. Finding someone to represent you can be more difficult than finding a publisher, because the established, reputable agents and reps are as selective about new clients as publishers are with new authors, if not more so. They have to be selective because usually they'll be representing all of your work, while you might work with two, three, or even more publishers over the course of a few years.

> **Playground Stories** _____
>
> Agent Sandy Ferguson Fuller of the Alps Arts Co. says:
>
> I think the decision whether or not to contract with an agent is a very personal one. In today's market, it is probably advantageous to have an agent to "get in the door" if you're able to convince a reputable, experienced agent to take on your work. …
>
> That is *not* to say that a writer can't tackle the market without an agent. If an individual has the time, desire, and savvy to research potential publishers, make the contracts, and submit in accordance with guidelines, many publishers still can be approached without an agent.

In fact, many of the best reps and agents will admit to having a "referrals only" policy on new clients, meaning their doors are closed as tightly as the doors of the publishers you want them to open for you. They'll only look at someone who comes to them with the endorsement of an existing client or publisher. These same agents and reps often go on to insist that they are still open to someone with unique qualities—if you can get that referral or personal contact. Before you start to feel irritated with this apparent lack of helpfulness, consider the sad fact that most agents and reps have as many clients as they can handle and may receive thousands of contacts annually. This is partly the result of closed doors at publishers. People are now trying to use agents and reps as the entry point to publishers, even when they are not ready for one. One agent I know tells me that she gets about 200 queries from possible clients per week—and she'll maybe take on a handful of new clients this year. Agents can't do their job for the existing clients if they don't close their doors; they'd end up spending all their time dealing with their mail and e-mail.

The situation is somewhat different for authors and illustrators, so consider the following before you decide what to do.

Now or Later: Authors

Your ability to find an agent may depend on the kind of writing you do. Nonfiction, especially for the institutional market, does not earn large advances and get high sales numbers, so many authors in this area represent themselves. Picture book authors, because they split royalties with an illustrator, are also less likely to have an agent. Conversely, good fiction writers are relatively more attractive to an agent, especially if their work is strong enough to garner interest from multiple editors—possibly leading to an auction, which agents love (you'll love them, too, if one of your books is auctioned).

Before trying to land yourself an agent, it's important to ask yourself if you are ready for one. Do you have several publishable manuscripts complete and ready for submission? Agents want to represent someone with a career in front of them, not a one-shot wonder. They particularly don't like being offered a manuscript that's dog-eared from making the rounds. Don't even bother to contact an agent if you don't have a good backlog of unsubmitted material. Are you ready to commit to working with an agent over the course of several years? Unless you are a bad personality match, or have conflicting ideas about what approach to take, expect to work with your agent for some time. Don't expect an agent to take you on a trial basis. They want to help you build a career and to share in the fruits of that effort.

But I'm an Illustrator!

The situation is somewhat different for illustrators. Illustrators may need to be represented more than authors do, and more published illustrators do seem to have reps.

The main reason for this is that the overall market for illustrators is different than the market for writers. Both work on trade books. But the textbook market is a much larger one for illustrators than it is for writers. Writing in textbooks is often done in-house or by teachers on a for-hire basis. And sometimes, excerpts from existing trade books are used. However, textbook publishers, when working on a major new textbook program, may want literally hundreds of pieces of new, high-quality illustration, done to often quite precise specifications, in a short period of time. They can't take the time to sift through the samples of individual illustrators, and so they tend to turn to artist's representatives, either directly or via the design studios doing the basic design work on the books. When this work is available, it keeps a lot of illustrators busy.

For the most part, though, you can't get this work unless you have a rep. A rep, when contacted by a textbook publisher, can suggest illustrators for a large number of different illustrations, and can vouch that each of them will deliver on time, and will deliver work that is as good as their samples promise. The textbook publishers like this because they know what they'll be getting, and they can take care of a batch of illustrations more quickly than by contacting illustrators one at a time..

Class Rules

In the textbook market, "SRO" is a hot term. No, it doesn't stand for "standing room only" or "single room occupancy," but for "school rights only." Artist's reps push for this with textbook publishers, to prevent them from re-using your original work in other types of books.

There is so much textbook work that even reps who spend most of their time marketing their clients to trade houses tell me that more of their income, meaning more of their clients' income, too, comes from educational projects than from trade ones. Educational illustration not only pays well, it can also be a good training ground for the more time-consuming (and let's face it, prestigious) work needed to create picture books.

So illustrators are well advised to seek out a rep, and you'll be pleased to know that they will mostly be prepared to work with you, even if you're just getting started. Do not contact them, however, unless you are ready for them. Here are some questions Christine Tugeau asks in an article on her firm's website:

- Can you draw and paint well? (I regularly see many who don't!)

- Is your work quality truly professional and competitive with what you are seeing in good picture books and educational program books?

- Do you have a style that reproduces well and easily?

- Are your characters uniquely yours, but also potentially appealing to the art buyers *and* the public?

- Can you afford to do your style for industry-norm pay scales? (If your approach is too time-consuming, you may not be able to make a living with it.)

♦ Do you have published work to show? (We don't make a dime if we don't get you work, and having *had* work is of practical interest.)

♦ Do you have at least 10 to 15 wonderful pieces for a portfolio, duplicates to send out, printed "keeper" cards/pages, and money to spend on pages in industry promotional books? (Reps get discounted prices and contribute something as well.)

♦ Do you have a fax and e-mail (essential) and can you send JPEG samples to the agent or buyers? (This is becoming more essential.)

♦ Are you good with specs, directions, and deadlines?

♦ Can you really listen to and accept criticism and revisions of your work and concepts?

If you can answer yes to all those questions, you may be ready for a rep.

Can You Keep a Secret? _____

Some illustrators have an agent, not an artist's rep. Why do they do that? As one of them told me, one reason is that "I write as well as illustrate. Agents deal with editors, reps often deal only with art directors .... Second is the potential for secondary rights and reversions to be sold through an agent. Most artist's reps do one-time sales, [and] do not follow up on other markets." She notes too that she is not interested in textbook or other for-hire work, and that she's a bit too "artsy" for most reps.

Whatever you decide, remember that the time you spend trying to find an agent or rep, a search that may not succeed, could be time spent on trying to find a publisher. For this reason, even if you do decide to try to find someone to represent you, don't stop contacting publishers directly yourself.

Getting to Solla Sollew

Looking for an agent or a rep can be like the Dr. Seuss book *I Had Trouble in Getting to Solla Sollew*. In that book, a very determined and angry character overcomes enormous obstacles to get to a place where there are no problems, "or at least, very few." When she does get there, she discovers that in fact the only problem is that she can't get in. It's easy to believe that if someone is representing you, all your troubles are over. They aren't. Your agent may not be any more successful at placing your manuscript or finding you illustration work than you were. You may not agree with the approach the rep is taking. The rep may offer you too little guidance with your work, or too much.

It's best to go into a relationship with an agent or a rep with your eyes wide open, and your expectations reasonable. Be sure to have a written contract with them. (Most will offer this as a matter of routine.) You are entering into an important professional relationship, one that's potentially closer than with any one publisher. You can work for several different publishers, but you're only going to work with one agent at a time.

Where *Are* They?

If you decide you want to have an agent, use resources such as *Children's Writer's and Illustrator's Market* or Ellen Shapiro's *Writer's & Illustrator's Guide to Children's Book Publishers and Agents* to locate them. Do your homework and be prepared to ask questions. But research them before you contact them. It's reasonable for you to ask them about what they will be doing for you, but only after they've expressed interest in representing you. Nothing turns off an agent faster than someone calling them and asking questions that they could have found answers to in a standard reference book or on the agent's own website. The Association of Author Representatives (AAR) has a list of questions you can use, as noted in the sidebar. Find out not only their commission structures but what costs they pass on to you. If they want to charge a reading fee before they'll look at your manuscript, run, do not walk, to the nearest exit. Agents can legitimately pass on some expenses, but those charging reading fees are not living on their commissions, which is what you want them to do.

Illustrators can visit the website of the Society of Photographers and Artists Representatives (SPAR), at www.spar.org/index.html, and find lists of artist's representatives.

Of course, you should also talk to other writers and artists, attend conferences, and follow other paths that may lead you toward finding the rep you want. That may be the only way to get in touch with an agent whose doors are otherwise closed. Just remember that having a rep won't land you in Solla Sollew.

Can You Keep a Secret?

When looking for an agent, ask about fees, about other clients, and if the agent belongs to the Association of Author's Representatives. There are reputable agents who choose not to belong, but the AAR's Canon of Ethics, suggested questions to ask of an agent, and member's list, all online at www.aar-online.org/, are useful resources.

The Least You Need to Know

◆ Agents and artist's representatives both send your work to publishers and negotiate contracts on your behalf.

◆ Artist's representatives charge higher commissions due to higher expenses.

◆ Carefully consider whether you need or are ready for an agent before trying to find one.

◆ An artist's representative can get an illustrator work in educational publishing that he or she could not otherwise get.

◆ Use book and web resources to help you with your search for an agent or rep.

Chapter 18

The Publishing Maze

In This Chapter

- ◆ The difference between a publishing house and its imprints
- ◆ Why you must submit manuscripts one at a time, not simultaneously, to imprints
- ◆ How to choose an imprint that's right for your manuscript or your illustration style
- ◆ Learning about imprints at a large publisher and a smaller publisher by analyzing their catalogs

Learning about publishing companies is like going into a maze of names. Publishing houses come in many sizes, shapes, and structures. Some have one simple name. Others have different divisions. Still others not only have divisions but also may have several "imprints" within each division. What's an imprint, then?

In this chapter, you'll learn how the larger publishing companies publish their books from different mini-publishing houses under the umbrella of the overall company. This knowledge is also put to practical use as you learn about the books a major publisher and a smaller independent publisher publish from an examination of their catalogs.

Companies, Divisions, and Imprints

It's overwhelming enough that there are hundreds of companies to learn about, but you'll quickly notice that many of them seem to contain separate entities with their own names. To which do you send a manuscript? To the company as a whole? To its children's book division? Or to even smaller parts of the company, which, strangely enough, all have their own names?

Dad, What's an Imprint?

Those small subdivisions are usually called *imprints*. What *is* an imprint? An imprint is literally the name that appears on the title page and spine of a book, such as "Dell Yearling," or "Viking Books." Both of those are parts of larger companies, in these cases Random House and Penguin Putnam, respectively. Each imprint usually has its own editorial staff, and sometimes its own marketing staff, but shares all the other resources of the company. Still, the company hopes that each imprint has a separate, recognizable identity, kind of like a brand name. When you think of Pepperidge Farm Goldfish, you think of a tasty crunchy snack. When you think of Penguin Books, what do you think of? Well, maybe imprint names aren't quite as well-known as snack foods!

Vocabulary List

An **imprint** is a part of a publisher with a distinct identity, name, and staff, usually concentrating on a distinct type or mix of books.

An imprint is not a division, which is usually a larger administrative body. Several imprints might make up the children's division of a larger company. Nor is it a "line." A line might be a part of an imprint; the easy-to-read line of Typical Children's Books, for example, which also has a picture book line and a nonfiction line. Note that a line is not the same thing as a series, because it might bring together books that do not share characters, subject, and theme. Sometimes an imprint is started from scratch, and given a name intended to reflect its identity. Sometimes it has the name of a noted editor, making it a "personal imprint," with books that reflect the taste of that editor. Other times it carries a name that used to exist as an independent company that has been absorbed into a larger one. In all these cases, the imprint has a name that is meant to give it an identity and its books credibility.

Still confused? Don't worry. It will start to make sense as you get to know the companies, and the in-depth look later in this chapter into two catalogs will help.

> **⚠ CAUTION**
>
> **Class Rules** _____
>
> The different imprints at a publishing company act independently of each other—except when they don't. Usually, they don't share manuscripts, and they have their own staff. But never send the same manuscript to two imprints at the same company. They can't both acquire it, and management at the company will prevent them from competing for it. On the other hand, it may be okay to send art samples to different imprints within the same company, if they do not share staff. A company's guidelines should help you decide how to approach different imprints.

One at a Time, Please

You need to understand what an imprint is because you send your work to individual imprints, not to the overall publishing company. Blue Sky Press and Cartwheel Books, for example, are two imprints at Scholastic—and very different, as you will see if you look at their catalogs. You would usually send one of the imprints your work (not Scholastic). If that imprint is not interested, they will return it to you, and usually won't share it with other imprints at the same company.

There are limits to the independence of imprints, however. Most companies do not want their imprints to compete with each other. People at most companies will accept your decision to send a manuscript to several different companies at once, but will feel you are being gauche if you send it to two imprints at the same company. For example, Dial Books and Viking Books are two different imprints at Penguin Putnam. Both publish picture books. You know that they won't be sharing manuscripts, but does that give you an opportunity to send the manuscript to both? No.

In the admittedly unlikely event that both are interested in your work and want to acquire it, the company will realize there is a conflict when both imprints bring it to the meeting at which they get approval to sign it up. At this point, one will be told to bow out, and all you will have gained is a group of people—the ones at the losing imprint—who are annoyed with you. Because publishing people move around, and because you may end up not publishing at the winning imprint for the rest of your career, this is not good.

There are also exceptions to the general rule that imprints have separate staffs, and that's another reason not to send manuscripts to multiple imprints at the same publisher. Charlesbridge, my former company, is both the name of the company as a whole and the imprint name for nonfiction picture books. Also at Charlesbridge are Whispering Coyote and Talewinds, both fiction picture book imprints, but each with a different emphasis. The same staff works on all three. If you sent a manuscript to Talewinds after Whispering Coyote turned it down, you'd just to be sending it to the same people again.

Door Number One ... Door Number Two

Now that you know what an imprint is, you may be inclined to sit down and send your manuscript or art samples to any imprint that publishes children's books, but slow down. One reason a publisher branches off into imprints is to specialize and narrow the focus of each. Imprints typically have tight guidelines about the "type" of books each produces, though in some case that type may be a specific mix—there is such a thing as an imprint's Swiss Army knife, which publishes everything from board books to young adult novels, with other "blades" of the knife perhaps being reference books, an easy-reader program, and photo-illustrated nonfiction.

I'll use a fictitious example to demonstrate why you need to carefully select the imprints to which you are sending your work. Say two imprints at one company both produce books with historical themes for children. You just wrote a young adult novel based on a boy serving in the Civil War. Your book contains facts galore about history, all woven into an edgy, realistic tale. At first glance, you think, "Hey, I'll send my manuscript to both imprints—one at a time, of course!"

Unfortunately for you, while you've learned that both imprints produce books with historical content by glancing through their catalog, the focus of those titles may differ greatly. One may only produce books for the institutional market, with an emphasis on historical fact. The other may only produce picture books based on history. Your young adult title, though extremely good, doesn't fit either imprint, and sending it to either of them wastes your time and theirs.

Similarly for illustrators, different art styles suit different kinds of publishers. If you work in a more painterly, fine art type of style, your home is likely to be in trade publishing. If your style is cute and cartoony, you might find that mass market or textbook publishing is the place to be. Investigate possible publishers before sending out mailings, and you'll save money and follow-up time by not sending materials to companies that just won't be interested.

To make sure that you choose the right imprint, you have to do research. Get the imprint's guidelines, which will usually start with a short statement about the kinds of books it publishes. Go to a bookstore and browse for books with that imprint's name on them.

 Class Rules

To find out what kinds of books a publisher produces, write to ask for guidelines. The guidelines will tell you a little about the imprint and how to submit manuscripts or art samples to it. And they may tell you how to get a copy of a catalog. Or try searching for the publisher online. Many companies now make their guidelines and complete catalogs available on the World Wide Web.

Even better, take a look at the imprint's catalog, which might be part of a larger catalog for the company to which the imprint belongs. You'll find more useful and specific information there than if you call and quiz an assistant in the department about the kinds of books they publish. The poor assistant will want to get you off the phone and will provide a brief and general description of the program. But the catalog will be full of information from which you can put together a detailed profile, as you're about to learn.

The Big Guys

As you learned in Chapter 7, publishing mergers and consolidations have created several large publishers in New York. In one way, they have narrowed the market for you, but fortunately, because imprints are independent and all of these publishers have several children's book imprints, you can still submit your manuscripts and art samples to each of them.

Of course, you can only send them materials if their doors are open. Writers often complain that they can't send manuscripts to these companies unless they have an agent or are published. Illustrators may find that their samples seemingly vanish into a black hole. Fortunately, not all the doors are closed. Look for the open doors and don't let the closed ones frustrate you.

What Are They Like?

You'll find that the big guys have a surprising variety of imprints. Some are personal imprints run by one well-known editor. Others are general-purpose imprints covering the gamut from board books to young adult novels. Some are known for solid nonfiction for the library market. Others are known for innovative picture books that get snapped up in bookstores. They all tend to be slow to respond to submissions, however. So it helps to get to know them a little better. We've talked elsewhere about the importance of targeting your submissions. This is one reason why: It will save you time in the long run if you can cut your list of possible publishers from 30 to 10. You'll spend less time waiting. How? Study their catalogs.

I've addressed writers in the following studies, but illustrators can do a similar analysis of a catalog to find out what types of books a company publishes, what range of art styles they use, and so on.

I'd Like You to Meet ...

I have a copy of the Simon & Schuster Children's Publishing catalog for fall 2000 on hand. (You should find the most current catalog you can; I offer this as an example, but surprisingly little has changed three years later.) It's a good example of a large, corporate publisher with several imprints to investigate.

Their catalog is pretty sizable, and lists six different imprints on the front. The catalog also lists two others, which we can ignore: Rabbit Ears is a book-and-cassette line, and Meadowbrook is a company that S&S distributes. Atheneum's section starts with a big splash about a picture book, and goes on to cover a mixed list of about 25 books, including picture books, novels, and both picture book and chapter book nonfiction. Some are designated "An Anne Schwartz Book," and there's a small section for "Richard Jackson Books." Make a note to find out whether these two personal imprints within Atheneum have separate submissions policies; the catalog doesn't say. I get a general impression of a high-quality list that includes such well-known authors as Eve Bunting and E. L. Konigsburg. Two books get two-page spreads with information about marketing and promotion being done, so the company is definitely aiming for the bookstore market with those, but mostly the books seem to be aimed at the review-driven library market.

Then comes Simon & Schuster; not surprisingly, because this carries the name of the company, this contains a large list of nearly 40 books. It's a more wide-ranging list, more middle of the market, and includes not only picture books and novels like those on the Atheneum list, but also a couple of celebrity picture books and gift and anniversary editions of famous books. There's overlap with Atheneum, but more of a focus on consumers, judging by the subjects of the books and, in several cases, by the emphasis on marketing campaigns that will help booksellers sell copies. Still, many manuscripts could fit at either one.

Margaret K. McElderry Books is a freestanding personal imprint (about which you'll learn more in Chapter 24). Of 10 books listed, some are picture books, a few are middle-grade novels, and there are also two books beginning an early-reader series and a young adult novel by Margaret Mahy, the famous New Zealand author. Browsing the pages, one sees none of the flash and promotional push we've seen earlier. All the books give the impression of being aimed quietly but firmly at children, and seem likely to sell mainly in the library market.

The other imprints in the catalog are quite different in focus from these first three, which all publish jacketed hardcover books. Aladdin Paperbacks publishes a mix of paperback series and reprints of previously published hardcovers, ranging from picture books to young adult novels. How do I know that some of these are reprints? In some cases, it says so in the blurb. In others, I recognize the book as one that came out a year or two ago. Check their guidelines, but this doesn't look like an imprint that is open to direct submissions.

Little Simon looks like a mass-market imprint, judging by the lower prices ($3.99) and presence of board books, pop-up books, and books with tie-ins to well-known cookie and cereal brands. Simon Spotlight seems similar to Little Simon, but all the books are tied to TV series and movies (in fact, to shows like *Rugrats* and *Blue's Clues*, which air on Nickelodeon, a cable channel owned by the same company that owns Simon & Schuster). Will either of these imprints be interested in an original story, using their characters? No, but they might hire illustrators and freelance writers to work to their specifications.

Can You Keep a Secret?

Look in the section under the price and ISBN for each book in many catalogs, and you'll see who owns and can license the subsidiary rights. If it says the publisher's name and "all rights," that book either came in as an author's submission direct to the publisher, or was commissioned. Some rights may be held by an agent, a foreign publisher, or a book producer. Checking this information helps you get a feel for how many books came as author submissions and how many came from agents or from other companies.

I've found three imprints that seem likely to take submissions, (but I'll have to find out if their doors are open) and three others who might be sources of freelance writing or for-hire illustration. That's not bad. I could dig even deeper into the exact kinds of books that each publishes, and I'll show how to do that in the following section, which looks at just one imprint.

The Little Guys

Look at any market guide and you'll find a lot of publishers who aren't part of larger companies but are pretty large on their own.

For the most part, these companies are more open to unsolicited submissions than what you could call the corporate publishers. Those that are open are usually quicker to respond to submissions (by quicker, I mean one to three months), and more likely to make personal comments.

What Are They Like?

Smaller, independent publishers are more diverse than the larger ones. This is where you'll find companies publishing for specific religious, cultural, and ethnic groups. You'll find companies with a regional focus, publishers for children with special needs, and publishers specializing in folktales, arts and crafts books, and the history of Williamsburg. (You can look it up on the Children's Book Council website—they're a CBC member.) You'll also find companies publishing for the general market, going head to head with the big guys, and sometimes with considerable success.

> **Playground Stories**
>
> Alexandra Siy, who has published with both kinds of publishers, has this to say:
>
> Working with Charlesbridge [an independent] has been wonderful. ... My experience with [an imprint at a corporate publisher] was much different. Once the books were published, it seemed that no one cared about them anymore. Even while working on them, there was far less dialog between myself and the editor, and I had no part in the layout of the book. My advice to beginner writers is to seriously consider small publishers (despite the lower advance) because they will probably be happier with their relationship with their editors and publisher and with the final product.

Why should you bother with these companies? They don't pay as well and they may not have as much marketing muscle as the bigger companies. But you are more likely to get personal attention at a smaller company. You may also find that, unless you're lucky or have a potential bestseller on your hand, a smaller publisher is more likely to take the risk of publishing an unknown, or the risk of publishing something a little different.

I'd Like You to Meet ...

For our case study of a smaller and independent publisher, let's take a look at Boyds Mills Press. Based in Honesdale, Pennsylvania, this respected publisher is part of the company that publishes *Highlights for Children*. And as you'll see in the catalog, that magazine is the source of some of their books. For our study, I've sought out both the fall and spring 2000 catalogs because they don't publish that many books in one season. There aren't many books, so I'll discuss them in more detail than in the S&S comments; you could do the same kind of detailed investigation of a larger company's catalog.

Both catalogs feature about 15 new books, published under just one imprint: Boyds Mill Press. There are some paperbacks, which we'll ignore, as they are based on already-published hardcovers. Looking at the table of contents of the spring 2000 catalog, we see a backlist section, organized by grade level. And that tells us that Boyds Mills sees teachers and school libraries as a good chunk of the market they are trying to reach, if not the most important chunk. We don't see the emphasis on promotional support we saw for the Simon & Schuster imprint. Because they are interested in the school and library market, we aren't surprised to find a good amount of nonfiction (four titles), two historical fiction picture books, and some picture books with learning components (one explores math concepts, and there's also a counting book). We also spot two collections of poetry, one made up entirely of originals, the other a compilation. Though there isn't a separate section in the catalog, the text about these books mentions an imprint called Wordsong. All of these are for children 12 years old or younger.

Can You Keep a Secret?

Use catalogs to find out about the *kinds* of books an imprint publishes, such as historical fiction or easy readers, not to study specific subjects. If a catalog includes a book about the death of a pet or an unusual summer vacation, that does not indicate a strong interest in that particular subject. Stories with such subjects could be published by any general-purpose imprint, because they address common childhood experiences.

The fall catalog is not a repeat of the spring one. It has more poetry collections, and I decide that I should get one or two of these from the library before sending in my own poetry. There are activity and craft books, but they seem to be connected to *Highlights*, so before shipping off a dog-eared manuscript of *101 Popsicle Stick Activities*, I am going to query to see if they accept these materials or just reuse them from the magazine. There is another novel for middle-grade readers. I am also interested to see three books with a religious connection: There's a picture book biography of Saint Nicholas, a history of Jerusalem, and a story of King Solomon. And there's a middle-grade collection of 15 biographies of athletes who "battled back" from something.

I've seen a diverse list aimed at the school and library market, probably not with much orientation to bookstores (no books by celebrities or brand-name connections, and they don't mention any big marketing campaigns). If you're writing historical fiction picture books, or collections of poetry, or middle-grade novels, this company is worth some more investigation. There seems to be a separate imprint for poetry books, so an author of poetry would want to inquire and find out if poetry is considered separately, perhaps by different staff. I didn't see any young adult novels or nonfiction, easy readers, or fantasy.

If you don't have access to catalogs, (you can send away for them or pick them up at conventions) you can use a neat feature on Amazon to find out about publishers. In the Books section, clicking on the Search tab in the row of tabs across the top takes you to an advanced search page. There you can do searches by publisher, format (this is optional), age level, and the year or years for which you want results. I did a test using Farrar, Straus and Giroux, age level of 4 to 8, and "During the year 2002," and obtained a handy list of 35 books from their spring and fall lists.

Could you divine all that I did from a catalog? Possibly not. I knew what to look for, and knew what it meant. But as you learn more about today's children's book market, and as you spend time reading catalogs, you'll become better able to get useful information from them. Once you've learned from a catalog, you can use the methods introduced in Chapter 19 to continue to investigate publishers.

The Least You Need to Know

- Publishing companies may have many different parts, but imprints are the ones a writer wants to get to know.

- Imprints are independent units within companies, and each has its own focus.

- Choose your imprint carefully, especially at large companies where different imprints will have very different programs.

- Catalogs are useful tools for figuring out the kinds of books each imprint publishes, and you should take some time analyzing them.

Chapter

Deeper into the Maze: Other Kinds of Publishers

In This Chapter

- ◆ The importance of picking the right publisher
- ◆ The magazine market
- ◆ Educational publishers
- ◆ Niche and regional publishers, and publishers in other countries
- ◆ Checking out new publishers, online and off
- ◆ Watch out for the subsidy publishers

So you've been knocking on doors at the big guys and the smaller guys and you're still not getting anywhere? There's more out there than you might think. After a quick reality check to ask whether you've been knocking on the right doors, this chapter will open even more doors—the doors to the magazine world, educational publishers (they don't just publish textbooks!), regional and niche publishers, and new publishers.

Sorry, I'll Try Next Door

You learned in the last chapter how to analyze a catalog to figure out what a publisher does—and what books they might want to see. As I said in that chapter, be careful what you do with what you've learned. If you learned that Publisher Q publishes picture books, but you didn't notice that all of them feature contemporary children, you might send them your poetically retold Middle English folktale, to no avail.

> **Playground Stories**
>
> Larry Dane Brimner sent what became his first published book to Clarion, only to have it be returned by an editor praising the manuscript but urging him to "'find the right publisher.'... Had I done a careful study of the Clarion list to begin with, I would have known that it rarely publishes sports-related nonfiction. My subsequent study led me to Franklin Watts because the book I envisioned, the book I'd written, was similar to books it published. My book would fit with the list."

You might send your manuscript to the wrong place if your knowledge of a publisher is superficial. Nine times out of ten, you won't hear from an editor that you simply chose the wrong house. You'll just get a standard rejection letter and be none the wiser.

So dig a little deeper before you throw up your hands—but not too deep! Sometimes at conferences, I have heard authors complaining that they wish they knew exactly which editor published which book, so that they could send that person their book, which happens to be just like it. You don't need to dig that deep. An editor who happened to publish a farcical story about a dog who learned the importance of good manners might not want to see another farcical dog story. If that editor went to another publisher, that company might not want to publish such a story. But either publisher could be open to a story with an animal as the main character. So it's more important to get the publisher's general focus and approach correct. Editors come and go, but unless they are sufficiently influential to change a publishing program, few change the company's focus.

Should you be concerned about a publisher's focus just because you don't want to waste the time of their editors? In these times of overwhelmed editorial staffs, maybe you should be, but let's not forget the purely selfish and practical point that you waste your own time if you send a manuscript to a publisher who isn't going to be interested in it. Yes, the publishing maze is confusing, but you'll save yourself time in the long run if you do enough research that you can target your submissions carefully and follow the publisher's latest guidelines.

CAUTION

Class Rules _____

Every editor has stories about wildly inappropriate submissions—novels for adults sent to publishers of picture books, picture book stories sent to publishers of library nonfiction for teenagers—and their mantra is "Find out more about us!" Emma Dryden of Margaret K. McElderry Books confirmed this point by heading a list of things she wishes beginning writers knew with these two items:

◆ I wish more beginning writers were familiar with our backlist and current titles before submitting their projects to us.

◆ I wish more beginning writers submitted their materials according to our specific submission guidelines.

Magazines

So you've followed my advice and tried every single one of the publishers that might be interested in your piece on bee behavior or your story about two children learning to take care of a puppy. What now? Either it's time to put it aside or it's time to try elsewhere. To start with, try magazines.

There are literally hundreds of magazines for children in North America; some—like _Highlights for Children_ or _Cricket_—publish for a general audience, while others focus on a very specific interest or audience. Some are for preschoolers, while others are for teenagers. Magazines can be pretty specialized, such as _Gball_, a girls basketball magazine, or _Pack-O-Fun_, a craft magazine. Whatever your interest, you are likely to find at least one magazine that matches up. In fact, given that magazines can more effectively target a small market than book publishers can, you'll find a wider and more varied range of opportunities among magazines than among book publishers.

Writing for magazines _is_ different from writing for book publication. If you mostly write for younger children, you'll see that a magazine piece needs (or demands!) fewer illustrations than a story for a picture book. If you write for older children, here's a market for short stories, mostly not published by book publishers. Or if nonfiction is your bag, there's great demand for short pieces or longer essays, quite different in form from what you'd do for a book.

To understand the difference, immerse yourself in it. Get your hands on some children's magazines in an area that you think interests you. If you write picture books for five-year-olds, for example, check out _Ladybug_. Type up a story from the magazine and compare it to yours. Is the length all that's different, or does the story develop differently? How about the vocabulary? Try reading several issues of a magazine and then several books intended for children of the same age, and reflect on the differences you notice.

Magazines work differently from books, too. Many magazines pay per word, or pay a flat fee per article. You can expect to receive anywhere from $25 for a very short piece to hundreds of dollars for a longer article. That doesn't sound like much, but it's a credit you can cite, and experience, and usually magazines only buy one use of your work, so you can sell it elsewhere. Check their guidelines carefully—some accept submissions generally, others want material for specific theme issues, while others commission work from you on the basis of your writing samples and stated interests. Magazines also specify how many words they want for certain kinds of pieces, where book publishers will ask for "long enough to tell the story." Follow those guidelines carefully.

> **Playground Stories**
>
> Sneed Collard writes for both books and magazines:
>
> For a long time, I viewed magazine writing as a way to break into books, but magazine writing has its own rewards. First, you can write about a topic without spending as much time on it as a book requires. Second, I enjoy the more journalistic, "snappy" approach that magazine articles allow. Third, magazine articles provide great "spin-offs" from books—and earn you additional income. Last, especially with the "testing fever" these days, several companies are gobbling up magazine reprint rights like crazy. I've now made more money from some of my magazine articles than I have from my books!

Magazines are a big market, and a great place to get experience. And who knows? You may decide this is the place for you, or at the least a great complement to what you want to do in books.

Educational Publishers

Educational publishers are another market worthy of investigation. They don't just publish textbooks. Schools today want all kinds of supplementary materials, from activities to poems to stories, in all curriculum areas. To meet this demand, educational publishers may buy the right to republish a book already sold in bookstores for their school audience. Or they may seek out original work.

When you are just getting started, it will be difficult to make headway at the really big companies such as Harcourt, Macmillan/McGraw-Hill, and Houghton Mifflin. Look instead for companies that produce supplementary materials. Companies such as Continental Press, Frank Schaefer, Mondo, the Wright Group, and Carson-Dellosa are producing series of "emergent-reader" books, grade-by-grade anthologies of stories to read, and poems, activities, and even games to go with math, social studies, and science curricula.

How can you find out about companies like this? If you're a teacher, you already know about them—they are the companies publishing the books you use. You will find them listed in some market guides, but to really learn about these companies, you should go to a national or regional convention of such teacher's organizations as the International Reading Association, the National Science Teacher's Association, or the National Council for Social Studies. You'll get a catalog listing all of the attending publishers and their addresses, and you'll be able to go from booth to booth to look at the books, gather brochures, and take notes about what they publish.

Educational publishers won't all want original material, and some only work on commission (they hire you to write something specific on a for-hire basis). But there is work if you look in the right places. For example, the Education Center, a teacher-resource material publisher, puts out calls for such things as "short-short" stories (525 words) for anthologies. This is a relatively unknown market, and one that might be just right for you.

Can You Keep a Secret?

How do you find out about the smaller educational publishers? If you can't go to a teacher's convention, Rozanne Lanczak Williams, who has built up a career working with such companies, suggests your local teacher supply store. Browse through the aisles and make notes on books similar to what you write. Contact those publishers and request guidelines.

Regional and Niche Publishers and Publishers Outside the United States

The publishers you are most likely to know are the ones that publish for the U.S. market. You'll find their books from Florida to Alaska (and probably in British Colombia and Newfoundland, too). They publish general-interest books for a wide audience. But what if you want to tell a story about a local hero or explain how the tide affects the bay? You might do well to find a local or *regional publisher*. What if you want to reach a child with a specific problem or background? Then you want a *niche publisher*. Both of these kinds of publishers do not try to reach every child in every part of North America; rather, they try to reach specific children. And what if you want to look beyond the U.S. borders, or if you are in fact living beyond them yourself? Then you have an entire world in front of you.

How do you find a regional publisher? You'll find them in the market guides (including a "Guide to the Small Press Market" available to members of the SCBW-I (Society of Children's Book Writers and Illustrators—see Appendix B), or online, but that may

Vocabulary List

A **regional publisher** specializes in subjects that are relevant to a particular part of the country, such as deserts in the Southwest or the Everglades in Florida, and sells its books locally. A **niche publisher** specializes in a subject that is of interest to a small group of people and sells its books nationally, but only in specialized outlets.

Can You Keep a Secret?

A great online source for information about independent publishers—not all of which are niche or regional publishers—is John Kremer's list of "101 Top Independent Publishers" at bookmarket.com/101pub.html.

take some sifting and sorting. Perhaps the most direct way is to go where the customers are. In your community, where would you go to buy a book like the one you have written? Go there, and look through the books on display. Note who published them. Call them up, or write to them, and find out if they accept submissions. If you live in Oregon and want to write a book about the art of the American Indians of the Northwest coast, you'll come across Sasquatch Books. If you live in Maine and want to do a story about life as a Maine fisherman, you would find that Down East Books is the place for you. Every region of the United States has one or more regional publishers.

To find a niche publisher, again, go where the customers are. In this case, that's not necessarily a bookstore. My website receives frequent questions from the authors of stories about children overcoming emotional problems or dealing with a physical disability. In the larger children's bookstores, you may find a special section for these books. But it might also be worthwhile to ask a child psychologist or school counselor to let you look through his shelves. If they do any "bibliotherapy," or handing children books to read that are tailored to particular problems, you may find a sizable collection.

Christian, Jewish, and other religious publishers also publish for a niche market—in this case, parents seeking books that speak to their particular faith or that more generally support values with which they feel comfortable. You'll find Christian bookstores in just about every community, and the Christian Booksellers Association has conventions at which you can investigate this market.

What other niches are there? There's one for just about every interest or lifestyle, though not always for children. Some publishers specialize in environmental themes, some specialize in craft books, and some in New Age values. Whatever your interest, there's likely to be a niche you can call home.

If you have a publishing home outside the United States, or want to seek one, the information here can get you started; however, you'll need to do some digging. For example, look into the Canadian market. If you are Canadian, be sure to consider Canadian publishers because many of them give precedence to Canadian authors and illustrators.

If you aren't Canadian, then that's a problem. Always look to your own country's publishers first. If you reside outside the United States, you might also consider the U.S. market because it is, of course, the world's largest English-language market.

> **Class Rules** _____
>
> English-language markets outside of the United States include Canada, the United Kingdom, Australia, and New Zealand. A useful starting point to research the Canadian market is the following web page, by Bev Cooke: www.underdown.org/canada.htm. For the U.K. market, look to this useful list of publishers at www.ukchildrensbooks.co.uk/pubs.html. You'll find other resources, too—for example, the SCBW-I has an active Australian branch.

New! New! New!

It's easy enough to get the idea that publishers are closing down and merging, and that the number of outlets for your writing is decreasing every year. The big publishers are certainly bigger than they used to be, but new publishers and imprints appear every year. For example, in the July 31, 2000, issue of *Publishers Weekly*, "New Hats in the Ring" listed nine new imprints—you'll find similar articles from time to time. Some are completely new companies, notably Handprint Books, Christopher Franceschelli's new company, founded after he left Dutton in 1997. More recently, McGraw-Hill launched Gingham Dog Press in the spring of 2003.

Other new companies already existed in some form before, and won't be much of an opportunity for writers. In that article, for example, three new imprints are packagers or British publishers that are now going directly to the American market, and so will not have much interest or room for new material. Three are editors moving to new houses or starting new imprints—Megan Tingley Books at Little Brown, or Richard Jackson's "return" to his personal backlist at Simon & Schuster. Such imprints do look at new writers and illustrators, but will stock their lists mostly with people with whom they have been working for some time. And the remaining two mentioned are tightly focused, drawing on existing material or authors: the *Family Heritage Series* of the Vermont Folklife Center, based on stories from their archives; and the *Everything Kids* series, a mass-market line spun off from a similar adult line.

Opportunities exist at companies like these, but are not necessarily an opportunity to clear out your drawer full of already-rejected manuscripts. New companies may be just as selective as old ones, so send them what they want. Keep your eyes open, read *Publishers Weekly*, read your favorite newsletter, and update your market guide every year.

E-Books and the Internet

Chapter 7 also mentioned electronic publishing. However, so far there don't seem to be many new opportunities for writers to publish books electronically; rather, much of this type of publishing consists of new editions of books that are already available in print form. And so far, those books are mostly novels and technical books because these translate more effectively to onscreen versions. It's more difficult and expensive to convert color picture books into electronic form. You can find plenty of freelance writing with online companies, but this is usually for short online articles, and earns you no more than a small fee.

Can You Keep a Secret?

For guidance to this brave new world, see *Writer's Online Marketplace*, by Debbie Ridpath Ohi (Writer's Digest Books, 2001). She founded the now defunct and much lamented www.inkspot.com. This book is a good guide to both the online market and electronic rights.

If you do work with an electronic book publisher, expect to be paid royalties, and do not expect to pay "listing" or "production" costs. (Companies that ask you to do that are just another kind of subsidy publisher.)

All Is Vanity? Paying the Publisher

With traditional publishing so difficult to break into, and the brave new world of electronic publishing not much help, you may be tempted to turn to publishers who don't pay you. These range from what are politely called *subsidy publishers* but are more accurately known as *vanity presses*, through certain electronic and *print-on-demand* publishers who set up your book for a fee, to a new twist I call "no advance" publishers. Authors and illustrators are often warned away from these. I'll explain why.

Vocabulary List

A **vanity press** produces books for you from your manuscript, usually without much editing and with no marketing, for a pretty sizable fee. **Print-on-demand** and some electronic publishers create a book file for you, which can be printed one copy at a time, or sold as an e-book, for a modest feel. That's all they do. And **no-advance** publishers don't charge you anything, but they don't pay you an advance, and expect you to do the marketing.

A Lot of Work in Vain

Subsidy presses are also called vanity presses for a very good reason—they rely on the vanity of those who want to see their work in print, even at considerable cost.

The money you pay will only buy you a stock of books, printed to uncertain standards, which you will likely have to market yourself. No vanity press in existence can get your book true national distribution or do the marketing needed to get the books sold.

One Copy at a Time

Now that publishing has become an electronic business, a new kind of subsidy publishing has emerged. It's possible to take a manuscript and convert it into an electronic form that's all ready to be printed. Instead of going to the expense of printing and warehousing a few thousand copies of a book, a company can use print-on-demand technology to quite literally print one copy of a book at a time. Per copy prices are reasonable, though the technology allows only for black-and-white printing at this point. This system can be used to prolong the life of books that would otherwise go out of print. It can also be used to produce books for aspiring authors for a fee considerably lower than charged by traditional vanity presses.

Another option is to use the electronic file as the basis for an e-book, and not create a physical book at all. Or you can offer both options together. The company providing the service pays the author for each copy sold, and you can recoup your expenses, if you sell enough copies. If you'd like to see how such a business works, explore the websites of www.xlibris.com and www.iuniverse.com. But please keep in mind that I'm *not* endorsing what they do.

Nothing Up Front

A recent step up from vanity presses are companies I'd call "*no-advance*, no-marketing publishers." These companies do pay royalties, but they don't pay advances, and they typically print a very small number of copies of a book. Authors are expected to market the books themselves, and may actually have to commit to selling a certain number ahead of time. So far these companies are only publishing nonillustrated books because they use print-on-demand technology. I'd examine such companies' contracts carefully, but they do seem to be a small improvement on the traditional vanity model, which has been around for a long time.

Going Solo

Instead of working with such companies, why not do what a publisher does and work directly with a printer, and hire all the other services needed to put a book out on the market? As you will discover in more detail later in the book, a publisher does a lot. If you are to replicate that and self-publish, it will cost you a lot of both time and money. If you only need to reach a local or specialized market and you can take the time to do that yourself, this could work. Otherwise, self-publishing might be a better option for you after you've gained some experience in publishing, as explained in Chapter 33.

And Why Not?

So, why shouldn't you pay to get your book published, or accept much less than you would expect from a traditional publisher? For one thing, the book won't turn out as good as it would with the help of traditional publisher's editorial and design staff, and it won't reach as many people as it would with the help of that traditional publisher's marketing staff. Perhaps even more important, you'll damage your credibility with editors at traditional companies. If that doesn't matter to you and if you just want to publish a particular book or a few books, and don't want a career as a writer, then it might be worth it for you to work with one of these companies. But if you hope to become a traditionally published writer, stay away from them. Keep your eyes on the prize, and keep moving forward.

The publishing maze is large and complicated. Carry a ball of string, and don't lose track of the different ways out of it.

The Least You Need to Know

- There are magazines for every age level and interest, and they can be great markets for writers.

- Educational publishers can be an opportunity—and teacher's conventions are a good place to find out about them.

- Smaller publishers focusing on regional and specialized subjects may be the home you need.

- New publishers come along every day. Read the fine print to determine how new they truly are, and what their needs are.

- There is a lot of heat and noise over electronic publishing, but so far few new opportunities.

- Don't be driven by the difficulty of finding a publisher to consider a vanity press.

Chapter **20**

So How Does It All Work?

In This Chapter

- ◆ Why publishers need you
- ◆ How to go beyond the basics and play the game the most effective way
- ◆ How to respond to an editor's interest
- ◆ The importance of persistence
- ◆ What goes on behind a publisher's doors, and why it sometimes seems like nothing is happening

By now you know the basics of getting your children's book published, but you need to know how to put it all together. You need to know how the system works—to the extent that it does. In this chapter, you'll learn why, even after the mergers of the 1990s, children's book publishers still need you, and how you can best approach them. You'll also learn what's happening behind the doors of a publisher when you don't get a response.

Publishers Need *You*

At this point you may not believe it, but publishers still need you. Without authors and illustrators, most publishers would not exist. Your creative energy produces works that are too distinctive to be created by in-house staff, and it's these creations that the trade market, at least, demands. Some publishers do seem to have little need for fresh talent, but every one of the people whose work they publish was a beginner at some point.

Publishing works on a never-ending cycle. Every publisher must create a minimum number of new books every year, or run short of income. A publisher releases two or three "lists" each year, grouping its books into fall and spring bunches, possibly adding a winter or summer group. Why? That's just the way it's always been done, though mass-market publishers tend to release books throughout the year. The publisher's business and budget is built around a certain number of books, be it 5, 10, or 50, that it must have on each list.

And that need for a full list is where you come in. Authors and illustrators leave even the most stable of lists. They get restless and move on, their editor leaves and they follow, they cut back their output, or they even die or move into another field. So every publisher needs some fresh blood from time to time. If they get it by luring someone over from another publisher, then *that* publisher needs to fill a space on their list. There is always some flux in publishing, and that change brings opportunity.

Play the Game by the Rules

To get anywhere in this business, you need some talent, persistence, luck, and an understanding of the way things work. The first three, you provide, and I hope you're finding the last one in this book. So far, you've read a lot of detailed advice. Now it's time to pull it all together and highlight important strategies.

The Union Makes You Strong

No union of children's writers and illustrators exists, of course, but there are national organizations to which you should belong and get involved with. It's been mentioned elsewhere, but it bears repeating! The occasional genius can go it alone, but the resources of the Society of Children's Book Authors and Illustrators (SCBWI) and the Canadian Society of Children's Book Authors, Illustrators, and Performers (CANSCAIP) (see Appendix B for more information) are worth getting access to, and local conferences are well worth attending.

But do more than that. Get involved for the local critique groups, for the support of other writers and illustrators, for the opportunity to have regular contact with editors. Go to one conference and you might get a chance to talk to an editor for a few minutes. Become an active member of your local chapter and you will get to know editors over phone calls and letters and at the conference.

That contact is valuable. Although I've met many authors and illustrators at conferences, the people I remember and keep in touch with are usually the folks who organized or helped out during the conference—not the person in the hallway who asked me if I would mind looking at her manuscript.

"" "" Playground Stories

Lisa Rowe Fraustino, author of *Ash* and *The Hickory Chair*, among other books, has this to say:

> Five out of the six books I have contracted to date have been with editors I met at conferences and developed a rapport with. And the sixth book is in a series published by the same house but a different imprint than one of my regular editors, and without my prior contact with the house I doubt my proposal would have been taken as seriously.

What she's not saying is that for years she was one of the organizers of a conference in eastern Pennsylvania, and that it was through that work that she met these editors, including me.

Catalogs, Conventions, and Guidelines

It's good to get to know editors. It's vital to get to know publishers. You've learned how to analyze a catalog. Do that for all the publishers who might be a home for your manuscript *before* you send it to them. You might end up dropping half of them from your list, saving yourself time and postage.

To get all those catalogs, you can write publishers and send the right size SASEs and wait for them to come back. Or you can go to a conference. National and regional teacher, librarian, and bookseller organizations have them every year, and in their exhibit halls dozens and dozens of publishers set up booths showcasing their latest books and giving away their latest catalogs. For booksellers, there's BookExpo America (BEA), and regional shows like the Southeast Booksellers Association show. For teachers, there's NCTE and IRA and NCSS and NCTM and their regional variants. And for librarians there's the American Library Association and regional conferences like the Texas Library Association convention. Often, the public can get in for the day to wander the exhibit hall, or if not, you can get a day ticket through a teacher or librarian you know.

Can You Keep a Secret?

The very best place to learn about trade publishers may be the convention of the American Library Association, where publishers display their latest books and give out catalogs. Held each year in January and June, ALA conventions move around—sooner or later one will come to a city near you, or to a city where you know someone. Find out more at www.ala.org/.

As suggested in Chapter 16, spend a day at one of these conventions. At the end of the day, you'll be exhausted, but you will leave much better informed about the latest in children's books than you were when you started.

Scope Out the Competition

Don't assume that your writing is so original that no one else has ever done anything like it. Find out what other books are out there that are similar, just so you can say in a cover letter how yours is different. It's not enough to say "I wrote this because I wanted to find a book on (fill in the blank) and there wasn't one at my local bookstore." Most editors won't believe this and may well be able to think of several books you didn't find. Anticipate them, and tell them about the similar books and the ways in which yours is different. This is particularly important for nonfiction, but you can do it for fiction, too. Careful searches on Amazon or a large public library collection, perhaps supplemented by a discussion with an experienced children's librarian, should get you the information you need.

Waiting Patiently—or Not

After you get your manuscript out there, be prepared to wait. Of course, don't just wait. Use that time to write another manuscript, to start research for a new book, or to read the five latest Newbery winners. When you do hear from a publisher, you most likely will get a form rejection letter, photocopied, without even an individual's name. Don't be disappointed. Every author starts out getting these. But check the rejections carefully. Don't leave your returned SASEs lying around unopened. There may be a golden opportunity inside, so open that envelope and be ready to spring into action.

Follow Everything Up

If you keep at it, do everything right, and have a little luck, there will come a day when you will hear from an editor. Most likely, 9 times out of 10, if not 99 times out of 100, your first actual contact will be a short rejection letter or maybe even a note scribbled on a form letter rejection. If you're an illustrator, maybe you'll just get a request for more samples. Do not be discouraged that this isn't a contract. Be encouraged that someone has taken the time to write to you. Respond, but be sure to respond appropriately.

When You Get a Nibble

The least encouraging positive response you can get is a short note scribbled at the bottom of a *form rejection letter*. It may say "We hope to hear from you again" or "Thanks for your submission" or "We don't publish this kind of story but we would like to see [something] from you." Notes like this may not seem like much, but at most publishers, very few manuscripts will get even this much of a response. The message? You are in the ballpark, and someone wants you to know it, even if you aren't ready to take the field as a starter. Submit work to this publisher again.

More encouraging is a short signed letter. Even if it's written in generic language— "Thank you for submitting XYZ. We enjoyed reading it, but are sorry to tell you that it is not right for our list"—you can be encouraged that an editor has put his or her name at the end of the letter. This is an invitation to write to that editor again, with a different manuscript. Accept this invitation!

Vocabulary List

A **form rejection letter** is a short, anonymous letter, usually photocopied, saying something like this: "Dear Author. Thank you for your submission. We appreciate your sharing your work with us. Unfortunately, your manuscript does not meet our current publishing needs, and we are returning it to you herewith." Anything more personal than this is encouraging!

A letter that rejects your manuscript but provides detailed reasons why should set off a celebration in your writer's heart. To write such a letter, an editor has taken a half-hour or more out of her busy day (or has asked an assistant to draft a letter and then reviewed it). This editor is interested in you. If she doesn't ask to see the manuscript again, do not send a revision unless you can see ways to deal with every single one of the concerns expressed in the letter. If she asks to see a revision, do your very best to think through what she says and make changes that not only do what she asks, but that also create a satisfying new whole. Don't be in too much of a hurry to get it back. That editor is not expecting to hear from you right away. She hopes you will take your time and reread what you've done, mull it over, read it to your critique group, and only send it back when you are sure it's ready.

Not Too Much!

After you have made contact in this way, this is not the time to clear out your drawer and send in every story you have ever written to this editor. She's not expecting it. Remember that it was one story that drew that response. Are you confident that a new story you've written is as good? If you are, send it. Can you say the same about that story you put aside a year ago, not sure of what to do with the ending? Probably not. Read it over. Do you really want her to read it? After all, you want this editor to think highly of you, and, realistically, she just isn't going to want to publish several of your stories right away.

So unless the editor specifically asks you to send her everything you've ever written, pick and choose and send her only your best work.

Not Too Aggressive!

At the same time, remember that you aren't the only author the editor's working with. She's juggling dozens of active titles and probably corresponding with dozens of other authors, on top of meetings and planning sessions and conferences. You are not going to suddenly start to get your manuscripts back from her within a few weeks. You should not call her a day after you calculate she would have received the manuscript to ask her what she thinks. Even if she read it when it first came in, she needs a week or two to mull it over. Let her get in touch with you. Even if she takes a couple of months, don't worry. There might be lots of other things going on. If you don't hear from her within the industry-standard three months, then a note or preferably a phone call is a good way to get in touch.

Class Rules

Want to know a sure-fire way to ruin a budding relationship with an editor? Deluge her with manuscripts, call her often when you don't hear from her, e-mail her all your latest ideas. Coming across as overeager or desperate won't get you better results, and might cool her interest in you. Strive at all times to be professional.

Publishing is a people business, and acting like a professional—dedicated, yet easy to work with—from the time you first write to someone through the time you see your book appear on the bookstore shelves is as important in helping you go on to another book as is the quality of your creative work.

You Can Get It—but You Must Try

Persistence leads to success. I make no guarantees—except to say that, without persistence, you won't get anywhere. Most published writers will tell you that they spent years learning, and going from form rejections to nibbles to regular correspondence and finally to publication. And even after that first book, they kept learning and growing and recovering from setbacks. Breaking through to a first book is no guarantee for a second or third. You have to write new manuscripts, they have to interest an editor, and your books have to do well enough that editors (and readers) want more down the road.

" " Playground Stories

Sometimes persistence goes right back to childhood. Writer Elaine Landau told us:

> When my mother was pregnant with me, a palm reader said that she would have a girl who was destined to become a writer. And my mother did give birth to a baby girl who showed a keen interest in writing. But she felt certain that I'd never make a decent living writing and tried her best to discourage me. I continued to fill notebooks with poetry and essays. When I went to college, she insisted that I take a practical major like business. I tried but after just one term I switched to an English and journalism major.
>
> Today I'm the author of over 150 children's books. If you have that dream, don't let anyone discourage you. Just keep writing.

What's Going On in There?

Sometimes, though, you don't hear back, or all you get is a form letter. Even a form letter tells you something, if you think about it. Whoever it was that read your manuscript decided that your submission did not warrant a personal response of any kind. You don't know if that's because the manuscript didn't measure up, or because you sent it to the wrong publisher. After trying several publishers and getting only form letters, though, you may want to go back to your word processor, or try another manuscript.

Why does this happen? Why can't publishers respond personally to *all* submissions, so authors and illustrators won't be left guessing? Let's look behind the office doors of a publisher to find out, and understand why persistence is so important.

Behind Closed Doors

It is not true that editors have a peaceful job, reading manuscripts, deciding which ones they like, setting them into motion as books, and then watching them bob away on the stream. Any editor is likely working on dozens of books at various stages of completion, all of which need her personal attention, and on top of that spending time in meetings. You'll get a peek into the lives of a few editors in Chapter 24, but for now, please take it as a given that no editor has much time to spend on reading the submissions.

At most publishing companies, assistants, junior editors, or retired editors come in one day a week to read the "slush." They then pass on the 10 percent or so that they feel might interest an editor. Don't worry—even if the reader is a new assistant fresh out of college, it doesn't take much training to weed out the poorly written, badly targeted, or just plain unoriginal writing, and pull out only what might be good enough. The editor will still reject most of what she sees, but at least she's not spending as much time sorting through it.

Help, I'm Sinking!

Unfortunately, the system doesn't always work this smoothly. Publishers also get completely overloaded, and then you may not hear at all, or not for a long time. The sad fact is that when people at publishing houses get busy, it's the slush pile that suffers. Editors can always read it tomorrow, or next week, but if a book is due at a printer, or a writer is waiting for comments on a manuscript, or an illustrator needs guidance, that must come first.

So manuscripts pile up on desks, in file cabinets, and in bookcases (and that's why it's called a slush *pile*). Typically a publisher will have a backlog of a month or two, and will deal with it in batches, between busy times. But it can get worse. If a company gets publicity in a writer's magazine or a staff person leaves, hundreds of manuscripts can pile up, and the publisher may resort to closing its doors to more submissions until it can get caught up.

> **Class Rules**
>
> If you don't like competing with thousands of other people, children's publishing is not for you. There are well over 10,000 members in the Society of Children's Book Writers and Illustrators, and plenty more who aren't members. Keep striving to do your best and most creative work so you can stand out in this crowd.

It's also true that more people are writing, and writing better. Ten years ago, a publisher might have received 2,000 manuscripts and queries in a year. That's a lot, but it's manageable. If three people each read 10 or 20 manuscripts a week, they can keep up with it. Today, that same company, with perhaps the same number of staff to deal with the manuscripts, is getting 6,000 manuscripts. That's scary.

Do I Know You?

Faced with this situation, and perhaps not needing to find many new authors, many publishers have thrown in the towel and stopped reading submissions unless manuscripts come in from someone they know, or from someone with an agent, or someone with a previously published book. A few ask you to "query first" (send a query letter) so they have the opportunity to judge if the book you've written even sounds like something they would publish. To many writers, it can seem that most publishers have closed their doors. That isn't true, as noted in Chapter 16, but certainly more are closed than used to be. And as more publishers close their doors, the ones who are left must deal with more mail. It's little wonder that it can be three, four, five, six months, or more before some publishers respond.

Lost in the Shuffle

A final reason that it can take so long to hear from publishers is that they are seeing more manuscripts that do not deserve an immediate rejection. Thanks to the work of organizations like the SCBWI, more manuscripts than ever are coming in that have possibilities. There are still plenty of manuscripts that can be rejected quickly, perhaps after reading only a few lines. But manuscripts that can be read all the way through, and need to be thought about, are the ones that take up a reader's time. And there are more of these.

As mentioned previously, the competition is tough. Keep at it and at the end of the process, after making contact with an editor and perhaps revising a manuscript several times, you may just have a contract. And then you are on your way to publication.

Can You Keep a Secret?

I once judged a contest for unpublished authors, in which I mostly read the first chapters of novels. Of more than 70 submissions, very few were easy to reject. Many, though perhaps after revision, could be published. In a competition this strong, sometimes it can be hard to get noticed.

The Least You Need to Know

- ◆ All publishers need fresh talent. You need to put your best foot forward when approaching them.

- ◆ Get to know publishers and editors at conventions and conferences.

- ◆ Be restrained when you first hear from an editor, at least in your response. Later you can celebrate all you want!

- ◆ Persistence is a key to success, but no guarantee.

- ◆ Publishers get swamped by manuscripts and often take months to respond.

Part 4

Working with a Publisher

You've made it over the transom, and now you're working with a publisher. Or at least you're about to be, because they've sent you a contract. So to start with, this part will help you understand the contract and then explains how copyright law affects what you do.

This part also introduces you to the revision process, as you work with an editor, and to what happens once an illustrator gets to work. You'll meet some editors and an art director. I'll also introduce the other folks who join the team.

Chapter 21

Oh Boy! A Contract!

In This Chapter

- What a publishing contract does
- How you will be paid and what you'll have to do
- The mysteries of subsidiary rights
- Legal terms and other arcane knowledge
- Negotiating tactics

At some point, if you stick it out and build your talent and have some luck, you will hear from an editor who would like to offer you a contract. The excitement generated by this phone call, e-mail, or letter might lead you to unquestioningly hand over your first-born child, if requested—but put on a green eye shade and negotiate the terms of a contract? You can't be bothered. You're going to have a book! But calm down and educate yourself at least a little about contracts. In this chapter, you'll learn what a publishing contract involves, and you'll learn what to expect and what to ask for.

You may not be able actually to demand much, especially the first time around, but it's good to understand what you are signing. So read on, and ask your editor questions if you need to.

How You Will Hear

The initial stages of the process vary. If an editor is interested in a manuscript—perhaps after corresponding with a writer about it, on first reading—she might have to obtain some kind of approval from the company to *acquire* it. At a minimum, this usually means getting several higher-ups to read it, and to approve the *acquisition* during a meeting known as a publishing meeting or an acquisition meeting. Financial analysis of the expected costs and possible profits may also be required, perhaps in great detail, and perhaps just as rough estimates. If the book is a picture book, an illustrator's contract always comes after the author's contract, possibly a year or more later.

Vocabulary List

To **acquire** a manuscript, an editor receives approval from the company, and then negotiates a contract with an author. Your manuscript is now (in a sense) the company's property. The editor has made an **acquisition**.

Quiz—What Do You Know?

Contracts are complicated and full of terms most people just don't know. To help you assess where you should start in learning about contracts, take this short quiz. Write down whether you think each statement is true or false, and then check the answers and see where you stand.

1. Copyright refers to the copy an author writes.

2. A royalty is a an honorary payment you receive for winning a literary prize.

3. Subsidiary rights are the rights of subsidiaries, or divisions, of a publisher to publish your work.

4. Joint accounting is a clause you want in a contract—it means that you and the publisher jointly track sales of a book.

5. An important negotiating tactic is to decide what you want before you start to talk, and then walk away if you don't get it.

And the answers are false, but all for different reasons.

1. Copyright is the right to make copies of an original work. Illustrations and text can be copyrighted.

2. A royalty is a percentage you are paid out of the money a publisher receives for the sale of a book.

3. Subsidiary rights are actually the rights a publisher sells to other companies, to make a paperback edition, audio recording, or some other use of your work.

4. You don't want this in your contract. You'll find out why in the following section.

5. This stance can be counterproductive. It's always possible to learn that you don't need what you thought you did, or that a compromise will get you something you hadn't even thought about. Negotiating a contract involves give and take.

How did you do? If you got all these right, you may not need to read this chapter. Otherwise, read on!

Tit for Tat

Publishing contracts exist for a very simple reason. You, as the writer or illustrator, are the creator of intellectual property. This property is not something physical like a house or a car; however, you can sell it, or sell the rights to make use of it. In short, you can sell the right to copy your work—that's your copyright. (The next chapter covers copyright in more detail.) A publisher can do many different things with copyrighted work, from publishing it once in a magazine to publishing it in many different ways over a period of many years. But first, the publisher must gain the right to use the property. It gains this right with a contract. The core of a publishing contract is the transfer of a creator's rights to their work to a company that (we hope) has the resources to use those rights in ways you could not. In return, you receive some form of compensation.

What can you expect to see in a contract? Contracts may be only a few pages long, or more than 20, but they all cover much the same ground. This chapter notes a few points that apply to illustrators only, but for the most part, author and illustrator contracts are very similar.

When you receive your first contract, the following information should help you navigate it. But if you run into something you don't understand, just ask. Your editor won't think you stupid for doing so—she may not even understand what you're asking about and may have to ask someone in her company's contract department. It would not be wise to sign your contract without understanding it.

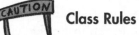

Class Rules

Don't hesitate to ask for an explanation of anything that you don't understand in a contract. Many contracts are hard to understand, or are vague, and you need to know what the contract means. If you don't understand it, how can you truly agree to it?

What You Gotta Do

Of course, you aren't just handing in your work and going on vacation. Publishers usually ask you to do more than that, and they'll spell out just what that is in the contract.

You'll be expected to revise to suit their standards. This can be sticky! What if they want you to make changes that you don't want to make? The contract may allow them to make them. Most publishers want you to be happy with changes, but almost all publishers put language in their *standard contracts* that allows them to decide on their own when a manuscript or artwork is truly finished.

Vocabulary List

A publisher's **standard contract** covers all the items they think they need in a contract, which won't all just be to their benefit—some items will be there because everyone will expect them. The terms in this contract are sometimes referred to as "boilerplate," implying they're just stamped on, like a plate on a boiler.

You'll also be expected to meet the publisher's deadlines. This may involve not only finishing the manuscript or illustrations on time, but also handling edits and other materials sent for checking at later stages.

The contract may even specify that you allow the publisher to use your likeness (a photo!), your name, and information about you to promote the book. Unless you are publicity-shy, you should have no objection to this. Publishers generally do not require that you actively promote your book, but they may encourage you to do so.

What Publishers Do

In return for your labor, and for the use of your creative efforts, publishers will do as little as possible other than publish the book. Publishing is a business, after all. On the other hand, you can expect certain things, or publishers couldn't stay in business.

Generally, a publisher will …

- Pay you royalties on book sales, usually twice a year, and usually give you some money up front. Sometimes, you get a fee only.

- Pay you a share of any proceeds from selling the right to do something with it, such as make a book club edition or a filmstrip.

- Agree to consult with you while the book is being developed.

- Send you free copies of the book on publication and allow you to buy more at a discount.

- Copyright your words or your art in your name.

In practice, a publisher may do more than this, such as send copies of reviews and consult with you even when it's not required, but they'll try to keep their contractual obligations to a minimum.

Illustrators should check to see that their contract includes a clause that covers care and return of art. Publishers return your art to you. Some actually agree to do so in the contract, and may even specify its value so as to be able to compensate you if any of it is damaged or lost while it is under their control.

Your Allowance

You live on the income produced by your creative work. Well, maybe you still have your day job. But you certainly want to make a living from your creative work, so the payment you receive for a book may be the most important part of any publishing contract.

How you get paid depends upon the publisher. Traditional trade publishers have long paid *royalties* based on a book's *list price*. Typically, the royalty is 8 to 10 percent for a hardcover book, which is split between author and illustrator for a picture book. Newer publishers or publishers in other markets often pay royalties based on *net price*, which is the amount of money they actually receive when they sell the book; these are often 10 to 15 percent, again split if an illustrator is involved. The percentage may be higher, but keep in mind that a publisher may sell a book to bookstores and wholesalers at a discount of 50 percent off list price, so it's always best to look at what you earn per copy sold rather than your percent royalty. Contracts usually specify a paperback royalty, which is lower than the hardcover, and may go into other kinds of books as well, such as board books and big books.

Vocabulary List _____

A **royalty** is a certain percentage of the price of the book times the number of copies sold. It may be based on **list price** (or retail price), the price marked on the book, or **net price,** which is the amount of money the publisher receives for the book. So that you will not have to wait until publication to be paid, a publisher usually pays an **advance** on the royalties, but you must wait for the advance to be recouped before seeing more income.

Cash in Advance

If you are paid royalties, there is usually an *advance*. This is money paid in anticipation of the money that will be earned from the book. For example, a writer might receive a $3,000 advance for a novel, and a 10 percent list royalty. If the book sells for a list price of $16, the royalty is $1.60 per book. The first $2,0000 counts against the advance, but after that, the advance *earns out*. In this case, the writer can realistically hope to receive more money in the future.

Vocabulary List

An advance **earns out** when the amount earned in royalties equals the amount paid out in the advance. For example, if you were paid a $3,000 advance on a picture book, and are receiving a 5 percent list royalty on a list price of $15, you get 75 cents per book and the book will earn out after 4,000 copies are sold. Up until that point, the money earned is charged against the advance. From that point on, you will be paid any royalties the book earns.

Sometimes, your advance is all you receive. Say a publisher pays an illustrator a $6,000 advance for work on a picture book, against a 5 percent *net* royalty. If the book retails for $16, and the publisher actually receives $8, 5 percent of $8 is 40¢ per book. The publisher would have to sell 15,000 copies of the book before it earns anything. It's possible that the book would never reach that level.

These two examples also illustrate a reality of picture-book contracts. Although the author and illustrator are generally paid the same royalties, the illustrator typically receives a larger advance. Writers find this annoying, but a picture-book illustrator cannot physically produce as many sets of finished illustrations in a year as a writer can manuscripts. Fair or not, it's a common practice.

Timing of advances is important too, because you don't receive royalties until after the book comes out. Some publishers pay an advance on the signing of the contract, which isn't just good for you—it also helps them to lock you in. If you want to get out of such a contract, you'll have to repay that money. Many publishers pay part or all of the advance when they approve the manuscript or artwork, which may require considerable work on your part. And some publishers pay part of the advance on publication. This isn't as bad as it sounds—that's still better than waiting to be paid royalties. Depending on the publisher and the type of book, advances for first-time authors range from $2,000 to perhaps $6,000, with illustrators receiving more or less twice that. Be sure you understand what you need to do to be paid your advance, or the different parts of your advance, and when it should happen.

Can You Keep a Secret?

Most publishers pay royalties every six months. For January to June, for example, you might get paid in September. Why the delay? Publishers are waiting to be paid themselves, because booksellers can take months to pay, and they are waiting for returns (unsold books). Returns sometimes come back in such numbers that a book has negative sales in a selling period.

Work-for-Hire

Some publishers use contracts that put you in a *work-for-hire* position, and pay you a fee instead of an advance and royalties. If the fee is a good one, this is not necessarily a bad option. It's common for illustrators doing jackets or illustrations for textbooks. Mass-market publishers, too, use contracts that put you in an employee role and allow them to copyright the book in their names.

Professional organizations such as the Author's Guild and Graphic Artist's Guild raise some red flags about work-for-hire contracts. Such contracts are acceptable if you are doing work such as producing material about a TV character according to the pub-lisher's detailed guidelines; however, they are not acceptable if you have created a truly original work. You want the world to know that you created that work, and you want to have the rights to your work when the book goes out of print. If your work is your own, not based on someone else's characters or a TV show or movie, try to keep the copyright in your name, and resist the publisher getting the right to re-use your work in different editions or other media without paying you an additional fee.

Vocabulary List

Work-for-hire contracts are common in many businesses, not just book publishing. If you do this kind of work, you are signing over ownership of your creative output to the company that hired you. The company can use your work as it sees fit, though you may be able to negotiate some limits to that.

Subsidiary Rights

As I will explain in more detail in the next chapter, your creation of an original work means that you have the right to dispose of a bundle of different ways in which your work can be used. The publisher will directly use the right to publish a book, but most publishers also want to acquire what are known as subsidiary rights—the other things that you can do with your text or illustrations. For the most part, publishers keep half of the subsidiary income, and the illustrator and author share the rest. However, some specific subsidiary rights may be divided differently. If the agreement is for your work only, you usually receive the entire half the publisher didn't receive. There are many different kinds of subsidiary agreements a publisher might make.

Some subsidiary agreements are for other kinds of books. Until recently, many pub-lishers sold the right to make a paperback of a book they were publishing in hardcover. Now, most publish their own paperbacks. But books are also sold by book clubs, school book fairs, and publishers in other countries, perhaps in translation, perhaps in English. Publishers usually work pretty hard to sell rights in these areas.

Magazine rights are licensed under the names of first serial (before publication) and second serial (after publication). Many publishers are generous with the proceeds from the first serial rights, on the grounds that a magazine article based on your book that came out before publication would do a lot to publicize the book. They might pay an author 80 percent of the proceeds if a sale is made for "first serial." That's not a given, but it might be worth asking for.

The use of excerpts from your work, or even from the whole work in a larger collection, falls under the umbrella of permissions. With the interest in using trade books in the classroom well established, this is perhaps the most reliable area for a subsidiary rights sale because textbook publishers seek out material, sometimes years after publication of the original book.

A book's content can also be enhanced in various ways, ranging from filmstrips and videotapes to plays, films, or even television shows. Don't count on sales in this area, but if they come, they can be lucrative.

Class Rules

If you don't have an agent, don't make a fuss about "giving" the publisher the right to do something with your subsidiary rights. As an individual, in almost all cases you would find it almost impossible to do anything with any rights you did keep. Let the publisher sell them: 50 percent of something is more than 100 percent of nothing.

And then we get to the tricky area of electronic rights. The hype has died down, but publishers remain interested in obtaining the rights to publish or sell rights in this area, while preserving the usual splits. The situation is still in flux, but don't expect to be able to insist on special terms. Publishers will drop a deal rather than give in on what they have set up as their standard in this area.

If you're just getting started, look at subsidiary rights as the icing on the cake. For your first few books, you can't expect much in the way of income in this area, and so seeking changes to the standard language may not be a good use of your energy. Understand what this is all about, but don't make it a big issue.

Legal Language

Get past the things you must do and the payments and splits you can expect from a publisher, and you come to a tedious and sizable part of the contract: the legal language. Here you'll find a thicket of clauses, many designed to guard a publisher against some pretty unlikely bad outcomes. Should you be concerned about these clauses? Well, are you concerned about being struck by lightning? No? That's about how concerned you should be about many of these, because that's about how likely some of these are to be activated—they may have gotten into the contract due to things that happened to the publisher's adult division (or even their TV or Internet division), or due to some reading in contract manuals that someone in the contract department did on a quiet day.

What basic clauses should you expect? That really varies. Typical clauses include the following:

♦ A guarantee that you actually control the rights that you are handing over—that you haven't already sold them.

♦ A warranty that you aren't infringing anyone else's copyright or saying anything libelous or otherwise illegal.

♦ What the publisher can do in the event of legal action against you and the publisher.

♦ How and under what circumstances the contract can be terminated or canceled.

♦ What happens when the book goes out of print.

♦ What happens if the book isn't published in a timely manner.

Can You Keep a Secret?

Need help figuring all of this out? Lawyers specializing in book contracts exist, but they are expensive. Instead of an agent or lawyer, published authors should consider joining the Author's Guild (see Appendix B). Members can get the services of the staff lawyers in deciphering a contract. Illustrators can join the Graphic Artist's Guild or consult their *Handbook*.

Should you understand these clauses? Absolutely. Just don't expect to be able to change them, with the possible exception of the final two. Unlike some of the things discussed earlier, these clauses are usually not ones your editor has any authority to change.

Ch-Ch-Ch-Changes

So what can you change? How much you can change in the terms offered to you depends (to be blunt) almost entirely on your leverage. If you're a first-time author, you have very little. If you have something of a track record, or have been lucky enough to have acquired an agent, you may have more leverage. But there will still be a limit as to how far a publisher will go. A publisher also may not see any need to make changes. They may already have offered you terms they believe to be reasonable, taking into account what their competitors do and what their own pay scale is from beginners to top-level authors. Sometimes, you just have to accept what is offered.

Regardless of just how much leverage you have, you won't get more by acting outraged or being inflexible. Start by offering a short list of changes you'd like. Discuss these with your editor. Be firm, yet polite and professional, and be ready to suggest or listen to alternatives. This approach, even in a negotiation in which you end up getting little of what you want, will earn you the publisher's respect and therefore increase the chances of improvements the next time around. Persistence can pay off too; in response to an initial "no" to a requested change, ask for something else, or ask the publisher what they could offer you instead. Keep talking. The longer the negotiations go on, the more the person you are negotiating with will feel invested in them, and they may continue to make concessions in an effort to resolve them. But if you do negotiate for some time, be careful not to add in new requests as you go along. As an editor who has been on the other side of such negotiations, I can tell you that it's annoying to get new issues suddenly thrown into the mix when you are trying to put together a package that will work for both sides.

Playground Stories

Agent Sandy Ferguson Fuller has this to say about negotiations:

> Don't try to tinker too much with advance amounts, but do insist on reasonable royalty rates. With a standard trade book, definitely try to negotiate a royalty-based instead of a flat-fee agreement, even if you must waive any advance and agree to a substandard royalty.

> Be sure that the various deadlines are reasonable. Don't be unreasonable in your dealings with a publisher—but don't be intimidated either. If a contract isn't equitable or negotiations turn sour, turn away—believe in your work, take a risk, and persevere—you will find a better deal!

If you want changes beyond the (usually small) ones you can get from a publisher when you aren't a big name, you need to be able to back them up with a reason. Tell them why they shouldn't be treating you as a run-of-the-mill author or illustrator. Be realistic. Having a family member who works for a movie studio, for example, does not justify withholding movie rights from the subsidiary rights section. Believing that your book is certain to be a best-seller won't get you a six-figure advance. If a clause in their contract is completely out of line with what their competitors are offering, a publisher might change it. But they might not. Sad to say, I've heard very few arguments in this area that really hold up—most people will do better by just asking for improvements.

Here are some goodies to ask for, beyond the obvious idea of a larger advance, or more free copies of your book. In the long run, you may be able to get what's called an escalator clause, which increases the royalty once a certain number of books are sold. You can ask for a flow-through clause, which passes through your share of large subsidiary rights sales (if your advance has earned out) when the money is received, so that you don't have to wait for the next royalty statement. Ask for a higher royalty on "special sales," which are deals made for large quantities of the book at a high discount, for which you usually receive less than your usual royalty. Keep asking.

As well as asking for goodies, watch out for no-nos. Following are some no-nos to watch for:

◆ Object to your royalty being reduced on small printings of the book. (Losing an increase in royalty from an escalator clause isn't so bad, so long as it doesn't go lower than it was to start with.)

◆ Avoid joint accounting, a clever setup that ties together one book's advance with those of other books, so that all of them have to earn out their advances before you see royalties.

◆ Make sure that the book is copyrighted in your name, not the publisher's name. You do not want to actually give up ownership of the copyright—you just want to let the publisher use it.

Literary agent Sandy Fuller has a somewhat different idea about what's important in a contract. So might you—and you should decide what that is. But no matter what you want, do not immediately walk away if you don't get it. Instead, try to do better. Even a publisher that won't make any changes at all to a contract may be worth working with for now, but go into all your negotiations with the attitude that the best contract is one with which both sides are happy. Be willing to compromise and to listen, and expect to be listened to and compromised with. If, time after time, you're unhappy with what you have when the negotiations are over, either you're working with the wrong publisher, or your expectations are too high. Find out by talking to other authors who are in a similar situation. Then, move on, or adjust.

The Least You Need to Know

◆ Contracts in publishing involve a creator (author or illustrator) handing over the right to publish a work in return for some kind of compensation.

◆ Publishers usually pay royalties to an author and will make other commitments in a contract, such as providing free copies to the author.

◆ Publishers don't just hope to publish a work—they hope to sell its subsidiary rights, and a large part of a contract will spell out just what's involved.

◆ Much of a contract is made up of legal language you probably can't change, but should still try to understand.

◆ Ask for what you think you want in a contract, but be ready to compromise.

22

They Might Take My Idea! Copyright Basics

In This Chapter

- ◆ What a copyright is and why publishers copyright your work
- ◆ How unpublished works are protected
- ◆ All about "ideas" and why they are not protected
- ◆ How folktales fit into the copyright world
- ◆ Why you really don't need to worry about a publisher stealing your work
- ◆ Avoiding plagiarism—intentional or otherwise

Invariably, we've all done it: worried about someone stealing our fabulous idea for a book. After all, few people surge with the genius necessary to come up with such a fine idea for a children's book! *Au contraire*—many people do. But that's okay, because ideas themselves aren't worth much on their own, at least under copyright law. Your actual created work, written down on paper, is worth far more. By putting an idea into written form, you can protect not only the work, but also that original idea. So let's take a look at the protection of anyone's created work.

A Tale of Two Ideas

Do you feel a little shy about sharing your idea for a children's book with anyone because you fear that whomever you share your tale with will move with it and "steal" your idea? Hey, it happens to the best of us—especially when we are unpublished and wanting desperately to write a book. But there's a difference between an unpublished work and an "idea" for a book. Consider the tale of the following two aspiring writers.

Both knew that Jane Pen-Name had published several books and numerous magazine articles. So each of them approached Jane, seeking advice about writing a book. Jane, wanting to help, asked each of them to describe what they planned to do. Writer A candidly talked about his book series idea. Writer B, however, had a funny look on her face, paused, and said, "Well, I want to tell you, but I'm afraid you'll steal my idea!" After Jane reassured her that her "idea" was safe, Writer B relaxed and talked about her book concept. Unfortunately, however, this "thievery" paranoia is common and can prevent you from receiving useful feedback by showing your manuscript to others. Some people even go so far as to worry about showing a manuscript to publishers.

Class Rules

Many writers believe that they must file with the copyright office before using the copyright symbol on their work, thereby giving notification to others of their rights as the creator of the work. In actuality, the use of a copyright notice *does not* require advance permission from or registration with the U.S. Copyright Office.

Vocabulary List

Your ideas become **original expression** and are, thus, protected by the copyright laws of the United States and many other countries when you take those ideas and actually create something—a book, a story, a sculpture, a symphony—from your idea that is completely true to you and absolutely original.

Here's the lowdown: Ideas are not protected by copyright laws. An idea is an idea is an idea (with apologies to Gertrude Stein), and that's all it is. You may be cursing the copyright office right now, but hold on. Think about it. There are very few original ideas. It's what you do with these ideas that matters. In fact, one of the most frequent questions I receive on my website and at conferences when I speak is, "How do I stop someone from taking my really wonderful idea?" My response? "Well, you can't!" But what you can protect is the *original expression* of your idea. Put it into finished form, and you can protect your own unique way of expressing your idea. The same applies to illustration.

Let's consider an example so we all get this concept perfectly clear. Gail Bigidea comes up with a great concept for a children's book about a girl and her horse. She tells her buddy, Claire Klepto, about her promising story line. Now that Gail has spilled the beans to Claire, Claire can use the idea and Gail has no recourse. But if Gail writes down her horsey tale—complete with the details of the singing ducks and talking trees—and then sees her story three years from now with the author as "Claire Klepto," Gail can come with the full power of copyright law behind her and lunge at Claire's throat (legally speaking, of course)! And that's "original expression."

You may be asking, "Why does my idea need to 'take form' in order to be deemed original expression?" For a basic reason: Most story ideas are *not* original. In fact, think of any famous story, boil it down to its "core idea," and it may not seem so original. Take *Where the Wild Things Are*. It's about a child and monsters. How many stories out there are about children and imaginary monsters? How many stories are there about a child and his or her first pet? A first day at school? Dealing with a new sibling? Dozens for each type, right? And, of course, people are constantly talking about the many sources for the *Harry Potter* stories; no, they aren't completely original, but J. K. Rowling did mix all of those sources together in a completely original way. Does this mean that everyone is "stealing" from an original story? No. In other words, it's not what you say, but how you say it.

"Mommy, What's a Copyright and Where Does It Come From?"

This leads us to how you protect your created work: with a copyright. The forefathers of the United States put copyright into the Constitution (Article 1, Section 8). It says, "To promote the Progress of Science and Useful arts by securing for limited Times to Authors and Inventors the exclusive Right to their respective Writings and Discoveries." This part of the Constitution protects what is known as "intellectual property," and is put into effect through the laws of copyright, trademark, and patents. Most countries have similar laws. Today we turn to the U.S. Copyright Office to ensure our artistic creations remain *our* artistic creations.

Copyright law matters most in publishing; trademark and patent laws are two other worlds, which are not discussed here. From that basis in the Constitution, a series of laws have set up the rules and time limits for copyright. Title 17, U.S. Code, provides protection to the authors of "original works of authorship." Meanwhile, Section 106 of the Copyright Act provides the possessor of the copyright several inalienable rights with respect to the copyrighted work. Basically, the copyrighter holds the power over the reproduction, distribution, sale, and performance of the work. So anyone wanting to use your work must have your permission, and if you require it, must pay you for it. As mentioned in the discussion of contracts, that is the basis of publishing as a business: You grant a publisher the right to use your copyrighted work in return for a payment.

Before we get any further, however, we want to point out that trade publishing is built on copyright—creative and individual expression. Much of mass-market publishing is built on another kind of "intellectual property," in this case *trademarks.* The stories in many mass-market books, though they may be copyrighted, aren't selling because they are blindingly original. They sell because the consumer recognizes the trademark, either the publisher's own, like Golden Books, or something from another medium, like Disney, Pokémon, or even Hershey's Kisses.

Safe, So Far

Now that you understand that copyright laws protect your creation—not your mere idea—what do you do about it? First, you need not register your work with the copyright office before sending it to the publisher for consideration. In fact, doing so will mark you as an amateur. If the publisher picks your work for publication, the house will automatically file for the copyright for you. Just denote somewhere on your manuscript the word *copyright* and your name and the date. There. Your work is now protected under copyright laws!

Some have suggested that to prove the date when you did this, you can mail a copy of the manuscript to yourself, and keep it unopened. The postmark establishes the date on which the manuscript took final form. This may not be accepted in a legal setting, however. It's best just to limit the distribution of the manuscript. Do send it to individual publishers. Don't post it on the World Wide Web—that's a form of publication.

But That's Not Fair!

You're relieved that your own work is protected, but what if you want to use someone else's work in some way? Should you just forget about it? Fortunately, copyright law doesn't protect everything. Some creative works aren't copyrighted, and even those that are copyrighted can be used—so long as you follow "fair use" guidelines.

The Trouble with Folktales

What if you are creating a work that essentially retells existing stories? Your work differs in the details from the source, but has more in common than the bare idea. This particularly comes up as a problem with folktales.

You may want to tailor a folktale you heard as a child or came across in your travels or research, so what can you do? After all, you know you didn't have the "original" idea. The good news is that, in many cases, the story is in the *public domain*, meaning that it is not protected by copyright law and may be used by other authors in any way they choose without permission. Copyright does not last forever (although the rules do change, and have as recently as 1998). Anything published before 1920 in the United States is almost certain to be in the U.S. public domain, and many other works may be as well. It may not be in other countries, though.

So look at your source or sources. Was your source published in a collection a long time ago? If so, you're in the clear. Can you find multiple sources for it, even if they are recent? That's okay, too. Cite all of them in your notes for the book, don't rely heavily on one of them, and go ahead and tell that story. Just like writers of historical fiction must check their sources, you—the reteller of a folktale— must check your sources, acknowledge them, and make sure that you aren't relying on someone else's copyrighted work as your sole source.

Vocabulary List

Creative work that is not protected by copyright is in the **public domain**. The author of that work is not entitled to any payment if someone else uses it, and does not even have to be asked for permission.

Class Rules

Using someone else's work as a source for your own telling of a folktale (or tall tale, biography, or work of history) is okay, provided that you've used at least three sources and that you explain how you used them in an acknowledgement or author's note.

Just because a story is in the public domain, or because you've been able to find several different versions of it, you should still do some careful work before using it. Do you know the culture from which it derives, or in which you want to set it? If you don't, you may create an inauthentic story, with details or a plot turn or a moral that no member of that culture would create. Also, do you understand how folktales work? As Aaron Shepard, a successful folktale reteller, says, "If you want to retell folktales successfully, it's not enough to be familiar with just the tale you want to retell. You have to know folklore in general. Otherwise, there's not much chance you'll handle it right." In fact, Shepard continues, confirming, "Usually this means knowing folklore better than most editors."

Making Pictures from Other Pictures

If you're like most illustrators, you work from visual reference materials. For a picture-book story about a contemporary family, perhaps you shoot a series of color photos to use; for a historical setting, maybe you have dug deeper and found references for the buildings, the clothing, the furniture, and even the style of glasses the main character wears. What's fair and what isn't?

Of course, you can use anything you create in any way you choose—although the scrupulous illustrator will obtain model releases from anyone who posed for you. As with folktales, if you create an original composition by drawing on several different sources, you are also home free.

Can You Keep a Secret?

Pictures and text on the Internet are just as stringently protected by copyright law as the same material in books is. Brad Templeton makes a valiant effort to explain this, and to counter the myths about copyright, in his article "Ten Big Myths About Copyright Explained" at www.templetons.com/brad/copymyths.html. He actually lists 11 myths, but I'm not complaining.

"It Was on the Internet" and Other Lame Excuses

Copyright law has a fairly simple core, but how it plays out in practice can get complicated. The situation isn't made any easier by the fact that there are some surprising misconceptions about copyright circulating in the general public.

One of them is the rather fuzzy idea that material on the Internet somehow isn't subject to the same rules as material in books. This just isn't true. You can't use a photo or a story from a website without the creator's permission any more than you can if they were in a book.

People also tend to have vague, and, let's face it, self-serving ideas about what *fair use* is. The common idea seems to be: "I'm using it, so that must be fair." The reality is more complicated. Yes, you can use material from copyrighted works, either in direct quotation or in paraphrase. What is fair depends not only on how much of another's work you use, but how you acknowledge it and make use of it. A properly attributed two-line quotation from a newspaper article is just fine. Use two lines from a short poem, however, and you've gone beyond fair use.

Vocabulary List

Copyright law allows an exception to the protection of copyrighted material. Under **fair use,** a modest quantity of a copy-righted work can be quoted in another work without permission or payment, provided that material is acknowledged. If a writer instead presents that work as his or her own, it is a case of plagiarism.

Because copyright laws can get complicated, the best thing to do is keep careful notes on any material you use that is not your own. Discuss this with your publisher early on in the process. They may run it by their legal department, and at worst, you might have to make some revisions. This is far better than receiving a notice that you and your publisher have been sued for copyright infringement.

"Dummy! Dumb-Dumb!" Why Stealing Is Stupid!

Right now, you may still have concerns about sending your manuscript to a publisher and having the publishing house steal your work. Or perhaps you're an illustrator and you're concerned that someone could use your carefully created sample illustrations without your permission. Stop worrying. We're here to tell you why stealing—by the publisher, by you, by anyone writing a book—is just plain stupid.

To start with, copyright laws are there to protect writers and illustrators. In order to steal your creation, the thief will literally need to take a recognizable chunk. In the form of a children's picture book, that might mean the entire story or some illustrations. Even taking extended passages from a book, or paraphrasing them in detail, is a copyright violation, and the victim, or their publisher, could go to court and win.

Publishers in particular have very little if anything to gain from "stealing" other people's creative work, yet have much to lose. Imagine you send a manuscript to a publisher. They advise you, "Sorry, not for us." Then three years later, you see your story, word for word, on the shelves at the local bookstore. A nightmare, but not likely to happen. Why would a publisher do that? The gains for the publisher would be minimal—perhaps a couple thousand dollars in payment to you. That's it! But the loss to their reputation could be monumental if this kind of deception came out. The publisher would lose its good name—and that's enormously important to the company. Other authors, writers, illustrators, agents, and even people working for that publisher would no longer trust that company. If those people don't trust it, the publisher won't receive good submissions, staff will leave, and eventually the company could fall apart.

On a final note, stealing is a pain in the butt! Publishers receive too many great stories from respected writers to need to connive to thwart the success of an unknown, previously unpublished writer by taking the writer's work and not pursuing a contract with that writer. Most publishing houses run on a schedule like a newsroom—harried and frantic. No one has time to steal your story. Of course, as we've all heard, stealing is said to happen in other parts of the media world, notably in the film industry. What's the difference? The big difference is that films often get go-aheads on the basis of an idea, with the screenplay worked and reworked to the point that no one author can claim it as his or her own (and because the studio owns the copyright, that's beside the point anyway). Thankfully, children's publishing—and most adult publishing— operates with more respect for the creator.

The Least You Need to Know

- Ideas cannot be copyrighted or protected, but work put into a final form can.

- You don't need to actually register your unpublished work with the U.S. Copyright Office in order to protect your work. Writing "copyright" and your name and date on your manuscript will suffice.

- If you plan to retell folktales, check your sources. Make sure the story falls within public domain or has multiple sources before proceeding with a manuscript.

- Like authors, illustrators need to be careful in their use of reference materials.

- Unless you are a lawyer and understand "fair use" law, look to your publisher for guidance in using copyrighted material.

- Don't fret about a publisher stealing your story; publishers stand to lose more (their good reputation) than they stand to gain (a few measly bucks) from taking your work.

Chapter 23

Make It Better

In This Chapter

◆ Why revision is important

◆ How editing helps with revision

◆ Different kinds of editing

◆ How to work productively with an editor

Once your book is under contract, and sometimes before that, an editor is going to want to revise your manuscript. Don't be embarrassed—it's not because you're a novice or a bad writer. Editing and revising are central to producing quality books. Ironically, the writing that seems the most effortless is probably writing that has been sweated over the most. In this chapter I'll explain the different ways in which editors may work with you to make your writing better, and give you some hints on how you can work with them more productively.

The Revision Process

Writing is *revising* and rewriting. Just about any writer will agree with that. The first words that you put down on the page will not be the ones you end up with. Some writers revise well on their own, and turn in manuscripts that need minimal editing. Others prefer to work with editors, often through multiple *drafts*. And others go through some of both, which can lead to box after box of revisions of a novel taking up space in their garages. (These do make for good visuals on school visits, though.)

The Best Part

Revision sounds like a lot of work, and it can be. True writers savor it, however. They know that getting something down on paper is the hard part. Then you can play. The pressure's reduced, if not gone. Once you have something to work with, you can tinker and think and try different ideas. It can only get better (or so you need to tell yourself).

Vocabulary List

To **revise** literally means to "re-see"; strive to see your writing afresh when you make changes. Each new version of a manuscript is called a **draft**. Your first draft is just that; a rough draft is one that needs polishing; and a final draft is the one you hope doesn't need to be revised again.

So revision is not only important—it's the best part of writing. But don't take our word for it. Jane Yolen, author of many picture books, novels, and books of poetry, points out that revision is what helps you actually recapture some semblance of that first, dazzling vision, which you then lost when you tried to get it down on paper.

Author Larry Dane Brimner agrees, saying that in writing, "The real excitement comes from wordplay. I simply enjoy writing a sentence and then seeing if I can make it sharper or clearer or more beautifully expressed. For me, the enjoyment and art of writing is in rewriting."

Playground Stories

Jane Yolen says this about revision:

The words in my head were splendid, of course. Once on the page they needed enormous reshaping. Isaac Asimov is reputed to have said that he never revised anything. Then he must have done all that work in his head. I have never written a sentence that couldn't be improved. Even my book *Owl Moon*, which I once heard described by Bill Martin—the dean of children's literature—as "the perfect picture book, not a word wrong," could do with some reworking. When I read it to kids, I revise on-the-fly.

On Your Own

Much of your revision you'll handle on your own, and as you become a more experienced writer you'll become increasingly able to polish your own work without help from others. Take this as far as you can, making sure to cover the different kinds of editing described later in this chapter, because the more finished your manuscript is when you submit it, the more likely it is that an editor will be interested in it, and the more rapidly it may go through the publication process. Manuscripts that need a lot of work won't be tackled until the editor has time to deal with them, and will end up on a list far in the future.

Writer and teacher Barbara Seuling says she revises many times: "I revise a gazillion times, and I love the process because I seem to get better in layers. I really do 're-see' each time. I find it invaluable." You don't have to revise quite so many times, of course, but go as far as you can on your own.

With Your Editor

Take advantage of working with an editor. Every writer, no matter how experienced, can use the help of editors when revising. An editor comes to your writing with a fresh perspective. It's not necessarily an objective perspective, just a different one, and perhaps one more akin to that of a reader reacting to your work the first time. Editors do much more than correct your spelling. In some ways, an editor is a very experienced reader, someone who can be conscious of her own intuitive responses to your work. Editors will notice gaps, and incomplete characterizations, and statements that are vague or awkward. They'll point out problems, and maybe even suggest solutions.

Ideally, when you and an editor are working on a revision, you'll form a partnership with the goal of producing the best possible finished piece.

Can You Keep a Secret?

Good editing can make a huge difference to your work. Don't lose a golden opportunity by refusing to listen to it. As Barbara Seuling says in *How to Write a Children's Book:*

Editors often see more clearly than the writer, who is close to his work, and they can point out areas for improvement …. If you are rigid about your work, unwilling to change words and sentences and paragraphs, and even characters, you may be sacrificing the success of the total book for the sake of a few well-crafted words.

The Writer's Reference Bookshelf

When you're revising, you'll find that there are certain books you'll want to have available for reference. Some are standard across the industry. Some are of greater use for writers of fiction or of nonfiction. As you develop as a writer, others will become your trusted companions, so modify the following list as you see fit and see Appendix B for more information about specific titles:

- *Webster's Third New International Dictionary*

- *The Chicago Manual of Style, 15th Edition*

- *Bartlett's Familiar Quotations*

- A standard almanac

- A compact print encyclopedia or CD-ROM encyclopedia

- *Words into Type*

- *Dictionary of Modern American Usage*

- *Roget's International Thesaurus*

But It's My Story!

A trap all writers fall into at some time or another is to fall in love with their own writing, and to believe that it is perfect, that not one word should be added or taken away from this divine state. You've labored over the work, you've revised, you've listened to your writer's group. It can be tempting to believe that you can't possibly improve it anymore. This is almost certainly not true.

You do not need to take the editor's suggestions literally, on the other hand. It's possible that a problem she points out can be solved by making changes she hasn't actually suggested. For example, if an editor comments that a quiet character acts uncharacteristically noisy at one point in a story, the problem might not be with that incident. You intended that character to act that way, and you need him to. So you don't want to change that, but you've discovered that you need to make a different change. Even though you intended all along to create a character that gets rowdy in certain circumstances, you neglected to establish that earlier on in the story. So this editor's comment on one spot in the story, if you have listened to it carefully, could lead to changes in entirely different places.

It's Wonderful! Now, Fix It!

Once you get started with revision, don't expect an editor to exclaim over the perfection of your manuscript while making only minor spelling corrections. That's not what an editor does. Unless your manuscript is in unusually good shape, you can expect editing at three different levels: the overall structure of the manuscript, the flow of the sentences and paragraphs, and, almost as an afterthought, corrections of spelling, grammar, and the like.

Hard work? Yes. Serious writers welcome it.

> **Playground Stories**
>
> Barbara Seuling notes that she much prefers editors who have something to say to her:
>
> I've had editors who took my manuscripts and never touched a word, or gave me any feedback. I didn't trust them. I've heard other writers say the same thing. You feel like you can't trust that someone will be there to catch you if you fall. We all need editors. Then there's the other kind of editor that makes you just about fall in love—who takes every word and every line seriously, and gets into the mind and heart of what you have tried to do and helps you to achieve it.

Structural Editing

Some manuscripts require changes in the way that they are put together. They may need to have characters dropped or added, they may need an additional chapter, or they may need to be reorganized. All of these kinds of changes fall into category of what we call structural, or developmental, editing. To do it, your editor may write you a letter, or she may just call you and ask questions, perhaps along the lines of …

- ◆ "What happens to William in the second half of the book? He drops out of the narrative."

- ◆ "Have you considered dropping the first chapter and starting in the middle of things with the second?"

- ◆ "Could you go into more depth on how jet engines work?"

- ◆ "In the conflict between Sue and Naomi, do you need all four arguments?"

- ◆ "What if this were told in the first person?"

- ◆ "Could you show us in what ways Paul is dependent on his father, instead of just telling us he is?"

We could go on and on, but we think you get the idea. Think these kinds of questions over carefully, and if you make changes in response to them, think again. Have your changes affected the book in such a way that you need to make additional changes in response? If you think they do, don't be afraid to make them, or at least to discuss them with your editor.

Even short picture-book length manuscripts can need structural editing. I was working on the manuscript of Larry Pringle's *Bats: Strange and Wonderful* when I noticed that a few lines that were a couple of paragraphs into the manuscript would actually work better as opening lines. I suggested this, Larry moved them and reworked them a bit to make them even better (the mark of a skilled writer), and now that book has an opening that has been singled out for praise by reviewers. Author and editor worked together well in this case. Try to do the same.

Can You Keep a Secret?

Write using active rather than passive constructions whenever you can. "Many soldiers were killed by the sudden freeze" becomes "The sudden freeze killed many soldiers." "The kitten was being petted by Calla" becomes "Calla was petting the kitten."

Do this stage of revision as thoughtfully as you can. All editors respect writers who respond well to revision suggestions.

Line Editing

Once the manuscript is in good shape, it still needs polishing. A careful editor will go through it line by line, with the aim of sharpening descriptions, getting rid of passive constructions, cutting out run-on sentences, and generally making it more of a pleasure to read.

Vocabulary List

In preparing a manuscript for publication, a **copy editor** carefully reviews it for style, punctuation, spelling, and grammar, and may also mark chapter titles, headers, and other design elements. Once the manuscript is typeset, the **proofreader** reviews the resulting proofs to make sure that they accurately follow the manuscript and the copy editor's annotations.

During this stage, your editor is likely to use some strange-looking marks and symbols. Mostly these are the standard marks that *copy editors* and *proofreaders* use. You'll see more of them later in the process, when the manuscript is actually copyedited. During editing, your editor will tend to use these marks, because she is familiar with them. You'll see marks in the margin of the manuscript, and right on the text. There aren't that many different ones to learn, and you'll find them useful yourself. I'm putting a table of the most commonly used ones here, but you can find a guide to all of the copyediting symbols in standard writing reference works like *The Chicago Manual of Style*.

Soon after this stage, you can expect your editor to declare herself finished with the manuscript. You aren't. The copy editor still has to read it. And you'll then get another chance to learn copyediting symbols.

Common Editing Marks		
What they'll write	**What it means**	**The result**
(cap) new york city	capitalize these	New York City
(lc) Please STOP shouting	lowercase these	Please stop shouting
(lc) TOO MUCH NOISE	lowercase all of them	too much noise
It was dark and stormy	run them together	It was dark and stormy
Up in the the air	delete this	Up in the air
A drink of water	insert something	A tall drink of water
dirty laundry	put in a space	dirty laundry
(break) Four score and seven	start a new line	Four score and seven
(tr) cats dogs and	transpose these	cats and dogs
The end	insert a period	The end.
Planes, trains and	insert a comma	Planes, trains, and
To sleep perchance to	insert a semicolon	To sleep; perchance to
Bring to an end	insert a colon	Bring to an end:
write off	insert a hyphen	write-off
(stet) Don't touch that!	ignore the mark	Don't touch that!

Here are some common editing marks and what they mean.

Fact Checking

For nonfiction manuscripts, and perhaps for historical fiction and folktales as well, many publishers will want to assure themselves that the research you've done is sound. In classic fact checking, the fact checker will work through your manuscript fact by identifiable fact, checking each in the sources you used and in others he locates.

Some manuscripts don't lend themselves well to that approach. If you've written historical fiction set in seventeenth-century England, the publisher will seek out a historian of the period. Or if you've done a poetic piece describing the ebb and flow of life in a small salt marsh on the coast of Oregon, your editor might want to send it to a marine biologist with knowledge of that area. In either case, the fact checker will comment on his overall impressions, but not necessarily check every fact.

Your editor will pass on comments to you, in some cases reviewing them first, though in other cases not. This may seem like a burden to you, but it can also be a great opportunity, a final check that may well turn up a note-taking mistake or a distortion that you meant to be a simplification.

Ask for It!

Working with an editor isn't all highfalutin' discussions about theme, plot, and turns of phrase, of course. Your editor, as you'll see in detail in the next chapter, is a busy person, probably juggling dozens of books and other responsibilities. Some editors are more active than others, too. So if you need something from her, you may need to ask for it, and you may need to ask for it repeatedly. Don't be bashful about this, but don't be obnoxious either. Just be politely persistent.

Editing

One of the shameful results of the increased amount of work an individual editor is expected to do is that some books don't get the editing they need. The situation in children's books is not yet as bad as in adult publishing, where we've heard that at many publishers' manuscripts come in, get a quick copyedit, and go straight into production. But editing, like writing, requires a kind of relaxed concentration, and long stretches of time. Both of these are hard to find in a typical office. Some editors find they can only edit effectively if they take a day to work at home.

What with the increasing workloads expected of editors, in some cases, if an editor thinks there isn't much wrong with a manuscript, and if he's got a lot of other things to do, he may be tempted to move it along without all the editing it needs. If you think that this is happening, don't hesitate to express concern. If there's something that's nagging you about your manuscript, tell your editor, and ask him what he thinks. Don't accept reassurances—tell him that's not what you want. Tell him you want his expertise, and be as specific as you can be about what you think the problem is.

Class Rules _____

When in doubt, communicate. If you want to know what your editor thinks, ask her. If you need two more weeks to finish the manuscript, say so. If you don't understand what an editor wants you to do, ask her to clarify. Editors are not telepathic, even though a good one may seem to understand what you are trying to do with a manuscript better than you do yourself.

My Paper's Late

Most likely you will be working toward a deadline as you revise, or perhaps for the actual delivery of a manuscript that was signed up on the basis of a proposal. That deadline is there for two reasons: to help the publisher maintain a stable program of so many books per year, yes, but also to help you finish. Deadlines are a useful spur. Are they absolute? No. We all miss deadlines, but we need them; very few books would get published without them. If you can't meet a deadline, ask for a new one. And try not to agree to a deadline you know you won't be able to meet.

No Guilt Trips, Please

In all your dealings with your editor, be professional. Nothing turns editors off faster than a writer who complains constantly of overwork or tries to wheedle payment of an advance before it is due.

The Care and Feeding of an Editor

Your relationship with your editor will go far beyond the editing of an actual manuscript. Editors hope that another manuscript is coming. And you also want to work with them on other ones. So let a relationship develop. Discuss ideas with your editor. Let her know that you're interested in hearing her suggestions for subjects for future books. Get to know her interests. You've got a lot in common. Make this a friendly relationship and you'll find that it becomes a more productive one.

Every relationship you'll have with an editor will be different, as noted by Pam Muñoz Ryan, author of picture books and novels:

> Over the years I've had 15 different editors. And like any 15 different friends I might have, each relationship has been different. Some have been simple affiliations where both of us seem to play our author and editor roles rather specifically with formal direction letters and no friendly chit-chat. The books ended up being okay. Other relationships have been more personal, collaborative, and sometimes even fun. Those books were more successful. A few of my author-editor liaisons have been disasters and didn't work at all and I and my manuscript became the bridesmaid of another editor and sometimes another. When that happened, I rarely got bridal treatment, nor did the book. Those titles usually ended up in the mediocre category. But I have been lucky enough to have had a few pairings that were epiphanies, where I had the opportunity to work with brilliant editors who were prophetic and inspiring. It is no surprise that those titles have won the most awards and are my best sellers.

Can You Keep a Secret?

Once you start working with an editor she usually won't expect you to follow all the submission "rules." Got an idea for a story? Call her up instead of querying her, and discuss it. Send her a few rough chapters and see what she thinks instead of waiting to finish a manuscript. Editors want to be involved in your work. Let them be. If they're too busy at some point, they'll let you know.

Like Pam, if you stick with children's publishing you'll have a variety of experiences, but make the best of whatever situation you're in, pull what you can from an editor with whom you may not be getting along, and make the book the best you can make it. And of course, enjoy the experience when you and the editor "click."

The Least You Need to Know

- Many writers think revision is the most enjoyable part of writing, and it's certainly the most important.

- Don't resist editing of your work. It will make it better.

- Structural editing, line editing, and fact checking are three different kinds of editing.

- Be sure to ask for editing if you feel your manuscript is being rushed through.

- Feel free to build a personal relationship with your editor, and make the most of it if it's a good one.

Chapter 24

My Editor Doesn't Understand Me

In This Chapter

- Some insight into "what editors are really like"
- The backgrounds of typical editors
- Editors' interests
- Profiles of several editors at different levels at different publishers

Now that you know a little bit about how you'll work with an editor, the question remains: What are editors like? Because writers typically don't get to know their editors very well at first, perhaps not meeting them in person until one or more books are out, it's easy to have all kinds of notions about them. This chapter makes some sweeping generalizations about editors, but ones that in my experience are accurate. I then provide detailed profiles of several editors, showing what they do and how they got where they are today.

What Are Editors Like?

While attending and speaking at writer's conferences over the past several years, I have heard some wildly differing ideas about what children's book editors are like. (Because I'm male and 90 percent of editors are women, I am an anomaly right from the start.) To some, editors seem to be nurturing-mother archetypes, who are lovers of books, committed both to the very best for children and to careful grooming of writers to be the best they can be. Others see editors as scary intellectual gods or goddesses who expect you to understand the difference between metonymy and metaphor. Still others see editors as skilled hacks dedicated to the smooth functioning of corporate machines. There is some truth to these imaginings, but it's a bit more complex than it appears at first.

The New York Ivory Tower

Editors have some typical characteristics. One is that they are still mostly based in New York. Publishers exist all across North America, but since the large publishers are mostly in New York, the bulk of publishing professionals reside there, too. I have observed that editors are college-educated, with degrees from Ivy League colleges or similar small, liberal arts colleges. Editors generally come from the middle class or above, and they don't go into publishing to make money. In fact, as assistants they often need partial support from their families until they reach a level where they can actually live on their salaries. Children's book editors are mostly white; though people of color are working their way up in the field, editing is still less integrated than most professions. Children's book editors are mostly young, in their 20s and 30s, until they reach the senior level. This is a job in which people move up or out. In short, editors don't "look like America," and may not look much like the writers with whom they work. Whether this has good or bad consequences is open to debate.

People Who Love Books

Why do people become children's book editors? For the most part, it's not because editors love children, or at least not in the way that teachers or pediatric nurses do. Editors may not actually have children; some of the great editors in children's publishing, such as Ursula Nordstrom and Margaret K. McElderry, never did. Generally, however, editors loved books when they were children, and they still do.

Their love of books is a sizable part of the reason why editors do what they do. They feel that they have a sense of what children will respond to in a book, because the editors themselves still react in the same way. And they want to be part of making more books like the ones they love. Editing is a great way to do this, because one's income is more regular than that of a writer, and one can be involved in so many more books at once. Some editors write on the side, but many do not—their creative side is entirely fulfilled by editing. The opportunity to work with creative people like writers and artists is also part of the attraction.

Outside of work, editors are a diverse group. Many do read books other than the ones they are working on, and not just children's books. Some read serious adult literature, mysteries, and romance novels. But editors don't spend their entire lives reading. Editors may pursue outdoor sports, from softball to cross-country skiing, or belong to a choir, or quilt or do woodworking. For the most part, editors don't dress in black turtlenecks and go to smoky bars where they can discuss Sartre. So yes, editors may live in New York, but you'll find that their interests are as varied as anybody's.

Can You Keep a Secret?

Nervous about holding up your end of the conversation if you meet an editor at a conference? Don't be. Just ask about the editor's favorite books as a child. She'll happily tell you, probably ask you about yours, and if the two of you somehow finish discussing those, just ask what she's enjoyed reading recently.

Cogs in a Machine

Editors love children's books, like writers, and like working with them (or most of them, anyway). But let's face it, you don't pay their salaries, or at least not yet. The publishing company for which they work does, and they would not be doing a good job if they didn't put the interests of that company first. That doesn't mean that they'll always agree with their immediate boss. In some cases, they will argue that doing something that in the short term seems to go against the publisher's interests, such as paying a writer a larger advance, may work in the publisher's favor in the long term, by making that writer feel more loyal.

It's unrealistic, however, to expect editors to always side with you or with difficult but exciting books. They know that they must produce books that make money for their publisher, or lose their job (or, in the case of a smaller company, risk the publisher going out of business). They probably understand that side of the business all too well, and that will mean that there will be times when they don't publish a manuscript they love, because they know it will lose money. Sometimes they will take risks, and that will be more possible at some publishers than at others, but not at every opportunity. They can't.

> **Playground Stories**
>
> Increasingly, editors work from home. Melanie Kroupa publishes her books at New York City's Farrar, Straus and Giroux while working nearly 200 miles away outside Boston. Many know that other well-known editors do the same, but may not know that editing is routinely becoming a satellite task, as publishing follows the trend in other industries. For example, Dana Rau worked at Children's Press as an associate editor on their early reader books. Wanting to spend some more time at home with her young son, she left to edit from 20 to 30 books a year from home.

We all would like to believe that children's publishing is different from other businesses. Over the past decade, we all learned that it isn't, when every publisher of any size laid off staff, closed imprints, merged with another publisher, or did all of those. The business, at least in New York, is more corporate than it used to be, and editors must be able to navigate those new seas. Editors can no longer just be passionate advocates of books for children. They must also be corporate infighters. I hope you find an editor who balances those two characteristics creatively.

Mass-Market Books for the Very Young—Bernette Ford

Bernette Ford until recently was the editorial director of Cartwheel Books at Scholastic, a position she'd held since she founded the imprint in the late 1980s. In May 2002, she left, and now packages multicultural picture books for publishers such as Scholastic.

> **Vocabulary List**
>
> A **novelty book** is any book with features added to it beyond the binding and pages: foldout, die-cut holes, lift-the-flap, pop-ups, or sound chips. Novelty books are similar to but different from *book plus* products, which are books packaged with something else, such as a plush toy. Both are mainstays of mass-market publishers.

While Bernette was there, Cartwheel published about 100 books per year, for babies up to 7-year-olds. A sizable number of these—35 to 40—were original paperbacks for 3- to 6-year-olds, including books for the "Hello Reader" program. About half are board books and *novelty books*. While at Cartwheel, Bernette also did some individual hardcover titles without jackets, such as the *I Spy* books and Robert Munsch titles, including *Aaron's Hair* and *We Share Everything!* And at the top end of her list were gift books for the hardcover market, such as *A Child Is Born*, by Grace Maccarone, and books Bernette feels strongly about, such as Miles Pinkney's *Shades of Black*.

Cartwheel is still operating, and as you might guess from the kinds of books Cartwheel publishes, its books sell mainly in the mass market. The bulk of their sales are to the big bookstore chains or to retailers such as Wal-Mart and Sears. Like other mass-market publishers, many of Cartwheel's books are produced on assignment, by writers whose work and resumés are kept on file, while others are created in-house or by packagers.

Scholastic started Cartwheel specifically to have a mass-market presence, and hired Bernette from Random House, where she had been working in their well-known mass-market division. At the time, Golden, Random House, and Grosset were the primary mass-market publishers for children. Now the big publishing houses have their own mass-market divisions, and Landolls (a major new mass-market publisher) has appeared, and the market is more competitive. It has also become more dominated by books tied to TV, movie, or other licenses, and at the same time less distinct from the trade market. There are now higher-quality mass-market books, and many mass-market books are versions of existing trade books—board books in particular are likely to be versions of hardcover picture books, rather than original creations.

While she was there, Bernette enjoyed the challenges of this market, and the shaping of each season's list from its beginnings to the point when she could look at it in the catalog and say, "That's a strong list." Fourteen full-time staffers worked with her to produce the list, along with a few regular freelance designers. Of course, because Cartwheel is a pretty large imprint and is also part of a large and successful publishing company, she had to spend perhaps three quarters of her time in meetings, and often found that she must take time to read manuscripts at home. Her decision to go into packaging is thus not surprising. But Bernette Ford's work at Cartwheel Books shows just how much impact one individual can have in developing an imprint, even one publishing for the more price-driven mass market.

Class Rules

Mass-market publishers like Cartwheel are not a good place to send manuscripts, because they often don't want original work. Many of them develop texts in-house or hire writers to write them to their specifications. If you want to work with them, you'll do best to check their guidelines, which will ask that you send them such materials as samples of your work and your resumé.

Successful at a Smaller Publisher—Regina Griffin

Regina Griffin came to Holiday House, the oldest children's book–only publisher in the United States, from the trade division at Scholastic. The company is celebrated as a publisher of quality hardcovers, publishing a little more than 60 books a year, two thirds of them being picture books, both fiction and nonfiction. The rest of the list consists of novels, mostly middle-grade level, and some older nonfiction. Their market is the reverse of Cartwheel's, as they make 80 percent of their sales to the libraries and schools market. Though Holiday House would like to increase their sales in bookstores, they have been able to rely on this market due to their reputation for quality. There are advantages to publishing for it, too; most notably, they don't get unsold books returned to them.

Holiday House is an independent company, owned and run since the 1960s by John and Kate Briggs, so Regina does not have to spend much of her time in meetings. She has a staff of only six, and must do without the corporate structure of a larger publisher; corporations may add paperwork and meetings to an editor's time, but they also take care of some tasks. As a result, Regina has to wear more than one hat, so her responsibilities as subsidiary rights manager (she is the one who licenses their books to book clubs, to audio and film companies, and the like), as managing editor, and as contracts manager cut into her editorial time. She gets much of her work done on the 30 titles or so for which she is personally responsible during regular hours. But she has to spend about 15 hours each week at home reading manuscripts.

Almost all the books that Holiday House publishes come in as submissions, either from one of the regulars on their list or from someone just getting started. Holiday House is known for its loyalty to its authors and illustrators, and so it comes as something of a surprise to learn that they make room for new talent. Perhaps a third of the titles on a list have a first- or second-time author or illustrator. To acquire one of these books, Regina simply has to decide that she cares enough about it to want to publish it, and then let John know about it. In many ways, Holiday House still does things the old-fashioned way, and Regina enjoys this, getting to work with straightforward people who care first about books.

Hearing about Regina's love of the independence of Holiday House, you might be surprised to learn that when she arrived there in 1995 her experiences had been mostly at larger publishers. When she was getting started, she had worked as an editorial assistant and for an agent, developed feature films for Disney, and handled some production responsibilities at Stewart, Tabori, and Chang, a mid-size independent publisher. At Scholastic, she started out by working as an editor for young adult paperbacks, especially those with movie tie-ins. Gradually she also started to work on younger paperback, general fiction, and hardcover books. Her experience with contracts and rights and production was just the mix needed for her to head the list at Holiday House, and to begin, cautiously, to innovate.

Successful at a Larger Publisher—Kate Jackson

As Associate Publisher and Editor-in-Chief of HarperCollins Children's Books, Kate Morgan Jackson oversees four imprints: HC Children's Books itself (hardcover books), HarperFestival (novelty), HarperTempest (YA fiction), Katherine Tegen Books (a personal imprint), and HarperTrophy and the children's part of Avon (both paperbacks). The heads of the other personal imprints—Joanna Cotler Books, Laura Geringer Books, and Susan Hirschman at Greenwillow—report directly to the publisher, Susan Katz. These 9 imprints together publish more than 500 titles annually, some of them paperbacks of previously published hardcovers. They publish more or less equal amounts of novels, picture books, and "other," which includes novelty books, audio cassettes, boxed sets, and the like. This is a diverse program, with different imprints concentrating on different parts of the market, from bookstores to price clubs.

With such a large program to oversee, meetings make up a large part of Kate's day. These include acquisition, editorial, marketing, and business strategy planning meetings, as well as individual meetings with the editorial directors of the imprints. She does still make some time each day for editorial work, and personally publishes three to five picture books per year. She feels that although she does less hands-on work than she did when she worked as an editor, she is still very much involved in shaping books—and the shape of HarperCollins's list.

As is the case at most large publishers like HarperCollins, most of their titles come in from authors and illustrators with whom they are already working or who have a track record elsewhere, or from authors with agents. They are also moving into the "brand" market, seeing brand names on books as a necessary way of getting the attention of booksellers and of children.

Some brands are of their own creation. HarperCollins has a rich and deep backlist, stretching back to the time of legendary editor Ursula Nordstrom, and recently supplemented by the acquisition of William Morrow's children's imprints, so they have less need than some publishers to create new programs from the ground up. Instead, they can mine their backlist; Kate was personally involved in developing one such initiative, the *Little House on the Prairie* program, an extensive line you may have seen in the bookstores, including picture books and paper dolls derived from the famous novels.

To reach her current position, Kate moved up within HarperCollins, where she arrived in 1991 after beginning her career at two college publishers. She feels very pleased to be where she is, and comments that although the company has changed and expanded from the company it was when Ursula Nordstrom was the head of the children's department, "our heart and soul is still the unmatchable backlist of books, authors, and artists that she cultivated." So HarperCollins may be a corporate publisher, but such labels miss the day-to-day reality of a place where every new person is assigned to read *Dear Genius*, the collected letters of Ursula Nordstrom, and where "her name is invoked on a regular basis in regard to what she did and what she would have thought and said." There's hope for children's publishing so long as such editors are remembered.

> ### 💬 Playground Stories
>
> Though the higher one goes in a publishing company, the more administrative work one does, people in managerial positions in children's publishing are still very much involved in creating books. As Kate Jackson says of her job:
>
> > I love the fundamental result of what I do—helping to create, and helping others to create, good book for kids. I feel strongly that what I do and what my team does makes a difference in the world. I love being around the creativity of the authors, the artists, the editors, the designers. I love being able to help shape and guide the direction of where this company and our list is going.

Getting Started—Jennifer Greene

Though a lot has changed in children's publishing, I discovered when talking to Jennifer Greene, an editor at Clarion Books, that at least at some companies things are still done the traditional way. She knew when she left college that she wanted to work in children's publishing, but her first two jobs were with companies doing books for adults. Her break came when she took a course in children's book publishing at New York University with Virginia Duncan, who told her about an opening at Clarion. She has been with Clarion ever since.

> ### Can You Keep a Secret?
>
> Don't let this get out to just anyone, but I'm encouraged to have discovered that a number of publishers still work by having editors sign up the books in which they believe. That's how it works at Holiday House, Clarion, and Margaret K. McElderry Books, and I suspect it's true in other places as well.

The day-to-day details of Jennifer's job are encouraging to the many who bemoan the loss of proper mentoring in publishing. Clarion is carefully set up to have senior and junior editors working together. When she started at Clarion, Jennifer served as what is known as a backup editor on some titles, working with an editor so that she would see how they handle things, perhaps also taking care of some tasks, and most importantly knowing exactly what is happening with those books. She then went through a period of editing five or six books each year, some of which she had acquired, and some of which she had been backup editor for and inherited when the editor left. She is now an editor who handles about 12 books a year that she acquires.

Jennifer gets to work on a variety of books, as Clarion publishes a mix of picture books, fiction, and older nonfiction. They are particularly well known for their historical fiction and their biographies. Like Holiday House, their sales are primarily to the school and library market, though they are selling more to bookstores. Clarion's books regularly receive respected awards and their authors stay with them. Their system seems to work.

The Clarion way of doing things also means a lack of meetings. Jennifer does have meetings, but only productive ones, such as working with the art director, or a weekly session when the staff gets together and reads the slush. There's a minimum of paperwork, and Clarion doesn't even have publishing meetings. If she wants to acquire a title, she discusses it with other editors, and then gets an okay from Dinah Stevenson, the head of the imprint.

In this idyllic setting, she finds time to write thoughtful rejection letters. She loves finding new people, and has pulled manuscripts right out of the slush. Her hope is that she and the authors she discovers are setting off on their careers together. She also loves developing picture books, a deeply collaborative process involving her and the art director as well as the writer and illustrator, and working through the process that leads from the words to the pictures. Her only lament is that she wishes she could respond immediately to submissions, but she has too much to do. At least what she's doing is all satisfying. May there always be places like Clarion.

Fifty Years Later—Margaret K. McElderry

Having said repeatedly that so much has changed in children's publishing, I now must say that some things, happily, remain the same. One is that Margaret K. McElderry continues to edit children's books. She may be the last of the generation of editors with a background as a librarian, having started her career in publishing as Editor of Children's Books at Harcourt, Brace in 1945. Margaret now edits a few books from home while Emma Dryden oversees the Margaret K. McElderry imprint at Simon & Schuster.

Margaret K. McElderry Books today is a small imprint within a large company, publishing 35 or so books per year. Margaret personally edits five to seven of them, and Emma most of the rest. The list is about half picture books, some of them imported, and almost half middle-grade and young adult fiction, with a few poetry and nonfiction titles. Like Holiday House, they publish primarily for the school and library market and for the independent bookstores. Margaret comments that she continues to publish the books she cares about, unaffected by the wider trends in the children's book market.

What has Margaret always published? She's known as an editor who did a lot to bring in books from foreign publishers, starting with German, Swiss, and Scandinavian authors in translation—such works as Margot Benary-Isbert's *The Ark*. She's brought in authors from Britain and Australia, including Mary Norton, Margaret Mahy, Lucy Boston, and Patricia Wrightson. She is also known for working with and developing writers and illustrators such as Irene Haas, Carol Fenner, Sarah Ellis, Eloise McGraw, Louise Borden, and X. J. Kennedy. Though she didn't say this, books she has edited have won just about every award there is to win, from Caldecotts and Newberys on down.

How is it that she's been left alone to publish what she wants to? Perhaps it's because what she wants to publish so often seems to be what children want to read, and librarians want to buy. Or as she comments wryly, "It doesn't hurt to have a book that sells awfully well every once in a while." And so she has continued to do what she has always done, though perhaps now more very young picture books, reflecting the greater demand for them today. In her role as editor-at-large, she concentrates on editing, and leaves the administrative work to Emma, who reports that she, like every other editor at a corporate publisher I talked to, spends a good bit of her workday in meetings. Margaret gets to do what she likes best, working with "unusual and interesting people." In her long career, she's always felt that "it's a privilege to work with authors and artists." That humility and her lifelong love of books help to explain how she's been able to help so many people create their best work.

Class Rules

Margaret K. McElderry's tip for writers is a simple but powerful one: "Read, read, read."

In Good Hands?

So there you are, a peek into the lives of some editors from trade and mass-market publishing. We hope you'll agree that as long as such people are involved in children's books, there's hope that books children will love will still find a place at publishing companies, and that these portraits gave you a better sense of the person behind the name in the market guide.

The Least You Need to Know

- Children's book editors typically come from white, middle-class, college-educated backgrounds.

- Editors share a love of books, regardless of the level at which they work.

- Administrative duties at larger publishers can take up much of an editor's time, but editors still find time to edit.

- Editors at independent publishers and smaller imprints get to spend more of their time editing.

- Margaret K. McElderry, still active after a 50-year career in children's publishing, is one of the great editors of our time.

Chapter 25

Making the Pictures

In This Chapter

- ◆ How a publisher chooses an illustrator
- ◆ The steps in the illustration process
- ◆ What an art director does
- ◆ The limited role of a writer in the illustration process
- ◆ What an illustrator should keep in mind
- ◆ The magic that an illustrator brings to a book

The manuscript is done, and now it's time for the book to be designed and illustrated. In this chapter, I'll tell you how a publisher chooses an illustrator, the stages of the illustration process, and the role of the writer (or lack of it) in all this. I'll also point out some pitfalls before reminding you of the magic that illustration brings to a book.

It's Not Done Yet!

A book is only half finished when the manuscript is done. If it's a picture book, it will be illustrated throughout. If it's a novel, it will need a illustration for the jacket, and perhaps some illustrations inside, scattered throughout the book or opening each chapter. Other books get illustrations, too—you'll see a hen's tooth before you see a children's book without an illustration, even if it's only on the cover.

At this point, the writer's role suddenly diminishes. This can be hard to take. Authors may feel that because the story belongs to them, they should have a hand in visualizing it, too. Typically, though, the publisher not only picks the illustrator but gives her the freedom to illustrate as she sees fit, subject only to the art director's supervision.

If you're an illustrator, this probably sounds good to you. If you're a writer and it doesn't, I'll remind you that your skill is with words—an illustrator may well be able to take your story places you never imagined. As picture-book author Tony Johnston comments, "You have to trust whoever's at the other end." As for actually choosing the illustrator, with so much of the time and expense of creating a book being the responsibility of the publisher, it's no wonder that the publisher wants to be the one deciding who illustrates a book. And after all, they've probably got more experience than writers do in making that kind of decision.

Class Rules

Writers may expect a lot of illustrators, and illustrators expect the same of writers. Experienced illustrator Megan Halsey says this about the manuscripts she likes the best: "Most good manuscripts have crisp, clear visuals that I see in my mind's eye while I read. I look for an element of fun, a good story, and tantalizing visuals to illustrate." Illustrators build on what's already there, but often go beyond it.

If you're new to this, understand that creating a book is something of a team effort, with different people playing different roles, bringing different abilities to the challenge of producing the best possible book. Whether you are the author or illustrator, your job is to do the best you can in your role, and let the publisher manage the team.

Finding a Good Match

If the book is being illustrated, the publisher—either the editor or the art director—chooses and hires the illustrator. How the publisher makes the choice depends on many factors. Here are some of the most important ones:

- ◆ Finding a style that suits a book's intended audience
- ◆ Finding a good match for the "feel" of the book—cheerful art for a cheerful book, edgy art for an edgy book, and so on

- ◆ Availability of an artist—popular illustrators get booked up years in advance

- ◆ Preferring an illustrator already associated with that company

- ◆ Matching a "known" illustrator with an unknown author, or vice versa

Writers may be involved in that decision, depending the policies of a particular publisher and their relationship with their editor. If an editor does show a writer samples, she will listen to the writer's preferences, within limits. If as a writer you have very specific preferences, try to express them in a way that leaves your editor some room to move. Maybe you've imagined your story all along with the dignified oil paintings of Allen Say. You can suggest that style to your editor, or comment that you've always liked his work. You may not know about them, but there are dozens of artists working in a style more or less like his. Your editor can find them, if she agrees with your suggestion.

Playground Stories _____

I once did take an author's suggestion—because it was so obviously an exciting match for an unusual manuscript. I was finding an illustrator for Evelyn Coleman's *The Foot Warmer and the Crow*, a powerful folktalelike story about a man escaping from slavery. I showed samples to Evelyn of the experienced picture-book illustrator I felt was the best possible choice. Evelyn asked me to consider Daniel Minter, an unknown artist. I reluctantly let him send me a package of samples. When I opened it, I knew that the strong forms on Daniel's brightly painted carved panels were just right for the book.

If you are an illustrator and know that you are being considered for a book, be cooperative and hopeful, but don't count your chickens before they turn into a contract. Many, perhaps most, illustration assignments are made quickly, without a lot of agonizing over choices. If a publisher is asking for more samples (or, rarely, a sample done "on spec"), they may be looking only at you, and want to see more of your work to confirm that preference. Or they may have a stack of possible candidates and are trying to winnow them down.

Class Rules _____

"In most cases, [writers] have little or no say on the art, even if you are shown samples as a courtesy. In general, this makes good sense, since most authors think they know more about art than they do. Picture-book writers must keep in mind that a picture book is a collaboration between writer and illustrator." So says Aaron Shepard, picture-book author and folktale reteller, in *The Business of Writing for Children*.

Illustration is an act of interpretation, and there are many ways to interpret even the simplest of statements. If you'd like to see this in action, get your hands on *Mary Had a Little Lamb* as illustrated in three different ways: by Tomie dePaola in simple, bold paintings; by Bruce McMillan in bright color photographs; and by Salley Mavor in three-dimensional fabric art. If you can't find these books, ask a children's librarian if she can show you a folktale for which they have different picture-book versions. Examine the different versions. You may well prefer one, but can you really say that one is right, and one is wrong?

The Role of the Art Director

As already mentioned, when illustrations are called for, an art director (or A.D.) steps in. At some companies, this person works with an illustrator independently of an editor. At others, the A.D. and the editor work closely together. But just what is an art director, and how is this person different from a designer? Some basics follow, along with a profile of Susan Sherman, art director at Charlesbridge Publishing.

Design vs. Direct

Art staffs at publishing companies consist of one art director and some designers. But although the titles are different, both kinds of staff may do very much the same job. How can that be? Well, the term "art director" doesn't just mean that this person is the director of the art department. An art director is someone who provides *art direction*, much as an editor is someone who edits. The designer, on the other hand, deals with the other aspects of the book, such as the typeface used, the size and shape of the pages, and where the illustrations actually go. The two roles overlap, of course, and someone with the title of designer often does art direction, and vice versa.

Vocabulary List

Art direction involves working with an illustrator on just about every aspect of the work they are doing, including deciding what to illustrate, the sequence and pacing of illustrations, composition of individual illustrations, and color palette.

Introducing ...

To learn more about what an art director does, and what people like about such work, I'd like you to meet Susan Sherman, A.D. at Charlesbridge Publishing. Long based in Boston, she previously worked at Little Brown when it was privately owned, at Houghton Mifflin, and then at Little Brown again after it had become part of a larger corporation.

She loves doing what she does, and says that in some ways she is like a teacher. She wants to help make the book, and specifically the art in it, be the best it can be. To accomplish that, she has to find the best way to encourage or push or redirect people with very different personalities. When I discussed this with her, I was struck by how similarly she as art director and I as editor describe our roles. There are key differences—she might use sketches to get across an idea, while I would use words—but the roles of art director and editor are in many ways complementary, and their contributions are key parts of the "intensely collaborative" process that creates a picture book.

She comments that the role of the art director has not changed, though the job has at many companies. Just like the editors I profiled in the previous chapters, meetings are now a big part of the day at the larger companies. For this reason, she's glad to be working at a smaller, independent publisher again, where the staff work more collaboratively, and it's possible to be experimental and take a few risks. Another big change was brought by computers. Computer design gives a publisher more control over design, and a greater ability to make changes. Type, for example, is now generated by the computer. In the past, design staff had to send out to have type set, and changing a type face or even the size of type cost time and money. The other side of this, of course, is that more work is now done by (usually) the same number of staff. The publisher has more control but must do more in-house.

Regardless of the technology used, every book brings a new challenge. For Chris Van Allsberg's *Polar Express*, the challenge was dealing with dark art on dark paper. The Houghton Mifflin production staff had to find a company that could reproduce that accurately. David Macaulay's *Black and White* was one of the first books the company designed on the computer, which made it much easier to set the four different typefaces used in that unusual book.

Sketches and Dummies and Roughs, Oh My!

What happens during the illustration process varies greatly from one publisher to the next, and even from one book to the next. When the illustrator is signed up for a book, some art directors give very specific instructions, and then carefully oversee each subsequent stage. This is more likely with mass-market and educational publishers, who have to keep the very specific needs of their markets in mind. Others let the illustrators develop their own ideas. During the process, the art director steps in to provide feedback when needed, and generally does what she can to help the illustrator do the best possible work, and to ensure that the final art will be suitable for production needs.

Creating a picture book is the most demanding project for an illustrator, so I'll concentrate on this. First, the illustrator breaks up the text and plans the sequence of illustrations. To do this, creating a *storyboard* is a good first step. A storyboard shows all the pages of a book, laid out in miniature, starting with the single page 1, continuing through all the double-page spreads (such as 2/3, 4/5, and so on), and ending with another single page, probably page 32. This allows you to plan out the book and make sure you haven't left out a title page, a copyright page, or any other essential elements. Do a preliminary breakdown of the text and use your storyboard to plan the visual flow of the story. At this point, you may want to explore different alternatives to a particular illustration. You might toss off 20 or 30 versions, in the form of *thumbnails*, small, very loose *sketches*, which help you to explore possibilities. As Jeff Hopkins, an up-and-coming illustrator, puts it, "It's like brainstorming on a page." Once Jeff is more or less settled on one, he'll rough out what he is doing with each page of the book, and may submit this preliminary work to the publisher, again in the form of thumbnails.

Vocabulary List

Plan out all the pages of a book in a **storyboard,** which shows each page and two-page spread in miniature. Editors or art directors often ask an artist to send them **thumbnails.** Artists use these rough thumbnail-size sketches to try out ideas and develop the layout and pacing of a book before moving on to full-size **sketches.** See examples of both kinds of sketches online at www.underdown.org/cigthumbnails.htm.

Thumbnails are done mainly to look at different compositions or to see how the book will work as a whole, and so they can be very crude. Should a character appear in a particular pose? What are the scenes to show so that the book has a good pacing and illustration and text appear in balance on the pages? Visual pacing and page turns at the right moments in the story come in at this stage (though of course they may be rethought later on).

Class Rules

For the details of the composition process, there's no better place to look than Uri Shulevitz's *Writing with Pictures,* which goes into more depth than I possibly could here. You'll find dozens of visual examples of the different stages in creating a picture book, accompanied by the wisdom of a master of the picture book form.

Creating a picture book means thinking about the book as a whole, not as a series of individual illustrations. Some illustrators start telling the story visually on the title page or cover, for example. Pat Hutchins, in *Rosie's Walk*, uses the turning of a page to set up a series of predictable but enjoyable surprises: A fox attempts to pounce on a hen, but (page turn) suffers one setback after another. Or consider the farmer's hat in Nancy Tafuri's *Silly Little Goose.* Early in this simple story of a goose looking for a place to build her nest, the hat blows off the farmer's head and is seen in the background of most of the pages, until, after discovering that various other potential nesting sites are already occupied by other animals, the goose finds the hat and uses it. Our two-year-old was very excited when she noticed and followed this purely visual story. She'd enjoyed the story without it, but this added to it. Or reread *Where the Wild Things Are* by Maurice Sendak, and see what he does with the size the shape of the illustrations at different points in the story. There are many ways to put a picture book together—perhaps you can create a new one.

Next come the actual sketches, and some illustrators go straight to them anyway. These might look very finished, or they might look very rough—different illustrators use this stage differently. Do what works best for you. Some illustrators spend time sketching their characters in many different poses, while others go straight to rough versions of what they envision for a particular page.

Once the book is roughed out, the illustrator usually does a final set of full-size sketches. These show the complete book as the illustrator intends it to look, and may be put together into book dummy form. At this stage, the writer may get a look at the sketches. If so, writers are expected to comment on such problems as a visual detail that contradicts something in their text; this kind of thing is easily overlooked during the process of working on the art. Writers are not expected to comment on the art itself, and even if they do, their comments won't be passed along to the illustrator. With some publishers, mass-market publishers in particular, the writers may see nothing from the time they deliver their manuscript till they get copies of the finished book.

The editor and art director typically review the final sketches together. A copy editor often goes over them, too, checking to make sure that there are no discrepancies with the text. Once any changes have been made, and the sketches have been approved, the illustrator has to get to work on the final art. For some, this is the least enjoyable part of the process. Creating characters and imagining the illustration sequence is fun, but now the task is to follow what's been approved and create finished art that also retains the energy of their sketches.

Other Kinds of Books

Many books only have an illustration on the cover, or perhaps the cover and some small illustrations scattered throughout the book. These kinds of books are more typically handled by designers, and may be completely designed before an illustrator comes into the process. When an illustrator is brought in, he or she will generally be given instructions as to what is needed on the cover, and what scenes the publisher wants illustrated if there are interior illustrations. Some companies see jackets as being part of the marketing of the book, so they'll be more concerned with making an attractive cover than with making it accurately reflect what's in the book. The illustrator may not even read the entire book—or even be given it. Sometimes the illustrator gets detailed instructions from the art director, and a summary of the book's contents.

Helping Out with Nonfiction

As you know, nonfiction may be done a little differently than fiction. If a book is being illustrated with "stock" photographs, or photos gathered from different sources, the author is sometimes the person who does the gathering. (If not, a photo researcher at the publisher handles this.) But nonfiction may also be illustrated with art, and then the writer may be asked to help out, or even be required to do so. There's a logic to this. While doing research, the writer probably came across good sources for the illustrator to use, whether they are pictures of animals or period costumes. Why make the illustrator find them all over again? And if the writer hasn't found good visual references for specific scenes, maybe they don't exist. The publisher needs to know this, and the writer may need to rewrite the text so that it doesn't depend on illustrations that can't be done.

The writer may also have personal knowledge or experience on which the book is based, and this can help with the illustrations, too. Sneed Collard, the author of *Forest in the Clouds*, didn't read other books to write this picture book about a visit to a high-altitude "cloud forest" in the mountains of Costa Rica. He went there. And he took pictures. When the illustrator, Michael Rothman, was ready to get to work, Sneed passed on several dozen slides to him. Michael also did his own research in published sources, but those slides were a useful part of his visual references.

It's Not an Exact Science

The computer has transformed book design in general, and picture book design in particular, but even if you are now able to revise a book layout 17 times instead of twice, you still end up with a book that looks good and that fits within a multiple of 8 pages. If you are new to picture book illustration, be aware that there are still technical limits to what you can do, and be sure to discuss them with your art director before you put pen or brush or digital stylus to paper or canvas or pad.

If you are planning to do full-page art that "bleeds" off the edges of a page, meaning that it's not confined by a frame or set margins, be sure to ask your A.D. for page templates. These will give you accurate dimensions to work within, taking into account the exact trim size for the book, gutters, and bleed. The A.D. will also be able to tell you how much larger or smaller than the final size of the book you can do your art.

You can go "up" or "down" a certain amount, but art that's reduced too much gets dense and dark, while art that's blown up gets less sharp and can become washed out.

For the most part, you have much more freedom now than you used to. Once upon a

Can You Keep a Secret? _____

Colors shift to some extent when art is scanned and converted into digital files using the four-color CMYK system. Mostly they stay in sync with each other—most people think the full range of color is there and it only becomes obvious that it's not when you compare a printed book to the original art. Certain colors, though, just don't pick up well, and should be avoided in art being used for illustration: anything "neon," bright green, orange. Ask for a test scan of your art if in doubt.

time, art had to be on flexible paper, of no more than a certain size, so that it could fit on a scanner's drum. Now, if you want to do your art on inflexible wood panels, or create 3-dimensional illustrations, your publisher can most likely find a way to deal with it. But be sure to discuss what you want to do if you plan to do something out of the ordinary. Working with unconventional media does cost more, and some publishers may not be willing to accommodate your creative urges.

Letting the Magic Happen

The illustrator makes a picture book what it is, and is important to other kinds of books as well. Once the author has done his best with the manuscript, let the illustrator do his thing.

Let the magic of illustration happen. Time after time, I hear from authors, when a book

Playground Stories _____

Illustrators may bring not only their interpretation of a manuscript, but might add purely visual elements to the story. Tony Johnston's *The Quilt Story* includes a family that goes west in the nineteenth century. Tomie dePaola, the illustrator, put a cat in every picture until the point in the story when the family actually left. He knew from his own research that families heading west didn't take their pets. A reader may or may not notice that detail, but it's there, adding another level to the story.

is done, how pleased and surprised they are with the illustrations, and what they've added to the book. The authors might have had something in mind for the illustrations; they've ended up with more than that. The illustration process does not always go well, but most times, it does. Play your part in it as best you can, and watch the magic happen.

The Least You Need to Know

- ◆ Editors may or may not involve you in choosing an illustrator for your book. If they do, be professional and reasonable.

- ◆ Illustrators usually do thumbnails and sketches before moving on to do finished art.

- ◆ If you get to see sketches, comment on how they match up with your text. Don't be an art critic.

- ◆ By the time finished art is done, you, your editor, and the art director should have found any problems. If you see the final art, don't bring up new issues.

- ◆ You might be asked to provide reference materials for an illustrator of a nonfiction book.

- ◆ Illustration can be magic! Let the magic happen to your book.

Chapter 26

The Rest of the Process

In This Chapter

- ◆ Who does what after the manuscript is done
- ◆ The process that turns a manuscript into a finished, sellable masterpiece
- ◆ Why it takes so long—book production, step by step
- ◆ The difference between writing a book and publishing a book

Once a writer hands over a manuscript, a team of individuals all geared toward producing the best book possible takes over. The illustrator isn't the only person to step in. In the next months, there will be many others involved in designing, manufacturing, marketing, and producing a book. You may not work directly with any of them, but they play a valuable part in the success of your book.

Your Editor ... and Beyond

In other kinds of publishing, there are often two editors involved with a book. One, the acquisitions editor, acquires the manuscript, and the other, the development editor, does most of the actual editing. This division does not exist in most branches of children's publishing. Instead, one editor handles both (as well as other) functions. Most likely the writer works with this same person until the point at which the manuscript goes to the copy editor. Edits could be substantial or minimal, depending on many variables (as described in Chapter 23).

Then others start to get involved. Once the substantial editing is done, a copy edit occurs. After or at the same time as the copy edit, design and illustration begin, as I discussed in the previous chapter. All the while, a managing editor keeps track of the schedule and the materials for the book. Finally, a production manager gets involved in planning work with a printer. Then *galleys* or final *page proofs*, which you may see, arrive. The final checks on the book are *blues* (for novels and such) or *color proofs* (for picture books), which you probably won't see. And lastly, the printer prints and binds the book. Voilà! That's the cycle of production on your book, in broad outline.

Vocabulary List

Galleys are long pages of type, not set up into the actual book pages. **Page proofs** are set up like a book. **Blues** or bluelines are used to check the final film of the book. **Color proofs** are a check on color for picture books.

Here Some Copy; There Some Copy; Everywhere Copy, Copy!

Once the manuscript needs no further editing (in the judgment of the editor!) it moves to the copy editor. You may be thinking, "Yuck, another person messing with my words." But don't think like that. The copy editor gives your book polish—and makes you look even better as an author. The copy editor may seem picky and overbearing, asking a whole lot of questions and making changes to your sentence structure, spelling, use of capitalization, grammar, and other details. The copy editor might even question your choice of words. He or she asks all the questions and fixes any errors for your benefit, however.

The copy editor also makes sure your manuscript conforms to your publisher's *house style*, which may address such matters as when numbers should be spelled out and when they should be written as numerals. The copy editor makes sure you've spelled or capitalized a name the same way throughout, double-checks the front and back matter, confirms the accuracy of names, and generally focuses on all the little things that are easy to forget or overlook.

So although you need to check your manuscript thoroughly and turn in the best book possible, rejoice in the meticulous, keen eyes of a copy editor, which provide a further, objective check. Not many people in this world possess the patience or mind-set to accomplish this task. Bow down before the copy editor and praise him or her. The copy editor just may prove your best buddy on the team! And in the end, if the copy editor suggests a change you don't like, you don't have to go along with it; provided that you have a reason for wanting to do it your way and your editor agrees, you can overrule the copy editor.

Some publishing houses keep a staff of copy editors; other houses hire freelance copy editors. Sometimes, picture books get copyedited in-house, while longer nonfiction and novels go to freelancers. Either way, your book receives very focused scrutiny.

Your copy editor is an important member of the team working on your book, though you will almost certainly have no direct contact with him or her. Instead, your editor will send you the copyedited manuscript, with handwritten notes and Post-it tags. You address the comments and questions and return the manuscript with revisions—also written on the manuscript or on Post-it tags—to your editor. If you have questions or concerns about the copy editor's suggestions, discuss them with your editor. Ultimately, it's your editor who has the final say and must be satisfied, though she will defer to the copy editor on many issues.

Class Rules

If the copy editor is making changes with which you don't agree, you can say so—but you better have a reason. Needing to have your characters use slang so that you can capture the flavor of their speech is a good reason. Thinking it "looks better" to spell out all numbers below 100 when the publisher prefers to stop at 10 is not.

High-Fashion Time: Designers

The "look" of a book comes from the conceptualization of the designer and, if there is one, the illustrator. The designer brings the text of the book alive with the cover design, the width of the margins, the regular typeface, the display type (the type used for titles and headers)—everything. Especially in children's books, the tasks of the designer vary greatly. There remains a huge difference between designing, say, a novel and a picture book. But in a nutshell, the art director, who oversees the designer, and the designer or designers of the publishing house, create the actual design. They decide how all the various elements of a book (the ones reviewed in Chapter 8) will look on the printed page.

Usually the designer suggests several design possibilities. The editor, illustrator, and sometimes you sit down and choose the actual design. Today, the designer will implement that design using a computer program such as QuarkXPress. In the past, he or she would take the typeset pages or galleys from the printer and paste them onto thin cardboard, often called "mechanicals," to show how the pages would look.

If there are illustrations, they are incorporated into the design. Some publishers have high-tech scanning equipment in-house that allows the designer to generate electronic images from the original illustrations. Other publishers outsource this task to companies that specialize in fine-resolution scanning. When this is the case, the designer prepares the original art for scanning. When the scanned images come back, the designer incorporates them into the layout.

> **Playground Stories**
>
> Tired of reading about all the stages in the creation of a book in the abstract? Then jump on the web, and see a wonderful display of the various stages in the creation of *The Westing Game*, a novel by Ellen Raskin that won the Newbery Medal in 1979, at www.education.wisc.edu/ccbc/wisauth/raskin/intro.htm.
>
> This web "exhibit" concentrates on the writing and revision of the manuscript, but Raskin was also an artist and designer. Go to the "Book Design" page, and you'll find fascinating examples of the work that went into page layouts and jacket design.

Just the Facts, Ma'am

The fact checker—like the copy editor—looks closely at the text, possibly the illustrations as well, to detect any discrepancies that may exist, so this happens later in the process. Unlike the copy editor, the fact checker isn't concerned about grammar. He or she focuses specifically on factual information. Fact checkers play a role in nonfiction, but may also be called in on historical fiction. Are the names, dates, and places accurate? Are there any anachronisms? Are there any contradictions? Did this person really say that? Is the information up to date? So many questions, so little time. The fact checker then tracks down the answers to ensure your book does not carry any mistakes or omissions!

100-Proof

Haven't enough people looked closely at the book? Well, no. The proofreader takes the typeset pages and checks to make sure that the book as typeset actually follows your manuscript and all the little changes made to it in the copyediting stage. She also looks—another pair of eyes—for obvious or glaring mistakes before the book is shipped off to the printer for manufacturing. Look upon your proofreader as the last person in the line to make sure all is well. Sometimes everyone from you to the editor to the copy editor can miss something, and the new set of eyes of the proofreader catches it.

Lights! Camera! Action! The Production Manager

While the proofers, designers, checkers, and editors are working their magic, the production manager is scrambling to put the book into tangible form and to keep costs within budget. The production manager decides what printer will print the book, and when. The production manager literally finds and buys the paper on which the book is printed. Children's books oftentimes incorporate interesting design elements—like the sparkles on the rainbow fish in *The Rainbow Fish*. A production manager was the person who found the paper, the sparkles, and the printer to produce that book—all while keeping the costs within budget.

When the book is all done—with a complete design, all elements in place, from the art on the front of the jacket to the bar code on the back—the editor or designer hands it to the production manager. He or she sends it to the printer, and coordinates the rest of the process. The printer takes the files from the production manager and makes film from them, following the design and making sure that illustrations appear where they should. But checking that isn't just up to the printer. The publisher may have already produced proofs for checking, but the printer will do it again. First come blues, a blue-colored printing from the film, which are checked by the publisher. If the book has color art, the printer may also produce color proofs, showing what the art will really look like. Usually there isn't time for either author or illustrator to see these, so just your editor and the designer review them—and then the book is printed, and bound, and shipped. It will probably take a few weeks (if printed in North America) or a couple of months (if printed abroad) to make it to the publisher's warehouse, but it's on its way.

Can You Keep a Secret?

Don't complain to your editor if the grade of paper or type of binding for your book isn't what you envisioned. Paper and binding costs are a major part of the cost of a book. A production manager may search far and wide to find the grade of paper necessary for a high-quality, glossy picture book, but not be able to get it at the right price. Cost and quality always have to be juggled.

Why do publishers take the time to send books overseas to be printed? In a word: cost. Printing a full-color book isn't cheap, but it's less expensive in Hong Kong and other parts of the Far East, due to lower wages (and, so I'm told, less-strict safety regulations). When perhaps 20 cents per copy can make the difference between making or losing money on a picture book, the opportunity to save that much or more by printing overseas is hard to pass up.

So That's Why It Takes So Long!

Considering the process, no wonder it can take up to three years from the time an editor buys a manuscript until the book hits shelves! Especially with picture books, where illustration can easily add a year to the schedule (and that's only if the illustrator started work right away), don't expect a book to make it into stores with any great speed. Your editors will give you timelines for the production of your book. Be patient—the wait is worth it. When a book follows the correct process thoroughly and meticulously, the end result will be better. Better to take three years for a beautifully produced, well-selling picture book than a year for a slipshod, weak, and cheap book that no one wants to buy, right?

You can expect …

- Several months in the editing stage, once your editor gets to the book.

- A couple months for copyediting.

- A year or more for illustration and design.

- A few more months for proofreading and fact checking (if it's needed).

- Several months for layout (composition), printing, and shipping (distribution to the sellers).

That's a long time, though it can be shorter if your book is not a picture book—and it can be even longer if the publisher's schedule is full. But at least when your book is done you can go find it in the stores, right? Not exactly. The publisher first wants to get it to reviewers and show it to booksellers, as explained in the following chapters. So it's a few months more waiting while that happens. And *then* your book will be on the market. Woo-hoo!

The Least You Need to Know

- Where your writing was a solo process, you now belong to a team of individuals all working toward a common goal: the production of your book.

- Although the people working on your book may make changes, try not to take the changes personally. The editors are there to make your book the best it can be.

- Several people—the copy editor, fact checker, and proofreader—will check and recheck everything in your book. Get used to the constant queries.

- The designer and the production manager are the people who create the final look and feel of a book.

- Understand that producing a children's book may take up to three years from start to finish (beyond the time you took to write it). Be patient.

Part 5

My Book Is Published! Now What?

On that happy day when your children's book is published, you might think that your troubles are over. Well, not quite, because it still has to be marketed and publicized. In this part, you'll learn what your publisher will do, what she might do, and almost certainly what she won't do. If you want to play a role, this part gives you tips for how to do that productively, from doing your own publicity to putting on bookstore events and doing school visits.

Though they may not come with your first book, you'll learn about some of the awards and other forms of recognition you can expect, and this part gives you some guidance on building your writing career. If you want to publish additional books, you might want to know what you can do to bring in an income between royalty checks. If you haven't already, now you can take yourself seriously.

27

What Are You Doing for Me?

In This Chapter

- How sales, marketing, and publicity all fit together
- The scoop on publishers' catalogs and what they do for the sale of the book
- Who reviews your book and why it matters
- The kinds of periodicals that might discuss your new book—from newspapers to magazines, from local to national
- How bookstores handle your book's arrival
- The long-shot publicity machines your publisher may approach before the book hits the shelves

After you've spent all your time on the creation of your baby—your book!—and after the publisher has spent all that money and time on the actual production of your book, what comes next? You might hope that the publisher will launch a major publicity campaign and dole out the big bucks to get the word out about your book. In this chapter, you'll learn the lowdown on what you realistically can expect the publisher to do.

Marketing and Sales People

So far in this book, you've met the publishing people who help you turn manuscript and artwork into a finished book. If that's all that a publisher did, your wonderful book would sit on the shelves of their warehouse, unseen. To get a book out into the world, the publisher has staff dedicated to selling, marketing, and publicizing it. Their roles are different, but hopefully dovetail together.

Take This Book, Please

Months before a book is due to go on sale, salespeople fan out across the country to persuade bookstore buyers, library buyers, and others to order it. If you are a famous author or illustrator with a track record, their job is easy. The bookstore or library will want the book. The only issue is how many copies they'll take. If author and illustrator are not so well known, the sales person has a more difficult job. Maybe they can persuade the buyer that the book is so wonderful the staff will want to show it to customers and talk them into buying or reading it. Or maybe the buyer will want to know what the publisher is doing to help get the book off the shelves and out the door. This is known as "supporting" the book. So the sales person will talk about the publisher's marketing efforts and upcoming publicity.

Paying for Attention

Very broadly speaking, everything a publisher does to promote a book that costs money falls under the heading of marketing. This ranges from putting the book in a catalog to making give-away items to paying for a window display in a bookstore to buying national advertising. Being in the catalog is basic—people have to know the book exists. But beyond that, a book's marketing budget can range from nothing (in which case the publisher is hoping that great reviews will make libraries all over the country order the book, and paying customers flock to bookstores in search of it) to hundreds of thousands of dollars.

Free Attention

Reviews, as previously mentioned, cost a publisher nothing, or at least nothing beyond the cost of getting a copy of the book to a reviewer. Some publicity work is, like sending out review copies, fairly routine. A publicity campaign may be far more elaborate, however, and involve getting an author on talk shows and into magazine features, as well as the more usual newspaper reviews.

Good publicity and marketing support the sales efforts of the publisher, though the best sales and marketing and publicity work still don't guarantee that it will sell—a sobering thought.

I'm in the Catalog!

The first and most basic marketing of a book is its appearance in a publisher's catalog. Savor that first recognition you have that, "My goodness! I'm actually published. That's my book!"

For their part, publishers produce catalogs to showcase all of their new offerings each season as well as their strong backlist titles. You should expect your publisher to list your book in the catalog that covers the time period in which its publication date is scheduled. For example, let's say that your book has a *pub. date* of March 2005. You might expect the publisher to include it in its fall/winter 2004–2005 catalog, if it releases three catalogs per year. If it does two, then it will be in the spring 2005 catalog. (The other season being the fall.)

Vocabulary List

The **pub. date** of a book is the official (and somewhat arbitrary) date when a publisher says it will be available in stores. Reviews of the book are often timed to come out before the pub. date—but the book itself may have already left the publisher's warehouse weeks earlier, or may have been delayed.

Can You Keep a Secret?

What does catalog copy look like and what does it include? Typically, the catalog entry of your book will include all the necessary items that someone or some business might need to buy your book. These include items like …

- A picture of the cover of your book.
- The title.
- The author's and illustrator's names.
- A brief description.
- Biographies of the author and illustrator.
- The publication date.
- The ISBN—International Standard Book Number.
- The price.
- The trim size—the size of the book's pages.
- Recommended age level.

Elsewhere, the catalog will offer instructions on how to order the book, which might differ depending on who you are—a single customer versus a bookstore.

Catalogs are produced for a variety of people. Sales representatives within the publishing house use them when they go on sales calls to promote new books at bookstores, libraries, and to wholesalers. They'll be given away at conferences for librarians, booksellers, and teachers, and other venues. The publicity department may send catalogs to contacts within the publishing journalistic community or to book reviewers. And if a person calls the company and asks for a catalog, more than likely the publishing house will send one out. The publisher's catalog is the first step in getting the news out that your book is available.

The Big Mouths

Most publishers send out advance copies (if it's a picture book) or *bound galleys* (if it's a novel or longer nonfiction) of your book to major reviewers as a standard publicity effort. "Okay," you may say, "but who are these major reviewers?" Certain publications always receive lists and advance copies of your book. These reviewers and publications are the driving force in many ways for the sales of books, especially to libraries, who wait to see reviews before making purchase decisions. Some of the places your publisher will send notification and a copy of your book are ...

◆ *Publishers Weekly.* The review section of *Publishers Weekly* is called "Forecasts." You'll get more booksellers reading this than the others.

 Vocabulary List

Publishers may produce an advance version of novels and similar longer books, called **bound galleys** (from the old term for the long pages created when a book was typeset, before it was laid out in pages). This version, typically unedited and usually without artwork, is sent to reviewers who will write about the book before its arrival in stores.

Picture books sent to reviewers may just be copies from the print run, rush shipped, or **f&g's,** which are pages that have been **f**olded and **g**athered, but not yet bound, meaning they can be sent out a few weeks earlier than if company had to wait for bound books.

◆ *Booklist.* The publication of the American Library Association. Thoughtful, respected reviews.

◆ *School Library Journal. SLJ* reviews the most books per year, though the quality of their reviews varies.

◆ *Kirkus Reviews.* Slightly more selective then *SLJ* and more literary in approach.

♦ *The Horn Book Magazine* and *The Horn Book Guide*. Strictly children's literature. *The Horn Book Magazine* comes out every other month and doesn't have space for many reviews. The *Guide* comes out twice a year with more reviews.

These trade publications exist to report on the upcoming titles and the publishing industry. Booksellers as well as librarians read them. Sometimes, Hollywood producers and directors read them to gain rights to books they think will make good films.

The publisher wants these trade journals to review and write about your book, thereby generating sales. Think about it. Book people read *Publishers Weekly* (*PW* for those in the know), *Booklist, Library Journal, Kirkus Reviews,* and *Horn Book.* Good reviews encourage libraries to try books by unknown authors, and may spur a bookstore to place a book in a prominent display. In some cases, these magazines put a star or a pointer before reviews of particularly recommended books—if you get stars from more than one magazine, your book will do well.

The Other Mouths

But hold on there a minute—the big mouths aren't the only ones available to blab about your book. In many cases, a publisher will send an advance copy to a short list of other publications, ones that can be counted on as regular reviewers of children's books. They may also routinely send their catalogs to a larger list of possible review sources, and allow them to request the books they want to see. A publisher may also consider targeting local or specialized publications—and you shouldn't hesitate to make suggestions to your publisher's marketing department. If your publisher feels it's worthwhile, they'll send information and maybe a copy of your book to these places.

What a publisher won't do is send copies of your book to every newspaper and magazine in the country. Most of them, unfortunately, don't review children's books. So don't feel slighted if you don't see your book reviewed in the magazines and newspapers you read. That's just a reality of the business.

 Class Rules

Don't depend on your publisher to send review copies of your book to multiple media outlets—especially local papers and magazines. Check first with your publicist to find out if there are plans to blitz your hometown or appropriate national publications. If not, feel free to send a news release and a copy of the book yourself. Try to find a newsy "hook" for your story, so you don't get ignored by publications that are mostly aren't interested in children's books.

Local Yokels

What's the appeal of local publications, those papers and media outlets in your own backyard? They look for the local hook of any story. You possess, for example, a better chance of garnering publicity from the *Sacramento Bee* if you live in Sacramento than if you don't.

Though it costs money for a publisher to send out review copies of books, your publisher may want to grab this natural publicity opportunity and send copies with a release to the local reviewers of children's books. The best thing you can do is provide your publisher with a list of all the local outlets—television stations, radio stations, newspaper columnists, and regional magazines—with a contact name, the address, and a phone number. Then sit back and (you hope) watch the interviews and reviews roll in. The more organized publishers will request this information from you. Provide it whether you are asked or not.

Mommy Says I'm Special!

In addition to targeting local publications for review, sometimes a publisher will target specialty publications. For example, let's say you write a nonfiction book about gardening for children. Your publisher may want to send copies of the book to national, glossy women's magazines that include sections on activities with children—such as *Ladies Home Journal* or *McCall's*. Many parenting magazines might like to focus on the book or include the title in a roundup of gardening books for kids in a spring issue of the respective magazine. And don't forget the gardening magazines.

You get the point. Technically, these magazines are not child-focused. The connection between your book and the magazine may not be obvious. But for the publicity manager, the link may prove fantastic for the marketing machine.

For your part, if you believe you know of some unique ways to position your book in various specialty publications, share them with your publisher. And again, make a list with all the contact information for the marketing or publicity representative.

I'm in the Newspaper!

Up until now, I've been talking about your publisher sending out review copies of your book to prominent reviewers and targeted publications. But oftentimes, a publisher formulates a kind of secondary list of people and publications to which only a *press release* or a catalog and request for review copies goes out. There may be hundreds of names on such a list.

As an example, let's say that your publicity manager knows of a freelance journalist who frequently writes about children's books. This freelancer may receive a press release only—if the freelancer gains an interest in the book from the press release, then he or she can fill out a review copy request and receive a review copy. Many times, the publisher keeps reviewers from smaller media markets on this list. Though *The New York Times* may receive the f&g's of your cool picture book, *The Seattle Times* may receive only the press release and request form.

Vocabulary List

A **press release** alerts the media to the publication of a title. Beyond providing an overview of the title, a release may "tie in" to an event or a news angle—depending on the book— to garner further interest from the media. Press releases list pertinent information, too, like whom to contact for a review copy and the cost of the book.

Not on the Shelf, but in the Store

Publishers sometimes send advance copies of books to bookstores. Generally, bound galleys are too expensive to produce many of; only if there are enough galleys left after the "big mouth" reviewers get theirs will the publisher forward copies to bookstores. Or if the publisher is trying especially hard to generate interest in a book, they may print more. If this is done, select bookstores receive the copies. You may be wondering why these are sent at all, especially when the store can't even sell the book, as final copies may not be available yet. Quite simply, the mailing allows the booksellers to read the book and generate a buzz about the title. The publisher hopes that someone in the store will get excited about it, order more copies, and talk about it with their customers, thereby generating sales. For this reason, in children's publishing, an edgy, hip young adult galley is more likely to reach a bookseller than a picture book f&g is. The bookstore will still see the book when the salesperson calls on it, of course.

Going Long and Deep

What author or illustrator doesn't think of it—sitting on *Oprah* chatting with the queen of talk about a book? Come on—we all fantasize about that sort of huge publicity hit! I'm reasonably certain that visions of *Oprah* float in your head. Not to shatter your *Oprah* or other talk-show dreams, but publishers rarely send review copies of a title to a major talk show unless the book holds some kind of universal appeal (to adults) or news hook. Moreover, what publicists know is that the producers of these shows rarely handpick a book—especially a children's book—for discussion on a show. It's the author or the author's story that does it. So if you are Jamie Lee Curtis hawking your children's tale, you have an edge.

Nevertheless, sometimes your publisher will find a reason or hook to send Oprah your book. And sometimes you can help them out with suggestions. If you feel strongly about it, and provided that you keep your publisher informed, you might even launch your own campaign. Lori Mitchell, author/illustrator of *Different Just Like Me*, got her book onto *Oprah* and *Maury Povich*, as well as local television. For more information about her book, which will help you figure out what helped it get on TV, visit the website at www.differentjustlikeme.cc. This won't work for everyone, and it's a long shot at the best of times, but efforts in this area do pay off.

Publicity efforts are labor intensive. You can count on some basics but if you want something unusual to happen, you may have to do it yourself.

Can You Keep a Secret?

Want to increase your chances of having a producer for a national talk show choose your book as a focus for the show? Provide your publicist with (1) suggested show topics and (2) suggested interview questions. By doing this, you save the publicist time and make the producer's job easier.

The Least You Need to Know

- You can expect a basic publicity effort from your publisher to promote you and your book.

- Nearly all publishers send prepublication review copies of books to prominent review magazines, such as *Publishers Weekly*, *Booklist*, *School Library Journal*, and *Kirkus Reviews*.

- In addition to sending galleys to the major reviewers, a publisher may send them to local media outlets on your behalf, or to specialty publications, and will probably do a mailing to a secondary tier.

- Bookstores sometimes also receive advance copies of your book to generate a buzz about the title with booksellers.

- Don't count on your publisher automatically sending your book to national talk shows such as *Oprah*.

28

Fun Stuff and Bragging

In This Chapter

◆ Great freebies—but someone has to pay for them

◆ How publishers get creative with marketing

◆ The difference between a publisher's ads and co-op ads

◆ Ways in which publishers help bookstores market your book

◆ Why marketing does not necessarily make for a bestseller

In the last chapter, you learned what you can expect the publisher to do on your behalf in the publicity and book review arena. In this chapter, you'll learn about marketing: things that the publisher does other than seeking publicity, which the publisher may or may not do for you, depending upon the book. This chapter also gets into how ads are used in publishing and what it *doesn't* take to make a bestseller.

Freebies

You may have many ideas about how to market your book—how to showcase it at libraries, bookstores, and schools with freebies that are given out to generate interest in your awesome book. When you think of freebies, think of bookmarks with the cover of the book on one side and a brief overview on the other; posters of the cover of the book; or postcards, again displaying the cover and sent out as a notice of the impending release of your book.

First, the bad news: Publishers rarely go deep into their pockets for this sort of free stuff—free for the customer, that is—because the cost often outweighs the benefits of added sales.

Next, the good news: Sometimes a publisher does produce such giveaways to help market your book. In fact, when a publisher creates and produces a freebie, it does so to generate name recognition instead of sales.

X Marks the Spot

Bookmarks are probably one of the most common freebies that a publisher will produce. A publisher may produce bookmarks for bookstores, where they can be used as mini-advertisements, either stuffed in the bags at the checkout or put on a display table for customers to take. Sometimes the publisher will produce bookmarks for teachers and classroom use. Let's say that you will be giving a reading of your picture book to several classes of second graders. If your publisher has created bookmarks promoting your book, you'll be able to give them out to keep you and your work in front of the teachers and the children.

Put That Up!

Because posters are so expensive, publishers usually produce them only for "long-term" authors and illustrators and their titles. A publisher might produce a poster, say, for a book with longevity like *Where the Wild Things Are* or *The Rainbow Fish*. The poster is then used by bookstores in window displays, in libraries for decoration, and in schools to promote reading. Publishers give these posters out to booksellers, librarians, and teachers at conventions, and also mail them out on request.

Occasionally a publisher may produce a poster for a book that isn't by an author it has been working with over many books and years. This standout title may possess a lot of buzz or be one for which the publisher hopes to create buzz. In either of these cases, the decision to create a poster is made by the publisher's marketing department well before the book is published. You'll find that you won't be able to lobby for it (though your editor may have been lobbying for it behind the scenes). If it happens, accept it as the gift that it is.

Postcards from the Edge

Postcards are another way the publisher may generate interest in your book. They're a great way to invite people to an event surrounding your book. You may think this is an ideal way to provide the media and your pals information about your next local event, but find your publisher unwilling to foot the tab for the creation of the postcards. You may be able to make a deal with the publisher: You agree to buy the postcards if the publisher pays the postage bill.

Do It Yourself

If you find that your publisher won't budge on any of these marketing materials, you may want to produce some yourself. Bear in mind that endeavors like event kits and postcards require time and money. The efforts may not yield desired results.

Creative Genius

Publishers don't limit their marketing ideas to postcards and posters. In fact, marketing departments spend hours and days thinking up interesting ways to promote your book—as inexpensively as possible. At Charlesbridge, for example, they sent out lunch bags to elementary school teachers with cartoon bugs printed on them and the title of the book *Bugs for Lunch*. The paper bags proved inexpensive to produce and, thus, worthwhile for the publisher to manufacture.

Some publishers create complete party kits for the booksellers to run story hours by, or displays to showcase the book at the checkout stands of the stores—called dumps!

Class Rules _____

Before devoting yourself to postcard production and bookmark creation, consider how long it will take to complete whatever publicity feat you're choosing to accomplish. Then, factor in how much money you stand to make and whether your project is worthwhile.

For Teacher's Eyes Only

Because children's book publishing often has an educational focus, publishers may strive to gain the attention of teachers. Just as helping a radio show's producer with story ideas linked to your title may provide you with a publicity hit, creating materials aligned with a title that will help the teacher in lesson planning will win you advocates. Consider the teacher who comes across a kit for a book published about rain forests and he just happens to have planned on delivering a unit on rain forests. The kit includes a taped conversation with the author, and suggested review questions, handouts, and project ideas—all based on rain forests and the book.

> **Can You Keep a Secret?**
>
> Many publishers don't create teacher's guides for just one book. Instead, the publisher links several books by theme or content or author and produces one teacher's guide for several books. The same goes for marketing flyers. A publisher may list several holiday books, for example, on one glossy flyer and publicize all of them for the cost of one leaflet.

Buying Ads

Publishers think carefully before investing in advertisements—basically because there remain so many better income-generating marketing ideas than buying an ad. When they do buy ads, they'll buy them for their own reasons, so don't try to lobby for them. Nevertheless, ads sometimes work. Let's look at when or why a publisher might buy an ad.

The Bookstore

Bookstore managers, owners, and large chain buyers read *Publishers Weekly* (*PW*) religiously. Many purchases occur because of a review or ad seen in this trade publication. A marketing manager might be more inclined to drop the bank on an ad in a publication that reaches such incredible numbers of professionals in the publishing arena.

> **Class Rules**
>
> Two issues every year of *Publishers Weekly* are known as the Children's Announcement issues. The magazine publishes lists of forthcoming titles from every established publisher, and publishers typically buy ads in it to showcase their newest offerings. Get your hands on these issues to see what's new—and to see your book getting its own little bit of exposure.

But hold on! I am not saying that a children's book publisher will buy an ad for a single juvenile title as a standard procedure. Within the children's publishing world, ads are targeted according to special issues. Let's say *Publishers Weekly*'s editorial calendar calls for a children's book focus (as it does twice a year, when the new season's books are highlighted). Knowing that the magazine will devote page upon page to children's books may incline the publishing house to display some strong, upcoming titles in an ad in the special issue, or perhaps to list all their new titles in one comprehensive ad.

Another ad trick children's book publishers use is purchasing an advertisement featuring several books. Let's go back to the holiday theme. If a publisher decides to promote several Christmas, Kwanzaa, and Hanukkah books, the house may place an ad for all the titles within the pages of *Publishers Weekly*. Now buying an ad in *PW* becomes a very targeted—and cost-effective—way to reach numerous booksellers simultaneously.

Publishers hope that these strategically placed ads bring increased revenue and sales.

The Library

Libraries buy books. And if your book appears to be a title that librarians may snatch up and buy—perhaps an exciting nonfiction title—your publisher may place an ad in *Booklist* or *School Library Journal* to draw attention to the book amid all the other titles out there and get it noticed. Even after publication, if a book gets a starred review, or gets named to an award list, a publisher may take out an ad to point that out to that audience.

The Consumer

You've seen the ads for adult novels in the margins of magazines, but what about children's books or young adult literature? Quite simply, a publisher may—again if applicable and thoughtfully targeted—purchase an ad in a consumer magazine to promote your book. Let's say that the publishing house acquired the rights to all novels based on a popular teen television series. The show tears up the ratings every week. To piggyback on the success of the show, the publisher may decide to place an ad in a magazine such as *Seventeen*, a consumer publication. The ad targets the youth who actually read the novels.

Or a publisher may buy an ad in a consumer publication such as *USA Today* or a national magazine if a celebrity is associated with the title. Perhaps the celebrity is making an appearance in an area. The publisher may take the opportunity to place an ad in the local edition of *USA Today*, for example, to further position the book.

A publisher probably will not buy an ad in *The New York Times* or some other newspaper your friends read because the cost is so high, and the ad will not reach enough people who might actually buy the book. Don't feel bad if you don't get an ad in such a newspaper. An ad is an investment, and it has to have a good return.

The Teacher

And again, because many teachers use books as resources or tools in their classroom, children's book publishers may focus an ad campaign on teacher's journals and trade publications. Let's say you just wrote a great easy-reader book—it's imaginative, fun to read, and everyone at the publishing house seems to think it's the coolest book with built-in teacher appeal to hit the shelves in a decade. Well, then, an ad may find its way into a teacher's magazine or journal.

Do you see the point? Advertisements are rarely placed, but when they are, the marketing department thinks about the most appropriate venue—then targets it with an ad.

Ground-Level Marketing

You've now read about some pretty big ways to market—ads, freebies, teacher's kits—but other smaller ways exist to get your book out there, too.

Did Hennie Pennie Live in a Chicken Coop or a Co-Op?

Let's say you book yourself to read your latest picture book at Barnes & Noble during story time the following month. Wouldn't it be nice to place an ad in the local paper advising the public of your reading? Yes, it would and may be possible for the bookstore to place that ad through the use of *co-op money*. In this situation, the bookstore and the publisher share the cost of an ad—cooperatively.

Vocabulary List

Publishers will reimburse bookstores for the costs of ads, events, or displays through **co-op money.** The bookseller usually is limited to a percentage of their actual sales of the publisher's books; if they sold $2,000 worth of books the previous month, they may be able to spend $100 in co-op money.

Bookstore Giveaways

Sometimes a publisher will initiate contests on a smaller scale to generate interest in a particular title or titles. The contest may focus on either the consumer or the bookseller. A bookstore may compete, for instance, in a "Best Window Display Showcasing *If You Give a Moose a Muffin*" contest. The publisher appoints a winner who receives a prize, like a trip or a certificate. Consumer-oriented contests may include drawings for books during story time or discounts on certain titles.

Yet several more ways to draw attention to your title and market it to the public!

Making a Bestseller

You should know that marketing often makes for arbitrary results. You may think that if your book is good enough, and if your publisher will just buy that ad in *PW*, your book will make it to *The New York Times* bestseller list. Unfortunately, what makes a bestseller is often a tie to a celebrity, a tie-in to some sort of entertainment, or just the fact that it's another book in a successful series.

In fact, go check out *PW*'s list of top-selling children's books for the previous year. You'll find that in many cases, the bestsellers were part of a successful series, or linked to a famous person (sometimes a famous children's book person), a television show, or a movie.

> **Playground Stories**
>
> We analyzed the *Publishers Weekly* list of the top 20 best-selling new hardcover books in 2002. The bad news is that none of them were by unknown authors or illustrators. The good news is that unlike previous years, only a few were tied to a movie or TV show. Five were by celebrities such as Lynne Cheney or children's book celebrities such as Judy Blume and Jan Brett. Several were additions to well-known series (*Lemony Snicket and Junie B. Jones,* for example). And there was a dictionary and a compilation of picture-book classics. Marketing, not media tie-in, helped at least some of these books succeed. That's good news for when you get to be famous!

Please don't think that I'm saying your book will never sit among these bestsellers; it may, but that takes time, and a certain amount of luck. But on the flip side, if your children's book never sees *The New York Times* book review or bestseller lists, don't despair. Steady sales and full speed ahead. Please know you can still be a successful children's book author or illustrator without any of your friends and family realizing it and without seeing your name next to J. K. Rowling's or Maurice Sendak's. In fact, many children's book authors forge a highly successful career without ever seeing their titles on even a specialized children's books bestseller list. Getting there requires hard work and longevity in the business. Don't settle for one book. Just keep cranking out the masterpieces that children love.

The Least You Need to Know

- Many great marketing ideas exist—such as bookstore party kits and bookmarks—but it's questionable whether they actually increase sales.

- Advertisements can be expensive, so publishers specifically target particular publications for optimal exposure.

- In children's book publishing, rarely will you find an ad for just one book. Instead, publishers cluster several like-themed titles into one advertisement.

- Though most everyone maintains aspirations of having a best-selling book, best-sellers are typically connected to celebrities, TV shows, or movies when it comes to children's books.

Chapter 29

Hey, Listen to Me!

In This Chapter

- How to prepare your publicity campaign
- How to improve your chances that the publisher will take notice of your marketing ideas
- How to formulate an angle to generate interest in your book
- Ways to approach and target different media outlets

As an author or illustrator, you may want to go above and beyond what the publisher offers in the way of publicity. You may have a million and one ideas that you'd like to see implemented. Or you may not have a clue how to generate a buzz about your book. In this chapter, you'll learn how to nudge the publisher into doing the little extras, and how to do your own publicity, if you feel you need to do the little extras yourself.

Nudge, Don't Push

There is a fine line between bugging and harassing the publisher with your ideas and contributing constructively to the marketing and publicity of your book. If you do have ideas, approach the publisher in a professional manner. The publicist for your book *will* want to know of any ideas you have regarding the publicity for your book. Many publicists do ask authors to prepare a list of their publicity ideas. Marketing departments may also send a detailed questionnaire. If you get one, fill it out thoroughly. It will be the basis of publicity materials about you and your book.

Once you offer your ideas, let go! Publicists, like your editors, live a harried and hectic workday. The last thing your publicist wants to hear is your voice on three times a day. Instead, politely extend your list of publicity ideas and wait to hear from the publicist. A follow-up call about two weeks after submitting your ideas, however, is okay.

I remember a story from an author at a conference who thought that planetariums might be really great places to publicize her children's book about stars and constellations. The author went down to her local library and researched all the planetariums and natural history museums in the nation—about 2,000 in all. She took the list to her publisher, who put together a pamphlet about her book (and a few others) and sent out a mailing to all the establishments on her list. The mailing proved incredibly successful for the publisher and the sale of the book.

This author simply provided the publishing house with the tools necessary to complete the marketing idea. Though the endeavor took hours for the author—researching all the addresses and locations of planetariums and natural history museums, the work paid off.

Now let's pretend that the author made the suggestion of sending a pamphlet to planetariums, but didn't pursue it any further. Would the publicist have had time to sit down in the library and research the mailing list? No way. She's probably got her hands full with getting information about this season's 50 books out to the standard media sources. By going that extra mile for the publicist, the author helped the marketing idea come to fruition.

Class Rules

Publicists know that the best resource in a book's publicity campaign is the author or illustrator. Oftentimes, the author taps into a creative tie to the book that yields a huge response from the public. It behooves you and the publicist to work in unison. So get to know your publicist and give him or her your ideas—just don't bother the publicist with a million phone calls to share trivial ideas.

Likewise, let's pretend the author had told the publicist the great idea, did not create the list, then called the publicist every day to see if a marketing pamphlet had been designed and sent out. Yikes! Rude, rude, rude. More than likely, the publicist would have erased the messages on voice mail as soon as she recognized that voice. Don't let this happen to you; so nudge, don't push, and be ready to roll up your sleeves and help!

Lend a Helping Pen

Want to know a great way to move along a productive publicity campaign? Offer to write the press materials for the publicist. Consider this: A publicist will not have unlimited time to devote to your book, and may only be able to send it to a standard review list. If you want a wider campaign in such a case, offer to help. If you create the materials for the *press kit*, the time spared the publicist creating the items can then be used in follow-up calls or other marketing-related endeavors for the title.

Follow these steps when approaching your publicist or marketing manager about your ideas. Make an initial phone call and politely say, "Hi, I'm _____, the author of _____. I'd like to help you in any way I can and actually have some publicity ideas. Where might I send them?" If you feel comfortable offering to write the press materials, do it. Put together a packet of *clips*, your ideas, and any press materials you have written and mail them to the publicist. Remember to type! Keep in mind that you can use the materials if the publicist doesn't. Wait a few weeks before calling. Give the publicist a chance to look over the materials. Don't bug the publicist. If it appears that your ideas will not be implemented, start using them yourself if you have the time.

Vocabulary List _____

A **press kit** is a folder of materials about your book sent to the media—newspapers, radio and television stations, journalists, magazines—to alert these outlets to your book's release. The best press kits link the book with a newsworthy item or a hook.

Vocabulary List _____

A **clip** is a copy of an article that either you've written or has been written about you or your book.

The following are several items that may go in a press kit:

◆ **A press release/new book release.** This announces the publication of your book, briefly describes it, and contains contact information. If something about the book holds a topical element, weave that into the release. For example, let's say your children's book is about atomic energy and scientists just found a way to harness atomic energy to cure cancer! The release can touch on the newsworthy aspect of your book.

◆ **Biographies of the author and illustrator.** This is typically one page detailing your life and publishing career. Who better to write this than you?

◆ **Clippings from previous articles written about your book or you.** The press kit may contain the clip from a review in a magazine such as *Booklist* or *Publishers Weekly*—especially if your book received an outstanding review.

> **Class Rules**
>
> If you prepare elements for a press kit, save everything to a computer disk. This way, your publicist will be able to quickly make corrections or edit the documents. Otherwise, someone will need to retype each piece into the computer.

◆ **A mini-feature.** Written like an article, it actually contains much of the same information as the press release, just in a different format. Because it's actually an article, publications may publish it directly. For example, if your kit includes a short feature detailing your struggle to rebuild your home after a fire, which resulted in a children's book about fire protection, your local paper—which doesn't always have the reporter to spare—may use your feature.

◆ **Suggested show or event ideas.** If your book can spawn a demonstration that might prove of interest to a talk show, such as a morning show, you may list the ideas together. For example, your book shows kids how to care for pets. You may write a suggested show topic, detailing the devastating effect of animal neglect and offering ways to help kids really care for their pet and ensure a safe and long life for the kittens and puppies.

◆ **Suggested interview questions.** Again, if a journalist becomes intrigued by your book, the more work you can have ready for the journalist the better chance the writer will do the story.

"I Did It My Way"

Frank Sinatra crooned it in his tune "My Way." Once you learn where your publicist's efforts end, you then need to decide how much of "your way" needs to be implemented. Essentially, how much time and energy do you want to devote to publicizing and fueling sales of your book? If you want to self-publicize, take a look at what you need to do.

In the end, you may decide to let go of your book to the marketing department in a similar way to letting go of it to the illustrator. They know their business, and even if they don't do everything you wish they would, they will do what in their judgment is likely to pay off. So self-publicize by all means, but don't feel that what you do will make or break your book.

Playground Stories

Don't get too caught up in your campaign. Bruce Balan offers this comment: "I spent many years becoming quite well-versed in self-promotion. I've been interviewed by scores of magazines, radio programs, and newspapers. I've created brochures, flyers, and review sheets. I've sent mailings to bookstores. I've spent money to hire a publicist. I've thrown publication parties. I've traveled to, and spoken at, conferences, trade shows, schools, and seminars. And I've come to a few conclusions:

◆ If your publisher is not supportive of your book, it probably doesn't matter what you do.

◆ Even if your publisher is supportive of your book, there are no guarantees of success.

◆ The authors I most admire are those who write well. Not those who promote well."

You Gotta Have an Angle

In order to publicize a book, even a children's book, you need an angle. You need to make your book stand out in a crowd of hundreds of titles—both in the stores and for the media. An entire chapter is devoted to book events in stores (see Chapter 30), so let's look at the media here. First of all, the media offers readers and viewers information. In the case of television, the reporters also need to show something. Conversations with authors are okay, but it's usually better if you can "do" something. In order for a news program to generate a story, they need a news angle—or at least a human interest angle. So your first step in publicizing your title is conceptualizing a hook or an angle. Consider these two hooks for some "pretend" books—both a nonfiction and fictional book:

◆ You've written a how-to garden and plant book for kids. A huge storm sweeps through your town. Gardens are destroyed and trees felled. Your angle is the rebuilding of gardens, teaching kids how to help in the recovery process!

◆ Your picture book details the story of a little boy moving from the neighborhood he's lived in from birth to a new neighborhood across the nation and his integration into a new school. Find out the statistics on children changing schools and the psychological impact. Offer tips in your press packet for acclimating to a new school. Hook adults into buying the book to help their children; the media will want to offer this "good" information to parents.

◆ You've written a multicultural picture book based on an experience you had with your Polish grandfather. You possess a natural "hook" within all the Polish American clubs across the nation. Because a subgroup is represented, you can sell books to those with the same ethnic background.

So let your imagination go wild! How can you hook people to find interest in your book?

Local Yokels, Redux

Your first stop on the self-publicizing train is your local media. Because you live someplace and wrote a book, you're news. If you live in a town or out in the country, try the local papers, radio stations, and TV stations. If you live in a big city, don't expect the major newspapers to be interested (though it certainly doesn't hurt to try *The New York Times* or the *Chicago Tribune* or the *San Francisco Chronicle*). Go for the neighborhood papers, the free monthlies for parents, the local cable TV show, and so on. Where do you get your local news? Go there! Take those releases you've written and fire them off to the local media.

Moving On Up!

Once you've sent your releases and kits off to the local media, concentrate on bigger media outlets—but in many cases only if you can accommodate an interview or plan on traveling in the area. Let's look a little more closely at your publicity options.

Newspapers

Any paper outside of your area will want one of two things—a news link or that you will be appearing in their town. Contact the feature editor if the angle you have involves a trend or a newsworthy attribute. Contact the children's book review editor if you plan on a signing or an appearance someplace.

Can You Keep a Secret?

Want to learn more? Susan Raab, children's books marketing consultant, has a fantastic archive of her "To Market" column at her website at www. raabassociates.com/tomarket/ tomarket.htm. Elsewhere on her site, you'll find information on her book, *An Author's Guide to Children's Book Promotion* (which, in spite of the title, illustrators will find useful, too).

Radio

Radio programs are great for calling you and conducting live or taped interviews over the phone. Find a media directory in your local library and go through the listing of shows by content. If your children's book focuses on sports fitness for children, then pitch yourself as an interview on the morning sports show. Producers of talk radio are constantly scrambling to fill the airtime with interesting and informational interviews. Don't limit yourself to approaching only the book shows. Generally, these shows deal with weighty adult books anyway.

Television

Again, are you in town for an appearance? Television programs need to show their viewers something—you! And moreover, you should have some informational or newsworthy hook for the appearance. We've given several examples of hooks tied to specific book subjects, but you can make yourself the hook. For example, until he got to be known as an illustrator, David Wisniewski got more attention from having gone to clown school than from having created a beautiful book.

Self-publicizing can be a full-time job, or you might decide to skip it completely. Whichever direction you go in is up to you, but do consider your options.

CAUTION

Class Rules

Author tours are expensive, and children's publishers don't pay for them. Unless you have money to burn, don't put yourself on a six-city tour across the nation. Certainly, if business takes you to Boston for a week and time permits, contact the media about appearances. Otherwise, save the travel for a vacation some place fun!

The Least You Need to Know

- Offer your publicity ideas to the marketing and publicity departments of your publishing house—but do it gently.

- Any materials that you can put together to help your publicist and the book's publicity are much appreciated. Moreover, you can use them for self-publicizing your book.

- Don't devote all your time to the success of your book through diligent marketing and publicity—write more books!

- Conceptualize "hooks" for your book to generate interest in different media outlets and make your book stand out over all the others on the market.

Chapter **30**

Bookstore Business

In This Chapter

- ◆ Why and how bookstore events fuel sales
- ◆ Whom to approach about an event/book signing
- ◆ What sort of events work best and bring in the crowds
- ◆ What your part as an author is in the event
- ◆ Ways to fuel sales of your book the day of the event

Whether you plan to drive all over the continent or stay locally to publicize your book, you won't want to miss out on the bookstore connection. The fierce competition between mega-chains like Barnes & Noble and Borders against the independent stores actually benefits you and your book. How? Each establishment is continually looking for great ways to draw in customers. The latest trend in bookstore community relations is the book "event": Never do a "signing" if you can avoid it.

In this chapter, you'll learn how to navigate your way to the right person to book the event, what type of events draw in the crowds, and how you can help fuel sales of your book at the event. Get ready because we're having a party!

A Tale of Two (or More) Bookstores

Just about any author or illustrator has a story about doing a reading from his or her book, and then sitting at a table and signing books, for all of 17 people. I'm telling you up front: Don't do signings. If you go to work with a bookstore, make an event out of it. Bookstores want events—they've got competitors to contend with.

Once upon a time, the quaint bookstore up the street ruled the literary roost. People came from all over the neighborhood to buy the latest best-selling fiction title or charming child's picture book. But today, more and more independent bookstores are giving way to *superstores* stocked with more than 100,000 titles dispersed into myriad departments. *You've Got Mail*, the romantic comedy starring Meg Ryan and Tom Hanks, showcased a love relationship between an independent children's bookstore owner (Ryan) and corporate bookstore chain entrepreneur (Hanks). In the real world, you know who the big companies are: Barnes & Noble, Borders, Tower, Crown. Almost anywhere you go, you'll find a Borders and a Barnes & Noble going head-to-head. Now factor in the smaller bookstore chains and the independents stores; with so many choices, competition rages to draw in and retain customers.

One of the great ways these bookstores contribute to the community and then bring in a loyal buying base is through the efforts of community relations departments. Today, even bookstores possess a public relations person in each location. The PR manager of a bookstore chain may address the media over a controversial title, but more common duties include planning events around books and author book signings. Essentially, the community relations manager churns out a monthly calendar of events—everything from weekly story times to monthly book club meetings to author signings and informational seminars. By hosting these "free and open-to-the-public" events, the stores draw in more customers, thereby selling more books—more of your book! The best events—those that bring in the customers—are the parties and seminars. And nowhere are the book parties happier, bigger, or more fun than in the children's departments.

Vocabulary List

In the book business, a **superstore** is a large store typically stocking more than 100,000 titles. Some superstores even sell other products besides books, such as CDs, stationery, and toys. Two chains known for their superstores are Barnes & Noble and Borders Books and Music.

Kids love books, and love socializing at events that deal with their favorite book. Can you remember your own fascination with the *Little House on the Prairie* series or the *Hardy Boys* books? Wouldn't you just loved to have spent an evening once a month dressing up like Laura Ingalls, reading passages from *Little House in the Big Woods*, and learning how to make a treat that Laura probably made more than 100 years ago? Little girls today can enjoy activities like these by participating in numerous American Girl Clubs run out of bookstore chains. Beyond the clubs for kids based on series like *Animorphs* and *American Girls*, bookstores offer pint-size consumers and their parents other opportunities to love (and buy) books. From story time hours to character costume parties to parent/child book clubs, bookstores around the globe are clamoring for ways to excite children to read and their parents to purchase.

Thus, a great opportunity arises for you to self-publicize your book. And the best part? You can either hit only the local stores or travel as far and wide as you please. But having an event surrounding your book at one or several bookstores isn't necessarily easy. More likely than not, calling and asking a befuddled floor salesclerk about a book signing won't result in an event. You need a plan to get in good with the store manager and/or community relations coordinator/manager.

Making Contact

Let's say your book, *Giggles and Grins*, a pop-up book of funny faces and jokes, just shipped hot off the presses to bookstores everywhere. And in your hometown, three bookstores exist as possible event targets. The first thing you must do—before pitching a giggly-good event—is find out if the bookstore even offers customers a *calendar of events*. The smaller mall stores, for instance, don't have the room or staff to host events. Call the store first and ask an employee whether or not the store hosts book-related events. If they don't, don't bother the staffer anymore. Move on. If the representative says yes, ask who the events contact is, and ask to speak with them or leave a message.

Vocabulary List

Bookstores that showcase author signings, story times for children, book clubs, and other author-related events out of the store typically print a monthly calendar that details each event, including the date and time. A paragraph description gives customers a clear idea of what to expect. These flyers are usually called **calendar of events** or the **event calendar**.

Who You Gonna Call?

As mentioned earlier, many bookstores now employ a person to handle all book-related events and community interaction, often called a community relations coordinator (CRC) or a community relations manager (CRM). These employees are the ones who

Class Rules

Don't book a party or gathering in two competitive bookstores around the same time. You glut the market of interest in your book and the event. Pick your favorite store first and give it first priority. Then, later on down the road, book another event at the competition. There will be less confusion and more trust in you as an author by the stores.

can help you to publicize your book in a bookstore. The CRC in a typical store looks actively, if not desperately, for authors and illustrators like you to host events and fill the dates on their calendars. If the store you're hoping to book an event in does not employ a special community relations representative, then you'll want to speak directly to the store manager. In some cases, the person you need to reach isn't even in the store; Borders, for example, handles events through "area marketing managers," each of whom is responsible for several stores. So make sure you find out whom you need to contact.

Leave a Message at the Tone

Chances are pretty good that you'll get a direct number for the community relations coordinator. Chances are equally as good that you'll need to leave a message. Because of the sheer number of calls this employee receives—everyone from schools asking for donations to authors wanting to book an event—the CRC frequents the phone line and is also often out in the community working, too. Jenn Pfeiffer, a former CRM for Barnes & Noble stores in the San Francisco Bay Area, once lamented the 90 messages she received in the 2 days during the week that she wasn't working! "I had to check my messages both days and clear off as many as I could each time just to leave space for my mailbox. Otherwise, it would fill too quickly," remembers Pfeiffer.

Because these employees receive an inordinate number of calls in which the caller rambles on and on about his or her business, you will endear yourself and retain a greater chance of store support for your event if you follow these simple guidelines when making first contact:

- Begin your message with your name, preferably spelled, and your phone number. Many times, the CRM will log the calls. Then repeat the number.

- Give the title of your book and the ISBN.

- Include a time frame in which you'd like an event to occur.

- Indicate that you will send a press release about the book and any media clippings (if you have them) and a letter detailing the event you envision.

- Send the letter!

- Wait patiently to hear from the representative.

If you can include a review copy of your book, do it. If the CRC or CRM decides to schedule an event with you, he or she will need to scan the cover of the book for posters that may be displayed in the store before the reading.

Class Rules

Don't wait to call and attempt to book an event with a bookstore just weeks before your arrival in town. Calendars of events fill up three months or more in advance. The CRC or CRM actually writes the copy for the calendar a month in advance. And then the copy must go to the designer and the printer. Think ahead—at least three months into the future. If you don't, you're likely to hear, "I'm sorry, but my calendar is already full!"

Party Plans

Once you've made contact, you'll likely find that whoever it is you've contacted wants to see those ideas of yours on paper. It's up to you to sell the store on the event idea.

The CRC wants to throw well-attended events that bring in customers. If an event—such as a straightforward reading and signing by an unknown author—seems unimaginative and certain to fail, the CRC won't book it. Or if the CRC does book it, you may end up wishing he hadn't.

So put on your creative cap and come up with a plan—several ideas to pitch the store's way for fun events. Your options are only limited by your ingenuity, but you will need to work with the options available in the store. Let's look at the standard event categories that occur in the children's departments of bookstores for which you can design your event:

Class Rules

Unadorned book signings, in particular, can prove brutal for authors and bookstore personnel. Unless the author is a celebrity like Hillary Clinton or Arnold Schwartzenegger or a series is beloved (the *Harry Potter* books are a good example), the public won't show up. The author is left to sit at a table as people nervously walk by. Not an ego boost, for sure!

- ◆ **Preschool/school-age story times.** Most stores offer story times twice a week or more. Oftentimes, the children's department supervisor or another employee picks picture books at random and reads them during the story hour. Really great story time facilitators incorporate themes into the hour and sometimes even include finger-play games and singing.

◆ **Series club event.** Kind of like a book club for kids. Groups of devotees to a particular series gather at the store to meet and talk about their favorite books in the cycle. The *American Girls* Club or *Animorph* Clubs popping up all over are good examples of this kind of event. Oftentimes, the facilitator of the club will incorporate other works of children's literature into the activities of the evening. For instance, if the *American Girls* Club focuses on the character living in the 1940s, the leader may showcase a display of old radios from the era and show the girls other books they may like to read to further explore the role of women during World War II.

◆ **Character parties.** Always a favorite event with the little tykes! At these events, your children's beloved storybook characters make an appearance—like Clifford the Big Red Dog, or the Mouse from *If You Give a Mouse a Cookie*. Then several of the stories from that character's repertoire or from the author who created the character are read to the kids. Sometimes treats are passed out, too, to add to the festivities. If your book showcases a noteworthy character, you might want to make your own costume or even puppet likenesses of characters. Along with reading your book to the group, you may host a puppet show!

◆ **Author readings and presentations.** The author of the book reads directly to the kids. Sometimes, like in the case of David Carter, the famed author of those fabulous pop-up bug books, the author treats the kids to a *chalk talk*. In a chalk talk, the author/illustrator shows the audience of kids how the ideas become a book. Puppet or props (with practice first!) can also enhance a reading.

◆ **Activity event.** In this type of event, an activity focuses on a book. If you're an illustrator or author/illustrator, this kind of event could be for you. Show your audience how you made your book, and turn them loose on making their own.

You Gotta Have a Gimmick

Back to your plan. The CRC or CRM will help you more if you help him more. Meaning: Give him every possible idea you have for an event and offer to help publicize the event, too. Just as when you attempt to garner media coverage, you'll need to go the extra mile here, too. Send the CRC a press kit if you have one. With the press kit, include a cover letter identifying …

◆ Your name, your book's title, ISBN, and publisher.

◆ Where the publisher can get copies of the book if not distributed through standard means or self-published.

- ◆ The event you envision.

- ◆ The dates and times you are available to accommodate an event. (Remember: Think three months or more in advance.)

- ◆ How you plan to publicize the event and draw in book-buying crowds (see Chapter 29).

- ◆ A template for a press release/event announcement to send to calendar editors and various local publications.

Check with the store shortly before the event, to confirm that they have sent out the press kits, and that they are expecting you. The best-laid plans can go wrong! On the day, come early, introduce yourself to the staff, and then introduce yourself to customers. They won't all know about your event, but they might be happy to stay for it.

Do all of this, and you're well on your way to having a real *event*, not just a book signing or reading. Almost all the people coming to one of those will be loyal friends and family. You want to get people who don't know you to come. Plan and publicize an event, working closely with the bookstore personnel, and you will draw people.

Can You Keep a Secret? _____

Keep copies of event calendars that list your presentation. Moreover, keep copies of your event proposal letter and press kit that you sent to the CRM. The next time you are looking to self-promote your book through a bookstore, you can reuse your ideas and also provide the new CRM a glimpse into the success of your last event. The calendars also typically list phone numbers for the stores, so the CRM can easily call the store that already hosted an event with you and either find out what worked fabulously or refrain from repeating any mistakes, too.

And afterward, don't forget to write a thank you note to the CRM. With any luck, they'll remember you warmly, and that can only help when your next book comes out.

The Least You Need to Know

- ◆ Bookstores, eager to draw in a loyal customer base in the midst of fierce competition, host book signings and author events regularly.

- ◆ You can fuel sales of your book by booking an author event in bookstores.

- ◆ Your point of contact at a bookstore is either the community relations manager/coordinator or the store manager.

◆ Make contact with the community relations employee at least three months in advance of the date you'd like to host an event.

◆ Don't assume that a reading is all that's needed to draw in the kids. Plan either a themed event or an activity to engage the kids and their parents, and publicize your event.

Chapter 31

Back to School

In This Chapter

- ◆ What a "school visit" is and what you must do to set one up

- ◆ What to expect in payment and fees

- ◆ Some of the many possible kinds of visits

- ◆ Benefits that go beyond promoting your book

So far, you may be getting the idea that you can play only a limited role in the marketing and publicizing of your book. True—except for one key area. Going back to school, by which I mean doing school visits, can do lots for the sales of your books over the long term, and at the same time serve as a useful source of income.

School Visit Basics

School visits happen all over the country, at every level of school, for a simple reason. They work. Subject-area teachers want to generate excitement about science or math or American history, and English teachers, reading teachers, and librarians are always looking for ways to ignite a love of reading and writing. One way is through a visit by a successful author. Illustrators do school visits, too, though you may have to work a little harder to persuade a school that you can make your visit curriculum-relevant.

A school visit does not necessarily mean you go speak to a school assembly, or launch into a monologue in a fourth-grade classroom. A teacher or a school will most want you to visit if you produce some sort of learning activity or program. These can take place in classrooms or in larger groups. As you'll find later in the chapter, there are many possible kinds of visits.

Before going any farther, ask yourself if you are cut out for school visits. Are you comfortable with public speaking? Are you comfortable with a room full of children? Note that you shouldn't have to be keeping them in order—the teacher or librarian *should* do that—but can you keep them engaged? If you're not sure, start small, and try out your approach at your child's school or your neighborhood library, with a small group. Schools want dynamic speakers who will get children excited about reading or a particular subject, so don't go out into schools if that's not you. There are other ways that you can promote your books.

If you can do school visits—many authors and illustrators enjoy them—you'll find that they are a great way to promote your books. But note that they work best over a period of time. As you do more and more visits, you build up an audience for new books, and you inform people about your backlist. School visits, in fact, may be the single most effective thing you can do to keep your books in print.

The basic things you need to do for an actual visit are simple. You work out a plan for a visit with a contact person, being sure to get the plan down in writing. You visit the school and get the students excited about books in general and your books in particular. And you get paid for this. Yes, you can and should charge a fee for most kinds of school visits. Many schools have budgets for author visits, and might not take you as seriously if you *don't* charge a fee. Considering the time involved to prepare and travel, even as a beginner you should charge $200 to $300 for a 1-hour presentation, and several hundred dollars for a full day at a school. Experienced authors charge considerably more. Schools in rural areas or the inner cities may have less money at their disposal, so do waive fees when necessary. But remember that doing a school visit well is hard work, and that the number of books you sell is unlikely to compensate you for your time. You deserve a fee, negotiated in advance and paid on the day of your visit, and reimbursement of your travel costs.

> **CAUTION**
>
> **Class Rules** _____
>
> If you are at all interested in school and other visits, run to your local bookstore and order *Terrific Connections with Authors, Illustrators, and Storytellers*, by Toni Buzzeo and Jane Kurtz.

As you get ready to embark into the world of school visiting, don't set off without *Terrific Connections with Authors, Illustrators, and Storytellers*, by Toni Buzzeo and Jane Kurtz. If you take a cursory look at it, it seems to be for librarians and schools who want to have authors and illustrators visit them. But it's also the best (indeed, so far as I know, the only) guide for the authors and illustrators themselves. You just have to read it the other way around. As Toni Buzzeo commented in an e-mail to me, "Even though Jane and I wrote *TC* for teachers and librarians, we think that as many authors and illustrators own it! It really is a fabulous resource for those of us who are children's authors and illustrators. Not only does it give book people a comprehensive view of the experience from the 'other side of the contract' so to speak, but it examines, in great detail, the intricacies involved in the practicalities as well as really meaningful preparation." If any resource is indispensable, this one is—I drew on it heavily while writing this chapter.

Making Contact

If you want to make school visits and have ideas for some workshops or other learning experiences, your next step is to set some up. How do you do that? There are many ways. Whichever way you use, keep in mind that you may need to plan several months to a year ahead—if you contact a school in March, for example, the earliest you will actually visit is likely to be September.

When you are just getting started, contacting schools in your area and letting them know you are available is a good first step. If you are calling a school "cold," you can start at the top, and talk to the principal. Explain what you want to do, and ask who you should speak to. Some people find that it may be best to just ask to speak to a reading teacher or librarian—or to ask the school secretary who she thinks would be most interested in bringing an author or illustrator to the school. If someone is interested, follow up with him: get him copies of your book(s), or a proposal for your visit, as soon as possible.

Publishers also get requests from schools for popular authors and illustrators. Typically, the well-known ones get many more requests than they could possibly fulfill, and in such cases the person in the marketing department who handles school visits will suggest someone else. Let this person know that you are eager to visit schools, and you're on your way.

Contact local arts councils and see if they have lists of recommended writers and artists. If they do, get on the list; schools looking for speakers may well use those lists. Similarly, join organizations both local and national that work in children's books and literacy, and see if that leads to some referrals.

And of course, talk to everyone you know, ask other authors and illustrators for referrals, write articles on children's books, volunteer in your local library, and generally get involved in your community. Many school visits come about because of personal contacts.

Can You Keep a Secret?

In a number of states, the state arts commission sponsors grant-based programs to help school districts pay artists such as writers and illustrators to come do programs of varying lengths. Typically the artist registers with the arts commission, which then produces a list for school districts to draw from as needs arise. Contact your state arts commission or education department to find out what opportunities exist.

If you develop a good program, and if you have a steady flow of books coming out, soon you'll have more requests than you can handle.

"Well, No One Told *Me* You Were Coming"

Talk to any veteran of a school visit, and you will hear stories ranging from the horrific to the totally wonderful. One horror is to go to the school office and be met with a blank stare from the school secretary when you attempt to explain why you are there: "Well, no one told *me* you were coming." Another is to discover that none of the students in the classrooms you are visiting has read even one of your books. And then there's being told, after three days in a school: "Oh, by the way, we found out that we can't pay you, so here is a bag of cookies to show our appreciation."

On the other hand, people also tell stories of arriving at a school that has been decorated to reflect the content of one of their books, of the excitement of being in a room full of children who have read every single one of their books, and of being dazzled with wonderful artwork, plays, and student-crafted books, all done in preparation for a visit.

As Toni and Jane emphasize in their *Terrific Connections*, preparation is important. They went so far as to craft a two-page "wish list" to use with schools. You might want to create your own, because you've got to try to make sure that the school is as prepared as you are. This could become the basis for the written agreement that details what you will do and when. If you've carefully crafted a lively presentation for fifth graders that shows the stages your manuscript and book went through, you would have a hard time adjusting it on-the-fly for a first-grade class you weren't told about. Be professional, but be sure to ask questions about what the school is doing and what they expect of you. You should even make sure that you have breaks and lunch time in your schedule. Cover all the practical issues: If you are going to do a book signing, make sure that the books have been ordered well in advance. Don't let the school assume that you will bring them. And again, get this all down in writing, and then make sure that someone at the school signs off on that document before your visit.

With the practical side nailed down, get to work making sure that you will have the best possible experience with the children, and that what you will do in the school won't just be a fun break from routine, but a learning experience that will feed into the regular curriculum. When planning a school visit, Toni starts by creating "extensive, standards-based curriculum guides" about her books, and sends them to all the schools she visits, with tips on how to use them. She wants to make sure that all the children she meets have read at least one of her books before she visits. Strive to do the same, and make suggestions for follow-up activities, too.

You're in the Spotlight—Now What?

So after all this talk of planning, what should you do in a school visit? That depends partly on the kind of visit. You may visit one classroom for 45 minutes, or spend a week or more as an artist-in-residence. You may be the only book person visiting, or be part of a month-long children's literature festival. Keep in mind the age level of the students you are facing as you plan your approach: Second graders appreciate lots of visuals and a chance to interact with you, while older students may respond well to a short presentation followed by a group discussion. For either group, take "stuff"— books, proofs, marked-up manuscripts, the contents of your idea file—concrete materials that will help them connect to the somewhat abstract notion of creative process.

The following sections discuss some of the possibilities for school visits.

The Assembly

In an assembly, you address the whole school. This is not an ideal situation! In order for this to work, your book must possess appeal across all grade levels of the school— such as from kindergarten to sixth, or from ninth through twelfth. Or you must have something to talk to the children about in an exciting way, or to perform, that goes across all grade levels.

In assemblies, in particular, you can't stick to your identity as an author or an illustrator. You must be a performance artist engaging a diverse array of kids. As an example, let's say that you are a police officer by trade and you've written a book on safety issues for kids. You may bring your book and talk to a room of kids about safety measures and even demonstrate with audience participants how to escape a possible abduction or what to do if someone tries to harm them. Though this particular idea would work, it can be difficult to come up with creative, assembly ideas, so you should avoid them if possible. On the other hand, if you find this kind of challenge inviting, go for it.

Story Times and Reading

You may be asked to go into a classroom and read your picture book to the kids. Or if you've written a young reader or young adult novel, to read a passage from it. Don't settle for this if you can avoid it. Talk to the teacher and find out how you can tie into the curriculum she's teaching, and develop pre-visit and post-visit activities. At the very least, try to see to it that the children read some of your books before you arrive, and build an activity around them, with your actual reading time kept to a minimum.

Class Workshop

Sometimes, focusing on your book is enough. Classes involved in making their own books as part of learning the writing process, for example, may invite you to talk about how your book came about. Children are fascinated by the multiple drafts you go through, intrigued by a copy editor's marks (so similar to their teacher's comments), and especially interested in materials like color proofs, which you sometimes can get from a publisher after the book has been printed.

For teenagers or middle graders, writing workshops can feed especially well into a school's curriculum. If you're a mystery writer, for example, you might create mystery stories with ninth graders, starting with some exploration of the elements of a mystery.

If you feel more comfortable with a straightforward public-speaking approach, keep in mind that teachers are always looking for real-life examples for their high school students of English-related professions. You are a professional writer once you've published, so you are an excellent resource for a teacher—you can guest lecture in the class on everything from writing your book to your career choice.

Workshops don't have to be tied to school time. You may want to offer students through the district a weekend or Saturday workshop. Perhaps your book deals with horse-shoeing. Why not give a seminar or workshop on the "Lost Art of Shoeing a Horse" to all the 4-H students? Or if you've written a novel, you could turn your experience into a writing workshop and critique seminar for students. The ideas are limitless; in fact I urge you to brainstorm a few right now.

Storytelling

This category applies especially to folktale tellers. Storytelling requires a dramatic retelling of the tale. One's voice, gestures, accent, mannerisms, some props, and so on are all employed to enhance the story. If you have a flair for the dramatic, and are good at memorizing stories, this is a great option for you.

Don't forget older students. High school students relish a really well-told story as much as the next person—the performance art of *storytelling*. A skit, a telling of some folklore—these are other ways you can expose your book to the education system. Let's say that you've put your own spin on a relatively new African American folktale. You are also a storyteller by trade. Seek out the teachers and find out whether one class over the other teaches multiculturalism in literature. Then book yourself in the school.

Vocabulary List

Storytelling involves more than reading a book. A storyteller vividly brings the tale alive through interpretation, voice, and dramatics. You watch the book instead of read it when a storyteller becomes involved.

Carnivals and Other Fund-Raisers

Many schools hold carnivals as fund-raisers during the year. Always looking for interesting booths, the school might let you set up a reading/book sale booth at the carnival, for a fee or otherwise; here's a case where the school doesn't pay you. The school may require you to donate a percentage of sales.

Or you might work with a school that's planning a book fair, and offer to do readings to make the event more than just a book sale. Of course, you'll want them to carry your books and provide some signing time.

On Beyond Schools

Everything in this chapter focuses on schools, but you can apply this approach to other related venues. Libraries also welcome authors, both for individual sessions and as part of larger events, such as "Read Across America," Sponsored by the National Education Association and described as "the nation's largest reading event." You can find a place at local book festivals, young author conferences, and the like. The contacts you gain by being active in schools may ultimately lead to invitations to regional conferences and national conventions of educational organizations. You can even do virtual visits by having an online chat with a classroom of children on the other side of the country, or extend a visit by working with some students on a project to be posted on their school's website. Your imagination may be the only limit to the possibilities. Stay active, talk to people, and sooner or later you'll find yourself exploring some of these other options.

Playground Stories

One of the most active authors in visiting schools is Jerry Pallotta, known for such nonfiction picture books in an alphabet format as *The Dinosaur Alphabet Book* and *The Jet Alphabet Book*. He visits 150 schools a year, speaking to teachers as well as to elementary and junior high students. His program features a slide show that he uses to explain the process behind the creation of his books—a focus that ties in nicely to writing and reading programs. His constant traveling helps to keep interest in his backlist alive, and to build an audience for new books.

On the Road

How busy *do* you want to be? You'll have to figure that out for yourself. If your books are the kind that "work" in the schools, then you can be very busy with school visits, and doing so will not only sell an existing book but also create an audience for future ones. Imagine that you've successfully visited 100 schools over a 3-year period. When a new book comes out, teachers at all of them will be interested in hearing about it, and many of the students will still remember you, too. So make sure that all those schools know about the new book. And go on the road with a new program.

Being on the road is not a wholly positive experience. As Jane Kurtz says:

> Many authors tell me they were shocked to wake up one day and realize they were not living the life they dreamed of and worked toward when they'd decided to become an author. Travel can be draining—longer than ever waits in airports, for instance, and the occasional "conference center" that is suspiciously like a dorm. But I do think we are lucky. We have this opportunity to connect directly with our audience, to get our books into the hands of readers who had never heard of us or our books before we visited their school or town. Your publisher may long ago have written off your book as "old news," but when you hear the hushed whisper of that kid who says, "I loved your book," you sigh with joy and go happily back to confront the spiders in the dormitory bathroom.

School visits can become a full-time job, but only if you make them so! Generally speaking, school visits are a great way to gain recognition of your book. But most authors probably won't make an income able to support them on school visits alone. So take advantage of the benefits of school visits, but not to the detriment of your writing. Continue to write. Ultimately, more books will result in more income.

Finally, keep in mind that school visits aren't just a way to make some extra income and to promote your books. They are also a way to connect directly to your audience. It can be immensely satisfying—if not overwhelming—to be in a roomful of children, all of whom have read your book, love it, and are excited to be meeting, perhaps for the first time, a real live author or illustrator. Memories of such experience, or letter(s) from children received months afterward, will help to keep you inspired. You owe it to yourself to have these experiences.

The Least You Need to Know

- Many different ways exist to show off your book at a school visit—including reading the story, giving a presentation, or selling your books as a fundraiser.

- Work through the right channel—it might be a teacher, but it might be the library media specialist.

- School visits can pay very well, but you may need to charge less when getting started or waive your fees with schools that lack the funding.

- School visits can add significantly to the sales of a book.

- School visits also help you gain recognition and an audience for future books.

I Won a Prize!

In This Chapter

◆ What the really big awards are in children's literature

◆ National awards that you might hope to win

◆ Lists that make a difference in your reputation

◆ Why state awards mean something

◆ The effects of these awards or recognition

Right now, you may just want to get your gosh-darned book published and don't even fathom the kudos that may befall you, but listen up. Within the children's publishing arena many opportunities exist for authors to achieve recognition and awards. Not that winning a blue ribbon always gains you everything, but it sure can help provide longevity for your career and aspirations. After all, if you win one of the major children's book awards, consider your book a classic with almost guaranteed sales for future generations. Also, publishers will be a good bit more eager to do another book with you when your first book received an award like the ALA Coretta Scott King or the National Book Award. In this chapter, you'll learn about the many ways you can achieve recognition and the admiration of your colleagues.

The Big Ones—Newbery and Caldecott

Walk into any big bookstore (and certainly smaller ones, too) and you'll likely find an entire bookcase showcasing the Newbery and Caldecott Award–winning books. These two awards remain the Academy Awards of the children's book industry. Unlike other children's book awards, which may have little immediate impact on sales, these two also drive publishers back to the printers for tens of thousands of copies. Why? The public recognizes them, and the winners are going to sell. Let's take a close look at each.

Newbery

Each year, the Association for Library Service to Children (ALSC) of the American Library Association (ALA) awards the Newbery Medal to "the most distinguished American children's book" published the previous year. Just a little history here—on June 21, 1921, Frederic G. Melcher proposed the award to a meeting of the Children's Librarians' Section of the ALA and suggested that it be named for the eighteenth-century English bookseller John Newbery.

Can You Keep a Secret?

For a complete listing of all Newbery and Caldecott medalists and honor books, consult *The Newbery and Caldecott Awards: A Guide to the Medal and Honor Books,* published by the ALA. Or online, visit these web pages: www.ala.org/alsc/newbery.html and caldecott.html.

The Newbery holds special significance among all children's book awards because it was the first children's book award in the world. Although only one book receives the actual medal each year, as many as several noteworthy books, referred to as "honor books" also draw recognition.

Past popular Newbery titles include *The Giver,* by Lois Lowry; *A Wrinkle in Time,* by Madeleine L'Engle; and *Sarah Plain and Tall,* by Patricia MacLachlan.

Caldecott

The Newbery Medal certainly paved the way for more recognition of outstanding children's writers. However, the illustrators of children's books found no kudos thrown their way. So in 1937—to give illustrators the honor and encouragement they deserved for bringing tales to life in picture books—a second medal was created. The Caldecott Medal, named in honor of nineteenth-century English illustrator Randolph Caldecott, resulted, and is awarded annually by the ALSC, to the artist of the most distinguished American picture book for children. (Of course, the author deserves some credit, too, for creating the text that inspired the illustrations, but it's the illustrator who receives the Caldecott.)

Class Rules

In the terms and criteria for the Caldecott Medal, a note exists that reads: "The committee should keep in mind that the award is for distinguished illustrations in a picture book and for excellence of pictorial presentation for children. The award is not for didactic intent or for popularity." Just because a book sells well, doesn't necessarily make it a winner among the experts—keep that in mind for other awards.

Recent winners include Emily Arnold McCully's *Mirette on the High Wire*, Eric Rohmann's *My Friend Rabbit*, and Mary Azarian's illustrations for *Snowflake Bentley*. And just like the Newbery Medal, those books not chosen but deemed wonderful anyway earn the title "honor book."

Other National Awards

But just because you don't win a Newbery or Caldecott doesn't mean you'll never receive any recognition for your hard work. Myriad other awards exist to provide credit where credit is due—and offer an alternative list of noteworthy books besides those given kudos as Newbery or Caldecott.

The National Book Awards

First up: the National Book Awards. In 1950, a consortium of book publishing groups sponsored the first annual National Book Awards Ceremony and Dinner in New York City. The goal of the consortium was to enhance the public's awareness of exceptional books written by Americans and increase literacy and the joy of reading. For more than 50 years, the National Book Awards have conferred the preeminent literary prizes each year within 4 different genres: fiction, nonfiction, poetry, and children's literature. The winners earn "fat bank," a $10,000 cash award, along with a crystal sculpture. The children's book category was recently reinstated after not being included for a number of years.

I Have a Dream: The Coretta Scott King Award

The Coretta Scott King Award honors African American authors and illustrators for outstanding contributions to children's and young adult literature that promote understanding and appreciation of the culture and contribution of all races. Named after

Can You Keep a Secret?

We highly recommend you seek out titles of past winners and peruse them to gain an understanding about the focus on multicultural literature and the world. For a complete listing of all the Coretta Scott King awards since 1970, surf online to www.ala.org/srrt/csking/.

the wife of slain civil rights leader Dr. Martin Luther King Jr., the award, beyond honoring her courage and determination to continue his work for peace, also honors the late leader.

In 1999, the Coretta Scott King Award celebrated its 30th anniversary. The winners of this award for the year 2000 were *Bud, Not Buddy*, by Christopher Paul Curtis, also a Newbery winner, and for illustrations, *In the Time of the Drums*, illustrated by Brian Pinkney with text by Kim L. Siegelson.

Big Award from *Little House* Lady

The ALSC every three years confers the Laura Ingalls Wilder Award to either an author or illustrator whose books, published in the United States, have made, over a period of years, a substantial and lasting contribution to literature for children. Call this a lifetime achievement award.

Few children don't know who Laura Ingalls Wilder was. Her series of books beginning with *The Little House in the Big Woods* provides pertinent historical information, as well as entertainment.

Past recipients of this award include Russell Freedman, Virginia Hamilton, Marcia Brown, Maurice Sendak, and Ruth Sawyer. Eric Carle was named the winner in 2003.

Are these the only national awards? Of course not. As you spend more time in this field, you'll learn about others, from the Scott O'Dell Award for the best historical fiction, to the Golden Kite Award, given by the Society of Children's Book Writers and Illustrators to a member, to the Orbis Pictus Award, given by the National Council of Teachers of English to the best nonfiction for children. None of them have the impact of the two biggies, but they'll all help your reputation and may help backlist sales—continued sales over time.

Teen Angst Awards

Up until the 1950s, the concept of the "teenager" barely existed. One moved directly from childhood into the adult world because of the necessities of life. But with U.S. prosperity and the baby boomers, suddenly teens came of age. Teen angst, rebellion, rock and roll, and even teen entertainment emerged. With the myriad emotions rumbling around within adolescents, it's no wonder this group embraces books that speak to them. Once teenagers were noticed, it wasn't long before the "young adult" book category was invented. And in response to those individuals who really speak clearly to the teen audience two awards stand out: the Margaret A. Edwards Award and the Michael L. Printz Award.

Margaret A. Edwards Award

Established in 1988 and sponsored by *School Library Journal*, this $2,000 award recognizes an author whose work or works provides young adults with a window through which they can view their world and which will help them to grow and to understand themselves and their role in society. Most important, the award recognizes those books that help adolescents become self-aware and address concerns about their relationship within our society.

Playground Stories

Who was Margaret A. Edwards? She was an administrator of young adult literature at Enoch Pratt Free Library in Baltimore, Maryland, for more than three decades. Edwards believed in the need to bring young adult literature and library services to young adults and spent her professional career pioneering many programs for her purpose. She also authored *The Fair Garden and the Swarm of Beasts: The Library and the Young Adult*— a work that explains her philosophy for turning young adults into readers.

Past recipients of the award include such authors as S. E. Hinton for works like *The Outsiders* and *Rumble Fish*, and Robert Cormier for *The Chocolate War*.

The Michael L. Printz Award

With the new millennium came a new award that distinguishes the best of the best of young adult literature—with edge. The Michael L. Printz Award honors the highest literary achievement in young adult books for a novel published the preceding year. In 2000, Walter Dean Myers received the award for his book *Monster*, an emotionally charged story of a 16-year-old arrested for murder. Look for upcoming Michael L. Printz Awards. The recipients are certain to push the envelope and speak to young people in a language they understand.

Get on These Lists!

Earning an award such as the ones discussed so far probably takes as much luck as skill. Dozens may have a serious chance in any year, but only one or a few are chosen. Needless to say, you may not ever receive a Newbery or Caldecott. But that doesn't mean that you can't see your book on some noteworthy lists, lists that may not have an immediate impact on sales but do add luster to your name and possibly longevity to your book.

ALA Notables

To recognize the best children's books of the year, the ALA doesn't just pick a few select titles for its awards. A committee also compiles the list called "ALA Notable Books for Children," made up of 60 or 70—or perhaps a few more—children's books that the committee considers to be the best of the year. Unlike the procedure with many other awards, the committee discusses the books it is considering in a public meeting at the ALA's semiannual conventions. Getting on this list almost certainly means your book will sell better to libraries.

 Class Rules _____

It really is up to you and your publisher to help your book find its way onto lists and to be considered for awards. Each award, medal, and notable list requires a process. An editor or committee needs to see your book to know it exists. Check that your publisher is actively submitting your books to the awards previously mentioned. If not, consider researching the awards yourself and making your own submissions.

Children's Choices

Do you want to get past the gatekeepers and be recognized by children, your true audience? Then being named to the "Children's Choices" list, an annual publication sponsored by the Children's Book Council (CBC) and the International Reading Association (the organization for reading teachers), may be your highest aspiration. Children all over the country vote on books submitted by publishers, eventually creating a list of about 100 titles. Every year, you can find the latest list online at the CBC's website at www.cbc.books.org/.

Outstanding Science

Science teachers in the United States recognize the best trade books on science for children in an annual list chosen by a panel named by the National Science Teachers Association (NSTA) and published with the help of the CBC. More than 100 books on a variety of subjects appear. The list is published every year in *Science for Children*. Copies are available online at the NSTA website at www.nsta.org/ or may be ordered from the CBC.

Notable Social Studies

The National Council for the Social Studies creates a list similar to the science teachers' list, but this time with a focus on social studies. About 150 books come from such areas as biography, contemporary issues, history, and world culture. Published every year in *Social Education*, the list is also available online at www.socialstudies.org/ resources/notable/ or by mail from the CBC.

Parents' Choice

The Parent Council reviews books every month and lists recommended learning titles. Nearly 3,000 reviews exist online at the council's website at www.parentcoun- cil.com/. The council consists of teachers who are parents and emphasizes the value of the book as a learning tool. Making it on the Parent Council's recommended list or review category helps you sell more books to parents and teachers.

Can You Keep a Secret? _____

Starting to feel overwhelmed by all these awards? If you want one handy place to start, just go to the Children's Book Awards page on my website, www.underdown. org/awards2002.htm.

On the other hand, if you want to know a lot more, get *Children's Books: Awards and Prizes*, published by the Children's Book Council, from your local library.

Wowing Them All Over the Country

In response to literacy problems and to place an emphasis on the benefits of reading, many states now pass out their own awards for outstanding literature for young people. They may be sponsored by local branches of national organizations, by state education departments, or by state organizations. These outstanding books may be evaluated by teachers, by librarians, or by children. Authors from all over the country may be eligible, or only state residents. Getting named to one of the lists may not do much for your book. Being on a number of them will, because it makes it more likely that school libraries will purchase it. Some, like the Texas Bluebonnet Award, give a boost in sales just to books nominated, because children all over the state read and vote on the books, and so their schools must have copies on hand. Your publisher should take care of sending your book to the relevant committees. Be pleased if you hear you've been named.

End-of-Year Lists

What is it about us that likes to package things up and box them together at the end of the year? Closure, I guess. Regardless of the reason, your book might place nicely on an "end-of-the-year" list. The most influential of the annual lists of children's books are the *Publishers Weekly* roundup, the *Booklist* "Editor's Picks," and the *Boston Globe/Horn Book* "Best Books of the Year."

I've mentioned just a few of the organizations and magazines that give awards or that create lists of recommended children's books every year. Some will get you more recognition than others. Some will help you reach a specialized audience, while others speak to a national audience. Right now, making sense of them all may be difficult, so keep your eyes open, ask questions if you get an award or are named to a list you've never heard of, and check the resources listed here and in Appendix B.

The Least You Need to Know

- Many diverse and varied awards exist in the publishing world to give kudos to children's book authors and illustrators.

- The original and most esteemed award in the United States for a writer is the Newbery Medal.

- The original and most esteemed award in the United States for an illustrator is the Caldecott Medal.

- Beyond awards, lists of notable books abound; these lists remain a good way for you to receive recognition.

- In many cases, in order to be considered for all these awards and lists, the publisher must submit information or applications; if your publisher doesn't act, sometimes you can.

Chapter 33

Building a Career

In This Chapter

- ◆ Some of the challenges you'll face once you get published
- ◆ How to deal with books going out of print
- ◆ Ways to make money that aren't completely incompatible with your writing
- ◆ The importance of continuing to learn and grow
- ◆ Take yourself seriously, and never forget that you aren't just a writer

Once the first book is published, you might think your struggles will be over. You have the ear of an editor or art director, and your books will now flow steadily into the publishing pipeline and out into the world. The reality is a bit more complicated than that. This chapter reveals some of the challenges that still lie ahead and points out some possible solutions. It's a big world out there, and I want to give you a few more tools so you can succeed in it.

Becoming a Pro

By the time your first book is published, unless you are very lucky, you will have already spent several years working toward becoming a children's writer or illustrator. Inevitably, you've learned a lot, and have absorbed and built upon the advice and information in this book. You are becoming a professional. To be a professional, you need to think strategically about what you do.

Your overall challenge now is to balance writing and illustrating with the other things you must do to keep your career going. You can't spend all your time promoting your already published books, or bringing in income from other sources. Earlier, I covered promoting your book, and later in this chapter, you'll see some examples of what you can do to add to your income. Don't get carried away with either of these! You need to be sure to set aside time to work on what you most want to do, so that your other activities don't take over your life.

You need new projects because you want to have new books coming out regularly. Each new one will help remind readers of your earlier ones, and get them hoping for the next. Ideally, when one book is about to be published, you'll already have others under contract, and be starting to think about still others. Just like a publisher, you need to have a pipeline.

Can You Keep a Secret? _____

Some authors work with more than one publisher to ensure a steady stream of new books. It's best not to do this unless each is publishing a different kind of book, such as picture books at one, chapter books at another. Illustrators may find it easier to work with a few publishers at once, but don't get too scattered. And try not to hop from one publisher to another. Building up a backlist at a publisher will ensure that your books get more support.

Obstacles

Let's not get carried away. Many people only dream of having the "problem" of having to balance different demands on their time. After your first book comes out, the next ones aren't necessarily any easier.

The First One's Easy

Everyone is excited by something new and possibly different. Publishers with a book by a first-time author or illustrator are excited to have discovered fresh talent, reviewers are intrigued, and readers are curious to see if something really unusual has come along. Your book is the new kid on the block who everyone wants to meet. After that first book, reality sets in. If it doesn't do well, by which I mean meet expectations for sales and reviews, the next one will actually be harder. You're already a has-been, even if there was nothing wrong with your effort at all. The publisher might have expected too much. One reviewer might have had a bad day. Or the combination of text and art that everyone at the publisher loved didn't appeal to your readers. And bad luck with a second or third book can have the same effect. Your publisher can decide not to do another book with you.

What to do? First, don't blame yourself if something like this happens. Someone liked your first book enough to invest in publishing it, after all. Work to make your next book even better. If your first book isn't out yet, hope that your first few books all do reasonably well. After that, your reputation can stand an off day.

Censorship

It may seem hard to believe, but censorship is an issue in children's books. It's probably more of a constant pressure for textbook publishers, who must produce work that won't offend anyone, but because children's books are sold to schools and libraries, their presence on the shelf or in the classroom can be and is challenged. Most often, fantasy novels get challenged for their magic and witches, and realistic young adult novels get challenged for their language or handling of sex. But just about any book that contains any content that one particular parent doesn't want his or her child exposed to can be challenged, and may actually be taken off the shelves.

Should you be concerned that your career will be damaged by censorship? Probably not, because most trade publishers aren't bothered by a few incidents of this type. But your career can be damaged by self-censorship. Don't anticipate the objections and try to head them off. Children can understand and deal with almost any subject, if it's presented in an appropriate manner for their level of understanding and maturity. So if you want to write about a tricky subject, create a scary and sophisticated illustration, or even just use realistic dialogue in a family argument, follow your own sense of what's right. If you've gone too far, your publisher will tell you.

Class Rules _____

What do Captain Underpants, Tiger Eyes, and Harry Potter have in common? They're all characters in books that have been targeted for removal from libraries—books by Dav Pilkey, Judy Blume, and J. K. Rowling respectively. Censorship can affect you. Find out about the extent of the problem and how to deal with it at the website of the National Coalition Against Censorship (www.ncac.org).

Doubts

Perhaps the most difficult challenge to overcome is that posed by your own doubts. You might wonder, "Am I really cut out to be a professional? Did I just have one good book, and that's it?" If you're a writer, you may have lots of new ideas, but not know which to pursue. Or you may feel that you can't generate new ones. Illustrators can have similar doubts: You may freeze up when confronted by a new manuscript and wonder how you'll ever complete it. You may end up feeling that you aren't that good after all—that your editor or art director turned your work into what it was. Don't listen to yourself!

Remember that after your first inspiration, it took you a long period of revision and polishing before your first book was finished. Why should your next books be any different? Don't be embarrassed to go back to the writing ideas in Chapter 2. If you're an illustrator, look again at those picture books that inspired you. And do be sure to allow yourself time to write or sketch, even if it's only a few minutes to use your journal, or note down a few observations. Keep going back to the well, and sooner or later, the bucket will come up full, and you'll be off again.

Books and Their Untimely Deaths

One of the sad facts of life in the publishing world is that books don't stay in print. You want all your books to be available forever, so this can come as a rude shock, especially if it happens only a few years after a book was published. Today, sadly, books are going out of print even faster, sometimes within a year or two of their original publication. Don't take it personally—you might even find some comfort in knowing that you've made it to this point. After all, one definition of an established author or illustrator is that they've got more books out of print than yet-to-be published. Remember, too, that there are some actions you can take to keep your book available or get it back in print.

Going OP

Publishers keep books "in print," meaning they are available even if you don't see them in every bookstore, only so long. At a point when the cost of keeping books in a warehouse and in the catalog is greater than the income a publisher makes from selling them, or when the cost of reprinting a supply that would take no more than three years to sell is too high, publishers declare a book *out of print* (OP). Recently, many publishers require higher sales levels to keep books in print, with the result that more books go out of print sooner. This is very frustrating, when you suddenly cannot get copies of a book for a school visit or when you see backlist sales cut off before the list has a chance develop.

Out of print does not mean gone forever, so be ready to take action.

Vocabulary List _____

A book is **out of print** (**OP** or **OOP**) when it can no longer be ordered from the publisher, and the publisher has decided not to print more. If a publisher wants to leave its options open, it may declare a book **out of stock indefinitely** (**OSI**), meaning that although it has no copies left, it might still decide to print a fresh supply.

Get Your Books and Your Rights

If you get some warning that a book is about to be declared OP, don't try to keep it in print, either by promoting it frantically or by lobbying your editor. You probably can't do enough to generate sales to make a difference, and your editor most likely is not involved in OP decisions. In fact, at the larger companies, an inventory manager, who may not even be in the same building, makes the decision in consultation with the marketing department (can they increase sales?) and the production department (can the book be printed cost-effectively?). Your editor may not know that your book is out of print until after the decision has been made and books have been *remaindered*, or sold off at a discount.

What you can do is let your editor know ahead of time that you want to hear as soon as possible about any decision to declare your book OP. You need to know so you can buy as many copies of the book as possible before they're all gone. Publishers sell off what's in the warehouse at a greatly reduced price, perhaps not much more than the $2 or so it cost to manufacture it. You may be able to get hundreds of copies. Buy as many as you can afford, and then worry about finding space for them. This is a better dilemma to be in than not hearing until after the books are all gone, as happens all too often.

Get your rights back, too. Once the book is out of print, ask the publisher for a letter formally returning your copyright to you. Even if you are not entitled to this by your contract, ask. If you are entitled to it by your contract, press your case as far as you must. Sometimes, a polite letter from your lawyer will shake this letter loose. Don't accept an OSI status for your book, either. This can be a legitimate designation for a few months, while a publisher waits for orders to come in, but don't let it become a substitute for out of print.

Vocabulary List _____

A publisher may **remainder** a book and sell off all its stock when putting it out of print, or it may sell only some of its copies to reduce its stock. In either case, the books will usually end up on sale for less than half the regular retail price.

Back from the Dead?

Once you've got your books and your rights, what do you do? You can sell your books on school visits, and make them available through online booksellers or specialized services like Backinprint.com. This website provides a service to Author's Guild members, selling their stock of out-of-print books and even making print-on-demand copies available.

Putting the book back in print is more difficult. Publishers don't jump at the chance to republish a book another publisher let go. They assume they won't be any better able to reach other customers than the first publisher was. Though a few publishers do republish books, the numbers of books that come back to life in this way are small compared to the many hundreds of books that go out of print each year.

Do-It-Yourself Publishing

When I mentioned self-publishing earlier, I warned you against it. However, once you are published, and provided that you have the time and money to invest, this may be a viable option.

Self-publishing is a lot of work. To do it successfully, you have to act like a publisher and find people to help with editing, design, and production, then front about $20,000 for a print run of 5,000 books, and then find ways to sell, promote, and distribute. All these things can be done, but to be done well, you have to know how to do them, or be able to hire people who do. It gets a little easier if you have a book that has already been published, and for which you have not only gotten the rights back but have bought or been given the film used to print it. You'll already know about the people who are likely to be interested in your book, and from this book and other experiences you'll have some idea of how to reach them. With the film, which will only need small changes to places like the title and copyright pages, you'll be able to save some money when you go to press.

Self-publish when you can go into it with your eyes wide open, with a carefully thought-out plan, and with the time and the money not only for a first printing but for a second printing before you've sold the first. As Josephine (Joi) Nobisso says of her experiences:

> I'm beginning to get calls from aspiring publishers, as I always did from aspiring writers! Most of these ventures look like vanity to me (meaning, in this case, that these books are being done in vain—no marketing possibilities are built in to some of the concepts and/or planned execution of these projects), but I'm

quite sure that the route I'm currently taking will soon be a usual one for established and responsible authors who are itching to get pet projects out there and who are willing to do (or to hire out) the promotion to the right markets.

Playground Stories

Self-publishing worked for Josephine (Joi) Nobisso. With Gingerbread House, her own company, she began by putting three picture books back into print, and sold a total of 18,000 copies in hard- and softcover in her first season. Lucky? No. She used an experienced printer, did a mailing to children's booksellers, sent out hundreds of review copies, and set up a website (www.gingerbreadbooks.com). She presold 3,000 copies of one book to Scholastic Australia and Scholastic New Zealand Book Clubs. She found a "niche" (scrapbook makers) market for one title, *Grandma's Scrapbook*, and sold 1,500 copies there through a special offer. She sold hundreds more through writing workshops she did in schools. And she also found a distributor who would carry her titles, and it shipped thousands more copies. It was a lot of work, but she'd do it again.

Success stories like Joi's are not the norm, though you'll hear of one or two a decade if you are a regular reader of publishing industry journals. Many more self-publishing efforts fail than succeed, however. It's especially difficult to self-publish an original book when you are an unknown, and in fact I know of only a few successes since I entered publishing. The first was Richard Paul Evans, who self-published *The Christmas Box* in 1992, and Michael Hoeye, who self-published *Time Stops for No Mouse* in 2000. It's interesting to note that in both cases, these authors are now happily publishing with a mainstream publisher. They did not want to keep doing all the work themselves.

What to Do Until You Can Live on Your Royalties

The dream of most children's book authors and illustrators is to be able to live on the royalty income from their books. In reality, few writers end up being able to quit their day job or to stop relying on a spouse with a steady income and a health plan. Illustrators may be able to find a steadier income from their own work, especially if they like doing educational work. But writers can find jobs that are both flexible and relevant to what they want to do, which is write. As you know from Chapter 31, school visits don't just promote your book. They also can be a handy source of income, especially once you have several books on the market (and illustrators, don't forget that you can do this too, though schools may not know what to make of you at first). Here we give examples of other kinds of work that can be done on a flexible schedule and at home. You'll undoubtedly find out about other kinds of work you can do just by comparing notes with other writers at conferences.

Packagers

We mentioned packagers in Chapter 7 as a possible home for some kinds of series. They are also a potential source of writing work, perhaps closely related to the work you do. Companies such as Mega-Books, 17th Street Productions, and Parachute Press produce many paperback series for publishers, hiring writers to create the individual books from an outline and a guide to the series often called a "bible." To get this work, you need to have samples to show, and be prepared not to be credited on the cover for your work. Some nonfiction is also produced by packagers, sometimes by one-person operations. Often known as "work-for-hire," you may not get to keep the underlying copyright in such work, but in at least some cases you do get your name on the cover. For just about any type of children's book except the high-end literary titles, you are likely to find a few packagers who specialize in it, if you do your research in the writer's guides.

Writing and Editing

Over the years, as you've gone over manuscripts in critique groups and corrected your writer friends' grammar (while they corrected yours), you will have picked up some general writing and editing skills, which you can use either inside or outside children's publishing. Start by looking locally. Many businesses need help with manuals and press releases and newsletters. Local free papers may expect you to work for free, too, but you can gain some writing credits and move on. Magazine and book publishers all need proofreaders and fact checkers, and if you're local, you've got a leg up; you can be a face instead of a voice on the phone, and even come in and work in their offices or pick up and drop off materials.

But there's no reason why you can't look outside your local area. If you are willing to take some time researching writer's sites on the web that have job listings, you can tap into a national market. Have writing samples and a resumé ready, and if you're looking at specialized jobs, such as proofreading, be prepared to take a test (so learn the proofreading marks).

Can You Keep a Secret?

Helping freelance writers and editors make sense of the job market is the Editorial Freelancers Association. Based in New York, but with national membership, the EFA has a job line, an annual pricing survey, an educational program, and other resources. Find out about them online at www.the-efa.org/ or write to them at 71 West 23rd Street, New York, NY 10010.

Textbooks and Supplemental Materials

Chapter 19 pointed out that some educational publishers acquire manuscripts, either by submission or on commission. These companies also need workbooks and activity books, from straightforward drills to more creative mixes of experiments, arts and crafts projects, and other hands-on activity books. They need stories and activities written to fit a particular theme and format in a textbook, so they work with writers, often as packagers do, on a work-for-hire basis. In the market guides, you'll find companies such as Cottonwood Press, Dandy Lion Publications, Evan-Moor Publishing, SRA McGraw-Hill, and Teacher Created Materials. Look for others, too. Some accept submissions, so you must always check their guidelines.

Teach! You've Learned a Thing or Two

By now, you've learned a good bit about writing or illustrating from the time you've spent on your own manuscripts. Perhaps you've taken some courses or workshops and felt you could have done better. Well, we're urging you to consider doing just that. Contact local colleges with active adult education departments, and find out if they offer children's writing courses. If you're an illustrator, look into teaching illustration at local art schools. If they don't have such courses, suggest that you could offer one, and find out what you would need to do to set one up. You can also set up classes online or offer advice and manuscript consulting by mail. You'll need to find ways to let people know about yourself.

Keep Learning

As if you didn't have enough to balance already, I have one more pressing item for your agenda: Don't ever stop learning and growing. Many published writers and illustrators have told me that although they reach a good level of ability and confidence in what they want to do, they never feel that they can say they have nothing more to learn. You've got to stay excited by what you are doing if you are going to pass excitement on to your readers. You've got to keep an open mind about everything. Your readers do. So don't stop reading the latest books for children, don't stop debating them with your friends, don't stop trying new challenges, don't stop going to conferences. If you are going to sustain a career, you can't let yourself coast along.

Take Yourself Seriously

As you move forward, believe in yourself and don't let yourself be intimidated, either by an unfamiliar challenge, by a dry spell, or by a publisher. Keep moving, and you'll reach your happy ending. I think a story that Deborah Kogan Ray told me illustrates this point well.

Today, Deborah is an established, well-known illustrator with something like 100 books to her credit. In the 1960s, she was a novice illustrator, taking her portfolio to two publishers on her first trip to New York. Something about her art caught the attention of the legendary Ursula Nordstrom, still head of what was then Harper & Row.

In short order, Deborah had a contract and a problem. She didn't know how to produce preseparated art, which then was standard for picture books. With the help of some very patient design staff, she learned, and she was working away on the finished art for the book when her contract was canceled, with no explanation.

So she sued for the remaining $500 of her $1,000 advance. Harper settled before the case went to trial. Deborah picks up the story:

> I found lots of work with other publishers, but remained *persona non grata* at Harper & Row for eight years.
>
> One day, I received a letter and manuscript from an editor named Elizabeth Gordon [at Harper], who was not on their staff when my troubles occurred. She wanted to take me to lunch and asked if I would consider illustrating *I Have a Sister, My Sister Is Deaf.* My immediate question was, "Don't you know that I sued Harper & Row?" She wasn't concerned.
>
> I illustrated the book. It is still in print. The question of what caused Harper to break my first contract has never been answered.

Suing a publishing company is not to be undertaken lightly, of course! But the principle applies in other situations. If you need more space to write in your home, find a way to create it. If you are asked to make substantial revision, and you don't understand why, ask for clarification. If you haven't seen any reviews of your book, even though it's been out for six months, ask why. Take yourself seriously and work to be a partner with your editor and publisher.

That's what Deborah did. She not only won her case, she ended up working with Harper again, and she got something else from the experience: "As to the great settlement from my lawsuit: I took my $500 check and bought my first drawing table. It had a side table, a straight edge, a paper drawer, and big drafting board with a crank to move it up and down. It was the biggest, fanciest drawing table that I could find."

Out into the Big World

Publishing companies can seem like enormous and powerful entities to writers and illustrators. Taking one on like Deborah did seems like a David and Goliath story. But widen the focus a little more. Children's publishing, itself a large and complicated world, is just one part of the publishing industry, which in turn is a pretty small part of any country's economy. I hope you have come to understand it better, but I know that our beloved industry is at the mercy of forces beyond our control. As you travel on in your career, I hope you'll remember a lesson to be learned from a small boy, named (oddly enough) Harold.

I refer to Harold in *Harold and the Purple Crayon*, by Crockett Johnson (published by Harper & Row, now HarperCollins, in 1955). This particular Harold has a purple crayon with which he draws what he wants, conjuring up problems at the same time, which he then proceeds to solve. He draws a mountain so he can see where he is, but falls off the other side, and quickly draws a balloon, and on he goes. In the end, he gets to the place he most wants to be. You can read this just as an imaginative adventure, or as a story about dreaming, but I think it also has something to say about how to live in the world.

Harold (the character) doesn't settle for what's in front of him. He creates the world that he wants to live in. When some aspect of it doesn't work out the way that he had hoped, he finds a way to fix it. I often point out at conferences that we can be like this small boy. Like Harold (the character), we can work to make our world be the way we want it to be.

In fact, this is what those of us who care about children's books must do. We are a sizable community—illustrators, writers, editors, librarians, teachers, and, potentially, millions of parents. We all vote. We can lobby our local, state, and national elected officials for better library funding. We can support the use of trade books as well as textbooks in classrooms when the subject is debated at local school committee meetings. We create books with our purple crayons. But we can do much more. We can and should work to make this a world in which the kinds of books we care about continue to have a place—a larger place than they do now.

This may take a bigger crayon, but it's important not to lose sight of this bigger world, and the impact we can have on it. Use your purple crayon, not only to create your own worlds between the covers of a book, but to make the world we live in a more hospitable place for the books we love and the children who need them.

The Least You Need to Know

◆ Now that you are published, your next challenge is to build a career for yourself.

◆ Books go out of print more quickly nowadays, but there are actions you can take to keep them available.

◆ Working with packagers, educational publishers, doing other freelance editing and writing, and teaching writing are all jobs you can fit in around your writing.

◆ Self-publishing can be an option for you, if you have the time and the money.

◆ Keep learning, take yourself seriously, and never forget that you can have an impact on the world.

Glossary

acquire To make an agreement with an author to publish a book. This is called an *acquisition*.

acquisitions committee *See* publishing committee.

acquisitions editor The editor involved in signing authors to write books. The acquisitions editor generally manages the manuscript as it comes into the publishing house. The manuscript is then passed on to a development editor. These roles are typically combined at children's publishing companies.

advance Money paid by a publisher to an author or illustrator before the book goes on the market, in anticipation of sales. The advance is charged against royalties and must "earn out" before any royalties are paid.

agent A well-connected professional who places your work with publishers, keeps track of your royalties, and perhaps provides career guidance in return for a percentage of your earnings.

art director (A.D.) A publishing staff person who works with illustrators on picture books, providing art direction—guidance to the illustrator as he or she works; as a job titles, this person may be the head of the art staff.

artist's representative An agent for illustrators.

assignment *See* commission.

audience The people for whom you are writing. In children's books, this can mean a specific age level.

author's representative *See* agent.

back matter Supplementary material in the back of a book, such as a glossary, recommended reading lists, an index, or information about the book.

backlist Previously published books. A publisher's backlist is an important source of revenue, because backlist sales are more predictable and dependable than *frontlist* sales.

binding What holds a book together. A trade binding is usually sewn and glued. A library binding is more durable, with cloth reinforcement and often a different sewing method. Paperbacks are usually bound with glue only.

bleed Not what publishers do to artists and writers, bleed is a technical term referring to illustrations that extend off the edges of pages.

blues or **bluelines** A printing, in blue only, from the final plates for a book. This is usually seen only by editors and constitutes a final check. If changes are needed, they have to be made to the film, which is expensive. Some publishers no longer use blues.

board books Short, thick, square-shape (usually) simple books for infants and toddlers.

body The main part of the text of a work, not including elements such as the table of contents or index.

boilerplate Standard language in a contract.

Bologna Shorthand for the biggest international gathering of children's publishers, the Bologna Book Fair, held every April. Publishers go to buy from or sell rights to other publishers.

book plus A book packaged with something else, such as a plush toy.

book proposal Materials sent to a publisher to propose a book, including at least a description of the book or books, sample chapters, and an outline.

bound galleys An advance copy of a novel or nonfiction book, typeset but not proofread, and usually without the final form of the illustrations. Usually bound as a paperback.

chains Companies that own many individual bookstores. The two biggest in bookselling are Barnes & Noble and Borders. They contrast with the *independents*.

chapter books Books for older children. They may be illustrated, but tell a story primarily through words.

clips Samples of one's writing.

colophon An item in a book's front matter that gives information about how the book was produced, from typefaces to the kind of paint an artist used.

commission When doing work "on commission" the publisher hires you, tells you what to do, and usually pays a fee instead of royalties.

composition The arrangement of the various elements (figures, objects, background) in an illustration.

concept book A picture book that explores a concept instead of, or perhaps in addition to, telling a story.

conglomerate A large company with many divisions, increasingly common in children's publishing.

consolidation The process of combining companies, closing overlapping divisions, and laying off staff.

co-op money   Money a bookseller spends to promote a publisher's books, which is then reimbursed.

copy editor   The person who reviews a manuscript for style, punctuation, spelling, and grammar.

copyright   Literally, the right to create and distribute copies of a creative work. Under copyright law, you hold copyright in a work from the moment you create it.

cover letter   The letter that accompanies your manuscript.

critique   A thoughtful, usually written evaluation of a manuscript, concentrating on problems of structure, tone, characterization, and the like.

designer   The person choosing type, doing layout, and otherwise settling the design of a book. Some illustrators do their own design work.

development editor   The editor who actually edits a book. *See also* acquisitions editor.

development house   *See* packager.

draft   A version of a manuscript. The *first* draft is the first one written; the *rough* draft is an unpolished version; the *final* draft is the last one.

dummy   A manuscript laid out in book form, with sketches of all the illustrations and sample finished pieces.

early or **easy readers**   Books written with a controlled vocabulary for children learning to read.

earn out   To reach the point when the royalties on a book have paid back the advance paid to the author.

endpapers   The sheets of paper in a hardcover book that attach the cover to the pages; these can be plain colored paper, or have a design or illustration.

exclusive submission   A manuscript sent to only one publisher.

fair use   A limited exception to copyright law, allowing others to draw on or use excerpts from a copyrighted work without formal permission.

fairy tale   Like a folktale in form, but told specifically for children and involves more literary elements.

fantasy   A type of fiction in which the rules of the world are different; animals talk, magic works, and strange creatures exist.

fiction   Writing from the imagination, or writing containing elements of imagination, fable, or tale. Also known as "lies," or "something you've made up."

film   What most books today are printed from.

flat fee   A payment made as the only compensation; the opposite of an advance against royalties.

flow-through clause   A nice clause to have in a contract, this clauses obliges the publisher to pass on subsidiary rights payments when they are received, not when the next royalty statement happens.

folded and gathered (f&g's) A sheet or sheets from a print run, folded, cut, and generally made ready for binding, but not bound. F&g's are often used as *review copies* for picture books.

folktale A story, usually with a message, that has been passed down orally and may appeal to both adults and children.

Frankfurt Frankfurt is the site of the largest international publishing convention, in the autumn every year. Like Bologna, but for all publishers.

freelancer An independent contract worker who is employed by the publisher. This person doesn't work on salary or as a full-time employee for the publisher. Many writers find extra income by freelancing; children's publishers may send out design and copyediting work to freelancers.

front matter The material that is placed before the body of a book, including such elements as the title and copyright pages, a table of contents, or an introduction.

frontlist The books a publisher is releasing this year or season; the new books.

galleys Long pages of typeset text, not yet broken out into book pages, not much used today because of computerized typesetting and page layout.

glossary You are reading one.

hardcover A book produced with a hard, stiff outer cover, usually covered by a jacket. The covers are usually made of cardboard, over which is stretched cloth, treated paper, vinyl, or some other plastic.

historical fiction Fiction in a historical setting, in which the main character, and often many others, are invented, while the setting and other details are based on careful research.

imprint A part of a publisher with a distinct identity, name, and staff.

independents Bookstores not owned by large companies, usually free-standing or having only a few branches.

index An alphabetic list of topics and key words to be found in a book, with their page number locations.

institutional One of the markets in children's publishing, named for the institutions the books are sold to—schools and libraries.

IRC Short for International Reply Coupon: good for postage anywhere in the world. Send one or more to a foreign publisher along with a self-addressed envelope for the response.

ISBN The acronym for International Standard Book Number. This number gives the book a unique ID, like your Social Security number, for orders and distribution. The first part of the number identifies the language of publication ("0" for English), and the second part is the publisher's number.

jacket Short for *dust jacket*, this is the paper cover on a book. Originally intended to keep it clean, it's now used to catch the eye of the reader, through dramatic art and type.

journal A blank book to write in whenever you can; not just for recording events, but for exploring ideas and jotting observations.

kill fee   A final payment made to an author or illustrator when a project is cancelled.

layout   The arrangement of all the elements of a book's design, from text paragraphs and illustrations to chapter titles and page numbers.

license   The right to do something. In publishing, the right to publish a book or books, or to use something from one book in another product. An "audio license," for example, gives a company the right to produce an audio tape of a book.

line editing   Close, line-by-line editing of a book, concentrating on tone, style, flow, sequencing, clarity, and such matters.

lists   Semi-annual (or more frequent) groups of books produced by a publisher, announced and placed in a catalog together. A publisher's list is simply the books that company produces.

literary agent   *See* agent.

manuscript   A writer's work before it is typeset and printed; originally "hand written," as the word implies, now it is likely to be produced on a word processing program.

mass market   Books sold through general retail outlets, usually with wide appeal and low prices.

middle grade   An age category roughly corresponding to the middle grades of school, perhaps the fourth through eighth grades, to which many of the classic children's novels belong.

midlist   Books with reliable but not outstanding sales—the ones in the middle of the list.

model release   Written permission for the use of one's likeness in print. Needed if you take someone's picture for a book.

ms./mss.   Short for manuscript or manuscripts.

multiple submission   A manuscript sent to two or more publishers at the same time.

niche publisher   A publisher that specializes in a subject of interest to a small group of people and sells its books nationally, but only in specialized outlets.

nonfiction   Also known as an "informational book," writing in which the author retells historical events, crafts a biography, passes on knowledge, or presents activities or experiments.

novelty book   Any book with features added to it beyond the binding and pages; for example, foldout page, die-cut holes, lift-the-flap, pop-ups, or sound chips.

on spec   Work done without a contract, in the hope that one will be forthcoming: "on speculation."

OP   Out of print, meaning that the publisher has no copies of a book on hand and does not intend to reprint it.

option clause   An item in a contract granting a publisher the right to consider an author's next work.

original expression   What copyright law protects: your own unique way of expressing an idea, telling a story, or creating a work of art.

orphaned book   A book left behind by an editor's departure; the book could have been published or at any stage of publication.

OSI Out of stock indefinitely. This means the publisher has no copies of a book on hand, but may want to reprint it in the future, and so the publisher is not calling it out of print. If it did, it might be obligated to return the rights to the book to the author.

packager A company specializing in creating books up to the printing stage or the distribution stage; marketing and distributing the book is handled by the publisher. The packager's name may appear on the copyright page, but the publisher's appears on the spine.

paperback A binding with a soft cover, usually a light cardboard. A *trade* paperback is usually the same size as a hardcover book, and printed to the same standards. A *mass-market* paperback is usually smaller, designed to fit in a rack, and printed on cheaper paper.

pedantic Describes a story in which the moral or message the author wants to teach overwhelms the plot.

permissions Agreements from copyright holders granting the right to reproduce their work.

picture books Books for younger children, which have pictures on every page, and tell a story through words and pictures.

PP&B Paper, printing, and binding. The cost of producing a finished book.

press kit A folder of materials about your book sent to the media to alert them to your book's release.

prewriting The all-important work a writer does before actually starting to write. This can be as simple as jotting down ideas, as methodical as creating an outline, or as complex as doing character studies.

proofreader The person who reviews the proofs for errors before a book goes to press.

proofs The typeset pages of a book before it is printed.

pub. date The publication date; the date when a publisher says a book will be available.

public domain Not copyrighted, either because it never was or because the copyright has expired or lapsed; public domain material can be used without attribution or permission, though good writing practice means making a note of sources.

publishing committee Also known as the editorial board, this is the group that at some companies approves the acquisition of a book.

query letter A letter you send to a publisher to ask, or query, to see if the publisher is interested in seeing the manuscript.

reading fees Fees charged to read and comment on a manuscript. If this is charged by an agent to determine if he will represent you, it is not a legitimate fee.

regional publisher A publisher who specializes in subjects relevant to a particular part of the country, and sells its books mostly or entirely in that area.

rejection letter A letter turning down a manuscript. If it is an unsigned photocopy, you've received a standard response. If personalized in any way, assume this is a good sign.

remainders Surplus books sold at a steep discount. A publisher may remainder a book and sell off all its stock when putting it out of print, or it may sell only some of its copies to reduce its stock.

response sheet   A feedback device, on which a writer lists certain ideas, devices, or grammatical points for the audience or an editor to consider.

response time   The time it takes a publisher to reply to a submission, usually measured in months.

returns   Unsold books sent back to a publisher by booksellers or wholesalers. Unlike many other businesses, retailers can usually return books for a full refund. Returns often come back several months after a book is published.

review copies   Copies of a book sent to reviewers, usually before publication, and often in the form of bound galleys or f&g's.

revise   Literally to "re-see"; to rewrite, perhaps making extensive changes. Often, when a new edition of a book comes out, the author has revised the previous edition.

rights   The many different ways a book can be *licensed*, ranging from book club rights to movie rights and even theme park rights. Also called subsidiary rights.

royalties   Money paid to an author by a publisher on the basis of books sold. It may be a percentage of the list price, which is the price for which the book supposedly will be sold to a consumer, or of the net price, which is what the publisher actually receives (often 40 to 50 percent less than the retail price).

sales rep   Short for sales representative. An individual who represents a publisher to a potential customer, such as a bookstore or wholesaler. The sales rep can be a house rep, hired by the publisher; or a commissioned rep, independent, and paid a commission for every book sold.

SASE   A self-addressed, stamped envelope, included with all submissions and query letters for the return of the manuscript or a response from the publisher. When soliciting publishers to publish your work, you should include a SASE.

self-publish   An individual who does everything a publisher does, from editing to printing and distribution.

series   A number of books that are related to each in terms of theme, purpose, characters, style, or content, or all of these things. Series are often given special titles that encompass each of the books in the series. For example, *The Complete Idiot's Guide* is a series of books. These books are geared toward a specific audience (not idiots, of course).

signature   The smallest number of pages a particular printing machine can print; many books are printed on large sheets of paper, fitting 8 or 16 or some other number of pages. When folded and cut, each sheet forms a signature.

simultaneous submission   *See* multiple submission.

slush pile   The unsolicited manuscripts that a publisher receives from writers who aren't represented by agents.

softcover   *See* paperback.

special sales   Sales of a book to nontraditional outlets, such as gift stores, or for use as premiums. For example, a publisher might sell 10,000 units (books) to a corporation that wants to distribute the books to employees of the corporation.

spine   The center panel of the binding of a book, which connects the front and back cover to the pages and faces out when the book is shelved.

SRO   School Rights Only: the rights you want to transfer to a textbook publisher, instead of granting them all rights.

storyboard   An illustrator's plan for a book, showing every page at much reduced size, ideally all on one sheet of paper.

structural editing   Editing involving the structure of a manuscript, usually done at an early stage.

submissions   Manuscripts sent to a publisher by an author or agent. Submissions can be exclusive, multiple, or simultaneous.

subsidiary rights   *See* rights.

subsidy publisher   *See* vanity publisher.

superstore   Regarding bookstores, a large store with 100,000 or more titles, a coffee shop, and other amenities.

tear sheets   Originally samples of an illustrator's work, torn out of a magazine or other source. Now can also be a photocopy of such a sample.

thumbnails   Small, rough sketches done by an artist before full-sized sketches, which may be literally not much bigger than thumbnail size.

trade   The kind of publisher who sells books to bookstores, and also to some extent to libraries.

transparencies   Photographs or art on transparent material (like slides) rather than on opaque material.

trim size   The horizontal and vertical dimensions of a book's pages. A book with an 8-by-10-inch trim size is 8 inches across and 10 inches high. A hardcover book has covers that extend beyond the pages, so book size and trim size aren't always the same.

unsolicited submission/manuscript   A manuscript that a publisher did not solicit, or ask for, from an author.

vanity publisher   A company the author pays to publish a book, rather than the other way around. The name comes from the fact that such publishers rely on the vanity of people who want to see their words in print and are willing to pay for this.

work-for-hire   Work done for a publisher or other company to their specifications, usually paid for with a fee and with copyright signed over to the company.

young adult (YA)   The upper end of the age range covered by children's publishers, possibly starting at age 12. A separate YA category did not exist until the 1960s.

Appendix B

Resources

I could almost fill a book with the books, magazines, organizations, and websites I've come across while researching this guide. Unfortunately, I just can't fit all the good ones here. So here is a highly selected list of some of the best. An expanded version of this list, with updates, is on my website, The Purple Crayon, at www.underdown.org/ciglinks.htm.

Essentials

These are the basic books you'll want to acquire:

For Illustrators	For Authors
Children's Writer's and Illustrator's Market	*Children's Writer's and Illustrator's Market*
Essential Guide to Children's Books and Their Creators	*Essential Guide to Children's Books and Their Creators*
Writing with Pictures	Your favorite inspirational or practical writing guide

Read on for more details.

Books on Writing

There are many how-to books on children's writing. Only a few are listed here. If none of them sound quite right for you, browse through the selections in a well-stocked bookstore until you find a book that does.

The Business of Writing for Children: An Award-Winning Author's Tips on How to Write, Sell, and Promote Your Children's Books, **Aaron Shepard (Shepard Publications, 2000)**
Perhaps not the glossiest or snazziest how-to book on children's writing, but nonetheless a useful how-to guide, especially for picture-book and folktale authors, from a successful writer. He also gives sound advice on working with publishers and the process. This is a thin book, but it's packed with useful information.

How to Write a Damn Good Novel, How to Write a Damn Good Novel II: Advanced Techniques, **and** *The Key: How to Write Damn Good Fiction Using the Power of Myth,* **James N. Frey (St. Martin's Press, 1987, 1994, and 2000)**
Great resources for any writer of young adult novels in particular, regardless of experience. "These books offer solid, step-by-step advice and are funny and really fun to read," says Laurie Halse Anderson.

The Invisible Child: On Reading and Writing Books for Children, **Katherine Paterson (Dutton, November 2001)**
The author of such classics as *Bridge to Terabithia* discusses "what stories mean to kids" (*Booklist* review, August 2001). Read this to learn what books this revered writer loves and why, and to find out why she feels *story* is important above all.

Love and Death at the Mall: Teaching and Writing for the Literate Young, **Richard Peck (Delacorte, 1994)**
Peck analyzes what young people read and why in his book. The author tackles such notable teen problems of peer pressure and suicide and how social issues relate to the writing to which young readers respond. A good reference if you strive for realism in your writing.

Picture Writing, **Anastasia Suen (Writers Digest Books, 2002)**
Subtitled "A New Approach to Writing for Kids and Teens" this highly useful guide distills much of what she teaches in her highly respected online classes. This is a practical, not philo-sophical book, with exercises and other help for someone trying to find their way.

Take Joy: A Book for Writers, **Jane Yolen (Writer, 2003)**
Jane is to some a guru of children's writing. I know her not just as the writer of this book's foreword, but as a passionate and thoughtful speaker and a jaded but still engaged observer of the children's publishing industry. Her words on writing will inspire you, prod you, move you, irritate you—and get you writing.

The Way to Write for Children, **Joan Aiken (St. Martin's Press, 1999)**
This book gives an overview of what children's books shouldn't do—like prove boring or condescending—but also offers the obligations that children's authors have toward their audience—"to demonstrate that the world is not a simple place." Basically, the book is inspi-rational.

The Writer's Idea Book, **Jack Heffron (Writer's Digest Books, 2000)**
Do you find yourself unable to put words to paper? This book provides prompts to get your creative juices flowing and begin writing. Though not intended specifically for the children's book writer, the more than 400 prompts are certain to help spawn ideas for those interested in writing for children.

Writing Books for Young People, **James Cross Giblin (The Writer, 1990)**
A how-to by a master of nonfiction.

Writing Hannah: On Writing for Children, **by Libby Gleeson (Hale & Iremonger, 1999)**
Australian author Libby Gleeson shares the writing process within a journal for aspiring writers. A good look at how to write a children's book by watching a children's book writer actually write one.

Books on Illustrating

There is little available that focuses specifically on children's book illustration. You must have Uri Shulevitz's book. The others listed here may also inspire some great ideas.

Bookmaking: Editing, Design, Production, Third Edition, **Marshall Lee (W.W. Norton, 2004)**
I took a course in book design when I was still wet behind the ears, and the second edition of this book was the textbook. I learned a lot about the process of putting together a book and then printing it, and got some hands-on knowledge of book design. The emphasis is on unillustrated or minimally illustrated books, making it a useful companion to Uri Shulevitz's book, reviewed later in this appendix. This edition is updated to cover the use of the computer in design and book production.

Children's Book Illustration: Step by Step Techniques: A Unique Guide from the Masters, **Jill Bossert (Watson Guptill, 1998)**
This guide looks over the shoulder of a number of established picture book illustrators as they plan and execute a project. Illustrators include Jerry Pinkney and Emily Arnold McCully, and a variety of approaches are shown. A very useful introduction to the nitty-gritty of illustration.

Illustrating Children's Books: A Guide to Drawing, Printing, and Publishing, **Nancy S. Hand (Prentice Hall, 1986)**
A useful overview that looks at how some top-notch illustrators actually work, and may help you focus your style.

Picture This! How Pictures Work, **Molly Bang (Seastar, 2000)**
A noted illustrator takes the reader step by step through the illustration of *Little Red Riding Hood* and in doing so demonstrates how visual elements such as shapes and colors actually work in pictures, and how a sequence of pictures tells a story. A fascinating visual guide to the way that picture books, at their best, work, and very handy for giving to friends who don't understand what you do.

Writing with Pictures: How to Write and Illustrate Children's Books, **Uri Shulevitz (Watson-Guptill, 1985)**
I can't overstate how useful I think this book is to the beginning or practicing children's book illustrator. It covers how to tell a story in pictures, planning and roughing out a book, compositions of individual illustrations, technique, style, and the use of visual references. Through-out, there are copious illustrations showing such things as the evolution of a picture in step-by-step detail. Shulevitz has been working in the field since the 1960s and his *Snow* was a Caldecott Honor book in 1999. He knows what he's talking about. The only problem is that this hasn't been revised since 1985 and so concentrates on black-and-white and preseparated color art, which in picture books have largely been replaced by scanned color art. However, the principles and techniques he teaches remain essential—there's no other book like this available.

Books About Books

Learn more about the field of children's literature and find guidance in locating the books which will inspire you.

***American Picturebooks from Noah's Ark to the Beast Within*, Barbara Bader (Macmillan, 1976)**

A long-awaited revised edition of this classic and definitive history of the picture book in the United States now seems to be in limbo, due to the financial difficulty of Winslow Press, its publisher. Look in the library for this now out-of-print edition, and wait and see if the new one makes it into print. It had the tentative title *The World in 32 Pages: One Hundred Years of American Picturebooks*.

***Children & Books*, 9th edition, Zena Sutherland (Addison-Wesley, 1996)**

This massive "now-classic children's literature textbook" (*Booklist*) gives you a complete course in children's literature in 720 large-size pages, with plenty of illustrations. It includes a history of the field, an exploration of theoretical approaches, bibliographies covering 2,000 books, and information about awards, censorship, and more. Yes, it's expensive, but if you are like me and went to a college that didn't offer a course in children's literature, this is a great substitute, and a book that will serve for many years as a source of information and inspiration. See *The Essential Guide to Children's Books and Their Creators* (following) for a less-expensive and less-weighty alternative.

***Children's Books: Awards and Prizes*, Children's Book Council staff (Children's Book Council, 1996)**

This is an extremely comprehensive guide, and an expensive one. Use it in your library.

***Children's Books in Print/Subject Guide to Children's Books in Print* (R. R. Bowker, annual)**

These are a complete and massive reference set. Use them in your library, but for easier and more up-to-date research, learn how to use the advanced search functions on www.amazon.com; you can search by publisher and year of publication, for example.

***Dear Genius: The Letters of Ursula Nordstrom*, Leonard S. Marcus (author) and Maurice Sendak (illustrator) (HarperCollins Juvenile Books, 2000)**

Not a resource like the other ones here, in that it doesn't include recommended books or essays about books, this collection of letters by one of the preeminent children's book editors of the twentieth century is nonetheless an inspirational and educational trip into the creative process behind many books now considered classics—*Harold and the Purple Crayon* and *Where the Wild Things Are*, to name just two. (Nordstrom was the head of Harper & Row's children's department for decades.)

***The Essential Guide to Children's Books and Their Creators*, Anita Silvey (editor) (Mariner Books, 2002)**

It might be difficult to believe that a 542-page book is "condensed" from anything, but this wonderful and comprehensive guide to contemporary children's literature is a shorter version of the more massive *Children's Books and Their Creators*. It's the best alternative I've seen to more expensive reference books, such as *Children and Books*, described previously. This is a great starting point for learning about the authors, illustrators, and genres of today's children's publishing world.

From Cover to Cover: Evaluating and Reviewing Children's Books, **Kathleen Horning (HarperCollins, 1997)**
An excellent look not only into the process reviewers go through, but at the standards editors often follow. From the *Horn Book* review: "Each clearly written chapter enumerates the characteristics that make a book of a specific genre successful. For example, the chapter on easy readers discusses print size and word length, while the chapter on fiction gives examples of the ways authors develop character."

Valerie and Walter's Best Books for Children, **Valerie V. Lewis and Walter M. Mayes (Avon Books, 1998)**
A great general guide to books for children, organized by interest and ability level. Use it to become more familiar with the best books of today.

Ways of Telling: Conversations on the Art of the Picture Book, **Leonard S. Marcus (Dutton Books, 2002)**
A leading children's book critic talks at length with 14 authors and illustrators of picture books, including Mitsumasa Anno, Karla Kuskin, Jerry Pinkney, Maurice Sendak, William Steig, and Rosemary Wells.

Reference Books

This section includes both general reference books used in publishing (dictionaries and the like) and reference books specific to children's publishing, such as guides to publishers.

Artist's & Graphic Designer's Market, **Mary Cox (Writers Digest Books, annual)**
Illustrators who only want to work in children's books will want to stick to *Children's Writer's and Illustrator's Market* (following), but if you are looking for other illustration work, this is a useful, annually updated "yellow pages," with hundreds of pages of listing (the most recent edition was almost 700 pages).

An Author's Guide to Children's Book Promotion, **Susan Raab (Raab Associates, 2001)**
A concise guide from a children's marketing consultant, covering all the different aspects of book marketing and publicity, and including a useful list of contacts. Get more information and access to the author's marketing columns at the Raab Associates website (following).

The Chicago Manual of Style, 15th Edition, **University of Chicago Press staff (University of Chicago Press, 2003)**
The 14th edition of *CMS*, as it is usually referred to, is the standard reference work in publishing for matters ranging from capitalization to the construction of an index. Now it has been extensively revised, taking into account recent change in technology; new material includes information on citing online sources and editing electronic documents. Don't throw out your 14th edition, but you can expect this edition to rapidly become the new standard.

Children's Writer's & Illustrator's Market, **Alice Pope (editor) (Writer's Digest Books, annual)**
An essential and annually updated reference book, this compendium lists about 800 publishers, magazines, scriptwriter markets, and many other places that you can sell and publish your work. The 2004 edition is the first to include listings for Canadian and international publishers. A must-have on the desks of those who write or illustrate for children.

Children's Writers Word Book, **Alijandra Mogilner (Writer's Digest Books, 1999)**
Do you have a sense of what vocabulary is appropriate for seven-year-olds? For 12-year-olds? A "controlled vocabulary" may be required in educational publishing, but even in trade publishing this can be a very useful reference and source of guidance, especially for beginning writers who have not yet developed an intuitive sense of what works for different age levels.

Dictionary of Modern American Usage, **Bryan A. Garner (Oxford University Press, 1998)**
Children's book publishers can still be relied on, most of the time, for good copyediting, but that's no substitute for this comprehensive guide to usage and grammar. Use it to polish your writing and produce a good impression.

The Forest for the Trees: An Editor's Advice to Writers, **Betsy Lerner (Riverhead Books, 2001)**
The author worked for many years at a large New York publisher of books for adults; her book is an enjoyable and insightful distillation of her experiences. Not an essential book, but a unique one that lets you hover invisibly in the background while an editor works and interacts with writers.

The Graphic Artists Guild Handbook: Pricing and Ethical Guidelines **(North Light Press, 2001)**
Put together by the GAG, which brings together illustrators and designers from many fields, this is a useful reference for illustrators, particularly if you work in more than one field. Nothing this comprehensive exists for writers, so far as I know.

It's a Bunny-Eat-Bunny World : A Writer's Guide to Surviving and Thriving in Today's Competitive Children's Book Market, **Olga Litowinsky (Walker and Co., 2001)**
This guide by an industry veteran covers some of the same ground as my book. There is a more detailed history of children's publishing, a good chapter on self-editing, and an insider's account of what happens to a manuscript from acquisition to publication. The main thread is the story of an invented first-time novelist, and his experiences while trying to find a publisher and an agent, and then working with a publisher. If you write picture books or nonfiction, or illustrate, however, you won't find much in Litowinsky's book you haven't found in this book.

Literary Market Place **(R. R. Bowker, annual)**
Use this massive and expensive reference book at your library. It's the Yellow Pages of publishing and has information and addresses for publishers, packagers, and agents.

The Magic Years, **Selma Fraiberg (Fireside, reissued 1996)**
What is a classic book about the cognitive and emotional development of children doing here? It's here because none of us really remember what it was like to be a small child, and this book helps us to remember, and to understand. I encountered it when my wife and I were looking for books to help us be good parents of our first child, but I list it because I think almost anyone writing or illustrating *for* children will benefit from reading it.

Publicize Your Book: An Insider's Guide to Getting Your Book the Attention It Deserves, **Jacqueline Deval (Perigee 2003)**
By a former publicity director at William Morrow, this is a great general guide to publicizing a book. Even publishing insiders will find some ideas. Useful whether you want to supplement your publisher's efforts or are publicizing your own self-published book.

The Self-Publishing Manual: How to Write, Print, and Sell Your Own Book, **Dan Poynter (Para Publishing, 2000)**
If you want to self-publish, this is a good resource. Josephine (Joi) Nobisso used it (see Chapter 33).

Terrific Connections with Authors, Illustrators, and Storytellers: Real Space and Virtual Links, **Toni Buzzeo and Jane Kurtz (Teacher Ideas Press, 1999)**
This is the only book you need if you want to do school and library visits. It will provide guidance in finding and planning visits as well as what to do on a visit. I drew on it heavily for Chapter 31.

Webster's Third New International Dictionary, **Philip Babcock Gove (editor) (Merriam Webster, 1993)**
Yes, it's expensive and heavy, but you have to have this book on your reference shelf, or be willing to walk to the library to use it. *Webster's Third* is the dictionary used throughout publishing to settle spelling, hyphenation, and such issues; those enigmatic "W3" annotations made in the margins of your manuscript by copy editors refer to it.

Words into Type, **Marjorie E. Skillin et al. (Pearson, 1974)**
Do not be put off by the publication date. WIT is an extremely useful companion to *The Chicago Manual of Style,* as it covers grammar, word choice, writing style, and similar issues in more detail, and is easier to use. Get *WIT* instead of the better-known but overly general Strunk and White.

Writer's Market, **Katie Brogan (Writer's Digest Books, annual)**
This enormous (more than 1,000 pages) annually updated market guide is indispensable *if* you are a writer interested in publishing in the general market in addition to the children's. Includes a guide to setting fees and feature articles as well as listings of book and magazine publishers.

Magazines

Booklist
The most consistently thoughtful and inclusive review magazine. Published monthly, aimed mainly at librarians. Booklist, PO Box 607, Mt. Morris, IL 61054-7564; 1-888-350-0949; www.ala.org/booklist/.

Children's Book Insider
A helpful monthly magazine for writers, and the place where updates to *Children's Writer's and Illustrator's Market* are published. Children's Book Insider, LLC, 901 Columbia Road, Fort Collins, CO 80525-1838; 1-800-807-1916; www.write4kids.com/index.html.

The Horn Book Magazine
A literary review magazine for children's books, with in-depth feature articles and regular columns on subjects such as multicultural literature and young adult novels. Published bimonthly, with *The Horn Book Guide* semiannually. The Horn Book, Inc., 56 Roland Street, Suite 200, Boston, MA 02129; 1-800-325-1170 or 617-628-0225; www.hbook.com/index.shtml.

The Lion and the Unicorn
An academic journal on children's literature, and a good place to go for a different (sometimes difficult-to-understand) perspective. The Johns Hopkins University Press, Journals Division, 2715 N. Charles Street, Baltimore, MD 21218; 1-800-548-1784.

Once Upon a Time
A quarterly magazine by and for writers, with an inspirational and supportive focus. For information, write to Audrey B. Baird, Editor, OUAT, 553 Winston Court, St. Paul, MN 55118; members.aol.com/ouatmag/.

Publisher's Weekly
The weekly news magazine of the publishing industry, with reviews aimed at the bookstore market. The semiannual children's book issues are a must-see. Subscriptions are expensive, but much of the content gets posted on their website. *Publishers Weekly*, PO Box 16178, North Hollywood, CA 91615-6178; 1-800-278-2991; www.publishersweekly.com.

School Library Journal
Monthly, reviews the most books, but not always consistently. *School Library Journal*, PO Box 16388 North Hollywood, CA 91615-6388; 1-800-595-1066 (within the United States); 818-487-4566 (outside the United States); www.slj.com.

Organizations

Association of Author's Representatives
To get the AAR's Canon of Ethics, suggested questions to ask of an agent, and member's list, visit their website at www.aar-online.org/.

The Author's Guild
This national organization is open to published authors for adults and for children. Contact 330 W. 42nd Street 29th Floor, New York, NY 10036; 212-563-5904; www.authorsguild.org/.

Canadian Society of Children's Authors, Illustrators, and Performers
CANSCAIP publishes a newsletter and brings those concerned with children's literature together. To apply, contact 35 Spadina Road, Toronto, Ontario, Canada M5R 2S9; 416-515-1559; www.canscaip.org/.

The Children's Book Council
The trade association for children's publishers creates a lot of useful publications. The best may be their list of their members (also available online), available for a 6×9-inch SASE with 3-ounce postage and a check for $2 sent to The Children's Book Council, 12 W. 37th Street, 2nd Floor, New York, NY 10018-7480; www.cbcbooks.org/.

Society of Children's Book Writers and Illustrators
Get access to the SCBW-I's newsletter, free publications, and reduced rates for conferences by joining. Get an application form from SCBW-I, 8271 Beverly Boulevard, Los Angeles, CA 90048; 323-782-1010; www.scbwi.org/.

Society of Photographers and Artists Representatives
The professional organization for artist's agents. Find SPAR's member's lists and more online at www.spar.org/index.html.

Websites

Articles for Writers and Publishers
www.ivanhoffman.com/helpful.html
A lawyer's personal website, with dozens of helpful articles on various contract issues and on copyright. Clearly, you are getting one person's point of view, but his views don't seem controversial or idiosyncratic to me.

CCBC Publications
www.education.wisc.edu/ccbc/public2.htm
Useful lists of recommended books from the Cooperative Children's Book Center.

The Children's Literature Web Guide
www.ucalgary.ca/~dkbrown
Run by a librarian at the University of Calgary, this is the best place to start to find information and other websites on children's books and children's publishing.

The Children's Writer's E-Mail Group at groups.yahoo.com/group/
childrens-writers/
A lively and informed group that discusses a wide range of topics relating to the writing and illustrating of children's books.

Verla Kay
www.verlakay.com
Verla Kay is a published author who has made her website a hub for children's writers, with useful information and links, workshops, and chats.

The Purple Crayon
www.underdown.org
Don't forget my website. You'll find articles, interviews, materials from this book, and my personal selections of useful websites.

Raab Associates
www.raabassociates.com
Susan Raab is a freelance marketer specializing in children's books. This site promotes her business and also has a wonderful archive of the columns on marketing that she writes for the SCBW-I newsletter.

Aaron Shepard's World of Story
www.aaronshep.com/index.html
This is an author's personal site with useful articles based on his experiences. It's also a striking example of what can be done to promote one's books by developing and maintaining a personal site.

Smart Writers
www.smartwriters.com
A useful website for children's book writers, Smart Writers offers numerous links including a publishers directory, information on writing contests, articles, a kids' room, and much more.

Cynthia Leitich Smith
www.cynthialeitichsmith.com
Another personal site, this one features an astonishingly comprehensive and up-to-date collection of children's literature-related links.

The Westing Game
www.education.wisc.edu/ccbc/wisauth/raskin/intro.htm
This is a web exhibit of the multiple drafts of the manuscript and sample pages from the page and jacket design process, all contributed to the Cooperative Children's Book Center by the author of this Newbery Medal–winning novel.

Writing World
www.writing-world.com
Don't be put off by the heavy presence of advertising; you'll find plenty of useful articles on a variety of topics, including writing children's books and self-publishing.

Sample Materials

Welcome to this warehouse of samples! First are typical guidelines from a trade publisher, so you'll know what to expect. Actual guidelines vary a lot, so you should still write for guidelines from actual publishers. You'll also see samples of different kinds of cover and query letters, and a sample manuscript format. Study these and you can't go wrong. (Well, you can, but they'll help you make that less likely.)

For more examples of cover and query letters, including one amusing look at what not to do, take a look at Jackie Ogburn's "Rites of Submission: Cover Letters and Queries," online at www.underdown.org/covlettr.htm.

Sample Guidelines from a Trade Publisher

Following these writer's guidelines are sample guidelines for illustrators.

SUBMISSION GUIDELINES

for Children's Book Writers

from a Pretty Good Publisher, Inc.

Pretty Good publishes children's books for the trade market for children of all ages. We publish both fiction and nonfiction, but do not publish board books, reference books, or activity books.

Pretty Good reads all unsolicited manuscripts that we receive, provided that they are submitted to us on an exclusive basis through the mail. At present, we do not review or reply to submissions or queries made by e-mail or fax, in disk form, or consisting only of website addresses.

Manuscripts of fewer than 20 typed pages can be submitted in their entirety. For longer manuscripts, we prefer to receive a query letter, summary (not an outline), and three sample chapters. Please write "Query" on the envelope, and include a self-addressed stamped envelope (SASE) with your query.

Manuscripts should be typed double-spaced on white paper. We recommend that you make a copy of your manuscript before sending it, as we cannot be responsible for submissions lost in the mail or at our offices. Your name, address, and telephone number should appear on your manuscript as well as in your cover letter. Do not include illustrations.

Please submit your manuscript to the attention of the Trade Editorial Department at the address above.

Enclose a SASE with sufficient postage (not a check or cash) for our response and return of the manuscript, or for response only if the manuscript need not be returned. If you do not enclose a SASE, your manuscript will be discarded.

Please send only one or two manuscripts at a time. We make every effort to respond in three months, but cannot guarantee that we will be able to do so, due to the volume of submissions. For confirmation that your project was received, include a self-addressed stamped postcard.

Before submitting a manuscript to us, we encourage you to review some of our published books in a library or bookstore or to take a look at our website (www.pretty-goodpublishers.com). If you would like to request a catalog, please send a 9 × 12-inch self-addressed stamped envelope with $1.47 in postage.

Illustration samples should be sent to the attention of the Art Director. We prefer tear sheets or color photocopies. Slides and CD-ROM portfolios may not be reviewed. Samples are not returned; we will contact you if we are interested.

Questions about the status of a manuscript must by made by mail, in an envelope marked "Manuscript Status," with a SASE enclosed. Please do not contact us until at least three months have elapsed and do not contact us by phone.

SUBMISSION GUIDELINES
for Illustrators
from a Pretty Good Publisher, Inc.

Before you contact us, we suggest that you review our already published books through your local library, a well-stocked bookstore, or an online bookseller to get a sense of what kind of illustration styles we find appropriate for our young readers. You may also request one of our catalogs, (if available) by sending an 8 × 10-inch self-addressed, stamped, envelope with 4 ounces postage.

We have a portfolio drop-off day on _____. You may drop off a portfolio with the receptionist any time before 11 and pick it up again after 4. Please call ahead to make sure that the Art Director will be in that day.

You are welcome to mail any samples you would like us to review or keep on file. We will circulate them and individual editors or designers may contact you if they wish to see more. One to four samples are sufficient. One black-and-white (if you work in b&w), and three in color are preferable. Good quality photocopies are fine. You may send a book "dummy" if you wish to showcase your ability to create a picture book.

Do not send original art. Slides may be submitted, but are not as convenient to view as printed samples. Do not submit samples on CD-ROM or other computer format; even if we have the necessary hardware and software to view them, we may not have the resources. For similar reasons, we are not reviewing online portfolios or websites.

If your work includes the ability to illustrate various types of people, landscapes, objects, or if you work in various mediums or styles, please include a mix of these capabilities. (However, please limit your style submissions to two or three.)

Identify each sample sent with your name, address, and phone number. Also include a self-addressed, stamped envelope (in the appropriate size) if you request returns.

Comment: Most publishers post their guidelines somewhere on their websites, and all will send them to you on receipt of a SASE. Notice the item on illustration samples in the writer's guidelines, which I included because some publishers don't have separate illustrator's guidelines. That may be the only help an illustrator gets.

Three Sample Cover Letters for Unpublished Authors

Please use these with caution. These are not presented as perfect examples of the craft of cover-letter writing, but as examples of approaches. You should adapt, improvise, and generally find your own way to best present your unique work. These are all addressed to editors, but you can take a similar approach when writing to agents. The biggest difference is that agents will want to hear more about you and other manuscripts; they're not interested if all you have is one.

Your Address

Date

Some Editor
Pretty Good Publishers Books for Young Readers
1 Main St.
Anymetropolis, HC 00000

Dear Editor,

When I remembered the time I gave my little sister a bloody nose in the backyard five minutes after Mom had praised her report card, I knew that I had the beginnings of a story. *Mom! She's Bothering Me Again!* is the story itself.

I hope you'll agree that the humor and drama of it—and the unsentimental ending—make this a worthy new rendition of a perennial theme.

In keeping with your company's policy, I have submitted this manuscript exclusively to you. I look forward to hearing from you soon.

Yours sincerely,

An Eager Author

Comment: If you haven't been published, do like this author did and don't apologize (or even mention this fact). You still have relevant personal experience with which to hook an editor. Words like humor and unsentimental also suggest that you know what you are doing. Above all, keep these letters short and businesslike. A cover letter should make an editor want to read your story; now the story just has to live up to what you've promised! If you are writing nonfiction, personal experience is still a great approach, as the next letter demonstrates.

Your Address

Date

A Learned Editor
Informative Books for Young Readers
99 High St.
Middleville, PB 00000

Dear Editor,

You and I know that sharks are far less dangerous to humans than the average SUV. But these primitive yet efficient creatures still excite fascination and fear in adults and children alike.

I drew on my years of experience studying sharks at the Jaws Research Institute and my unquenched enthusiasm for the subject to create *Shark!*, dramatic nonfiction for a middle-grade audience.

How can this compete with the dozens of books on the subject already on the market? By providing up-to-the-minute information on sharks, told from a first-person perspective by a scientist active in the field.

I've seen the books that Informative publishes and believe that my approach suits your list. I enclose a SASE for my manuscript's return if you do not agree.

With best wishes,

A Shark Scientist

Comments: *In this example, the author is a scientist. But you don't have to be an academic expert on a subject to write about it for children. You do have to know the latest research and be able to communicate it. First-person experiences are almost always a good way to catch an editor's eye. So is knowledge of what's out on the market, but be succinct, like this writer is. You don't have to describe the competing titles and compare yours to each of them. Knowledge of a company's publishing program is always a plus; if can even become the basis of a cover letter, as it is in the next example.*

Your Address

Date

Some Editor
Pretty Good Publishers Books for Young Readers
1 Main St.
Anymetropolis, HC 00000

Dear Editor,

My six-year-old son never gets tired of the goofy humor in *The Gerbil Looks Unhappy*, or the rambunctious antics of Eleanor in your easy-reader series. Thank you for publishing them!

Because PGP Books seems to welcome such wild and wacky stories, I'm hoping that you'll enjoy the enclosed, *Where's Davey?*, an over-the-top adventure based on the (apparent) disappearance of one of my own children.

In the event that I'm wrong, I enclose a SASE for the return of the manuscript. I hope to hear from you soon.

With best wishes,

A Funny Author

Comments: *It impresses an editor if you display familiarity with a publisher's program, especially if you don't just mention such extremely well-known books as Goodnight Moon and Where the Wild Things Are, as you might if writing to HarperCollins. This isn't a form of name-dropping! It's also important to say something about the books, and to compare them in approach to your book. Do not focus on the subject of the book; it's not too insightful to claim that a publisher who's done one book on dogs will obviously be a good home for another one.*

A Sample Cover Letter for Published Authors

The three approaches used previously will work well for you, too. All you need to do is add a brief paragraph about your writing experience for children. This example simply reworks one of the previous examples.

Your Address

Date

Some Editor
Pretty Good Publishers Books for Young Readers
1 Main St.
Anymetropolis, HC 00000

Dear Editor,

When I remembered the time I gave my little sister a bloody nose in the backyard five minutes after Mom had praised her report card, I knew that I had the beginnings of a story. *Mom! She's Bothering Me Again!* is the story itself.

I hope you'll agree that the humor and drama of it—and the unsentimental ending—make this a worthy new rendition of a perennial theme.

I'm the author of *Wombats and Dodoes* (Informative Books) and *The Thing in the Closet*, just released by Conglommo, Inc. I've also had several stories published in *Cricket*.

I have submitted this manuscript exclusively to you. I look forward to hearing from you soon.

Yours sincerely,

An Eager Published Author

Comments: You can mention magazines as well as books, provided that they are nationally distributed, mainstream publications. Books for adults are not relevant. Really!

Letters for Illustrators

Life for illustrators is a little less complicated than it is for authors, at least when it comes to contacting publishers. When sending out a mailing of samples, you can actually not bother with a cover letter altogether, though a short letter demonstrating your familiarity with the publisher's program and mentioning any relevant work you've done doesn't hurt. But the samples are what matter.

However, if you're writing to an artist's representative in the hope that she will represent you, then a personal letter is a good idea.

Your Address

Your E-Mail Address

Date

Ann Artrep
Ann Artrep Agency, Inc.
99 Hope St.
Midsize, PB 00000

Dear Ms. Artrep,

You may remember that we spoke briefly during the Children's Publishing Basics workshop in Bigtown recently, and you suggested that I send you some samples of my work.

I've been working in children's books for five years now, ever since I graduated from Cal Arts. I've been pretty busy recently, working for educational publishers, as you'll see from the samples. I've also illustrated two trade books for Small Independent Co.; *Look Ma, No Hands!* by Alison Charming, which just came out this year, and *Wash Day* by Alda Animals, a funny nonfiction book on how animals keep themselves clean. That's due out next year.

I'm ready to get a rep to help me take the next step up in my career and feel that you could be one. I visited your website to get an idea of what you do and the kind of client you represent, and think I'd fit in well. I hope you agree. If you don't, I've enclosed a large SASE for the return of the samples.

Yours sincerely,

An Eager Illustrator

Comments: *An art rep I talked to about this sample had only a few comments about what she wanted to see and what she didn't—but they were forceful comments. Be sure to get the art rep's name right, and be personal, though professional. Letters with a mass mailing feel are a big turn-off. Mention how you heard about the rep, or who referred you to them, because so many reps are now looking only at people referred to them. And do give a short rundown of your career to date. The samples speak for themselves, but your letter helps to put them in context. Include your e-mail address so they can respond that way if they prefer.*

Two Sample Query Letters

Publishers often require query letters to reduce the volume of their submissions, particularly of longer manuscripts. Here you have to work harder to get their interest; with a shorter manuscript a reader will almost always glance at the manuscript, even if the cover letter is a downer. With a query letter, you have to make her want to request and then read the entire manuscript.

Your Address

Date

A Learned Editor
Informative Books for Young Readers
99 High St.
Middleville, PB 00000

Dear Editor,

You and I know that sharks are far less dangerous to humans than the average SUV. But these primitive yet efficient creatures still excite fascination and fear in adults and children alike.

I drew on my years of experience studying sharks at the Jaws Research Institute and my unquenched enthusiasm for the subject to create *Shark!*, dramatic nonfiction for a middle-grade audience. Eight compact chapters provide the latest information about the life cycle, special adaptations, and threats to the survival of the shark. I've also taken an in-depth look at human-shark incidents—and concluded that the shark often is the loser. A guide to shark species, book and web resources, and a diagram of shark anatomy round out the book.

Through personal contacts, I can also put together a complete set of full-color illustrations, and I enclose a sample of what's available, along with an outline and two chapters. The complete 76-page manuscript is available.

I've researched the market, and I believe that there's no book on this popular subject that not only provides up-to-the-minute information on sharks, but also is told from a first-person perspective by a scientist active in the field. I'm confident this approach will suit your list. I enclose a SASE for your response.

With best wishes,

A Shark Scientist

Comments: Compare this to the earlier cover letter about this hypothetical book. You need to include more information about the manuscript, because it's not in front of the editor. Because this is nonfiction for older readers, and potentially photo-illustrated, the author also lets the editor know that she can help to gather those materials. Another plus is that the entire manuscript is available. Getting a contract offer for just a proposal is a possibility for nonfiction, if you are published, but if you aren't it's better to complete the manuscript before trying to place it.

Your Address

Date

Some Editor
Pretty Good Publishers Books for Young Readers
1 Main St.
Anymetropolis, HC 00000

Dear Editor,

Do you remember the bully in eighth grade? Many middle-schoolers are confronting a contemporary version of that terrifying figure, as Josh does in this passage from my novel, *The Gauntlet:*

> "Hey, kid! Think you're cool, don'tcha, all dressed in black? How's that black gonna look with some red on it?"

Josh stopped dead in the hall, looked quickly behind him. No one. He'd have to face Steven on his own.

You know these issues. Dealing with difference, and dealing with the reactions of those angered by it, are major challenges for our society. We can stand back and talk about them. But they are all-too-real, concrete problems for my protagonist, as he navigates the halls of a large public school.

The sample chapters I enclose will show you that *The Gauntlet* is no message-driven polemic, but a gripping story about Josh. There are many YA novels on this subject, especially recently, as we struggle to learn from Columbine. But there's little for the middle-schooler, and I believe there needs to be. I hope you agree, and I enclose a SASE for your response.

Yours sincerely,

A Determined Author

Comments: *An actual excerpt from your manuscript, provided it can stand the scrutiny, can be an effective lead-in to a query letter for a fiction manuscript. My example doesn't hold up—do better! As with the nonfiction query letter, work hard to get across what's unique about your manuscript. Make the editor want to read all 100-plus pages of it.*

Sample Manuscript Format

Here's a sample manuscript, set up to both show and tell you what to do. I know it disturbs the nice clean look of the page, but be sure to include your name and address on the first page of the manuscript. If it gets separated from your cover letter and SASE, the editor will still be able to contact you.

> Your name (optional—word or page count)
> Street address
> City, state/province, and post code
> Telephone number
> (optional—e-mail address)
>
> *(leave a break of at least four lines)*
>
> Your Title
>
>
> by Your Name
>
> *(leave a break of at least four lines)*

Start your manuscript here. It should have margins of at least 1 inch on the sides, top, and bottom. Indent your paragraphs. Double-space between lines. Do not be tempted to save on paper by single-spacing a long manuscript. This will make it harder to read, and you want the editor's reading experience to be the best you can make it. For the same reason, use a common, easy-to-read typeface, no matter what your word processor offers.

You can number your pages, starting with the second page, in the upper-right corner, if your manuscript is longer than a picture book.

You can put "Copyright © (year) by (Your Name)" on the first page, but this is no longer necessary. Unpublished works are protected by current copyright law, even without this notation.

For presentation purposes, you can create a separate title page, starting the text on the second page, but this is not necessary for short manuscripts.

Index